Plain Once Seen

By

Lance Hurley
and
Virgil Hurley

BLACK FOREST PRESS
San Diego, California
October, 1999
First Edition

Plain Once Seen

By

Lance Hurley
and
Virgil Hurley

PUBLISHED IN THE UNITED STATES OF AMERICA
BY
BLACK FOREST PRESS
P.O.Box 6342
Chula Vista, CA 91909-6342
1-800- 451-9404

Printed in the United States of America
Library of Congress
Cataloging-in-Publication

ISBN: 1-582750-07-6

Lance's Dedication:

To my partner, my encourager, the love of my life -- Darla
To my three constant sources of illustrations -- Jared,Luke,Logan
To my church family at CCM -- thanks for encouraging me and my
creativity

Virgil's Dedication:

To Lance, Brooks and Scott. As Christian boys they raised and, as
Godly men, exceeded our expectations.

TABLE OF CONTENTS

FOREWORD

The co-authors certainly qualify to write such a book. For the past five years Lance Hurley has consistently used these very visuals in preaching to audiences ranging from church members to nationally-known church planters. He has found that people remember what they see as well as the truth they're taught.

Virgil Hurley brings a broad academic and journalistic background that deepens the visuals and makes them excellent teaching tools. From his experience in ministry, teaching and study he is able to provide a wealth of spiritual lessons and applications that can help develop Christian maturity. Their collaboration offers unique perspectives that put a bounteous harvest of ideas within the reach and in the grasp of pastors, teachers and small group leaders.

Dahk Knox
Ph.D., Ed.D.
Author, Academician, Publisher

PREFACE

In *Plain Once Seen* we sacrificed complexity in methodology for in-depth **Applications** suggested by the **Subject Idea** (one-word summary of the visual); **Scripture** (relating to the subject idea); **Truth Stressed** (theme or proposition of the visual); and **Procedure** (merely suggestive, though tested by use). This allows the visual to be a true teacher, not simply an object lesson.

For example, **II Corinthians 7:8** stresses the potentially-damaging effect rebuke can have, or the life-changing response it can evoke. All our experience impacts us, and we may not immediately know its long-term results. Like the punctured pop container, we can be left with the appearance bereft of the substance of Christ.

The **Index** opens the entire book to use on any of the subjects. For example, the Christian's need to witness for Christ is found, not only in *Evangelism*, but also in *Discipleship, Church, Jesus,* et al – each with a differing perspective. The Index allows the leader to broaden the base of already-provocative applications.

Many of the illustrations offer full-length lessons; others hint at that completeness. However you use the material, may the Holy Spirit help your audiences *see* the Christ as they're *taught*.

ADVERSITY

Optimistic faith in adversity spins "straw into gold". Its creative resourcefulness energizes solutions and minimizes obstacles, whatever the sex, age group, nationality or time. No one disputes how savage adversity can be. But if we see it as speed bumps, not brick walls, we'll learn to approach it gently and go slowly over, without bouncing ourselves silly. If we react angrily and race at the adversity, we'll be jerked and jolted and ricocheted—and may be shattered! In these illustrations are an encouragement to let God, not circumstances, dictate the way we respond to misfortune.

Subject Idea: Effect

Scripture: II Corinthians 7:8

Visual Item: Aluminum pop can

Truth Stressed: Life can slowly destroy our joy in Christ.

Procedure: Prior to use, make a small nail-hole in the can's bottom; drain the pop out (you may need to make another hole for air). Be sure it's empty. At the presentation, describe the delight of cold soda when you're thirsty. Without explanation, pop the tab and hold the can upside down.

Applications:

1. Unfortunate circumstances can puncture our lives, leaving only a small wound, but large enough to drain our confidence, joy and contentment, leaving us empty of what should fill us. Adversity won't necessarily bring us closer to God, and Satan tirelessly uses it to drive us farther away.

2. We need to periodically appraise the impact that negative experiences have on our relationship with God. Have they distanced us, left us unaffected or developed greater faith? Of the three possibilities, two are negative, since having a neutral impact means we've stopped adversity short of God's goal. People often lose their faith, not by

having their reservoir of trust suddenly breached, but by developing small leaks that, over an extended period, drain commitment empty. Unable to identify their source, we unmistakably see their result, by breach or by leak: trust in God and joy in the Holy Spirit gone!

3. Just as air remained in the can with the fluid gone, form can remain in life once the substance of faith has disappeared. We won't notice the difference in the can while it's on a shelf, unused. But try to get liquid from it, and only air results. Many erstwhile strong believers, having been bludgeoned by adversity, have gradually lost faith, and no one knew, perhaps not even they. But when they called for faith, only doubt answered. When they wanted joy, only despair. When they wanted to praise God, they cursed Him. We all experience circumstances that deplete our hope and peace drop by drop until they're gone! And later, when we return to find hope and peace, we're bitterly disappointed to find unbelief and despair!

4. Let us be forewarned: the life God intended to be filled with Christ's love can be emptied drip by drip if we don't plug the holes! It can lose the substance, leaving only form!

⌘   ⌘   ⌘   ⌘   ⌘   ⌘

Subject Idea: Testing
Scripture: Matthew 26:75; 27:5
Visual Item: Toothpick
Truth Stressed: Trials test our maturity.
Procedure: Say you have an important tool for the baker—pull out a toothpick. Ask how many have used a toothpick to test whether the cake was done. Did they ever feel guilty puncturing it to see if it had baked sufficiently?

Applications:

1. As a toothpick's puncture determines a cake's usefulness to us, life's adversities determine our maturity. And as, if the cake isn't done, particles will cling to the toothpick, the remnant of ruins will emerge when adversity hits the immature or vulnerable.

2. The toothpick can't be blamed if it withdraws particles of cake; if, after it should be done, it isn't, the toothpick simply shows that the cake needs to bake longer. Yet, adversity gets blamed when we pout, shout and complain after its visitation. Both the toothpick and adversity are neutral forces whose impact merely proves what they uncover, whether in the cake or us. What was the difference between the Jews who said the Holocaust had cost them their faith in God and the Jews who said only prayer kept them alive and in control during the Holocaust? The maturity of their religious faith!

3. Adversity merely reveals what we are; it doesn't automatically make us better or worse. A lady recovering from a lymphoma told a class of 11-year olds that her problem probably sounded scary to them, but she had decided not to be afraid! Adversity had punctured her life, only to find courage. She had what Dr. Scott Peck calls character—the ability to confront crisis early and head on! While captaining the steamer *California*, Captain Cleveland Forbes had a lung hemorrhage, imperiling his life, bringing physical pain and costing him charge of his ship. Still, in his personal log on February 4, 1849, he noted his attendance at divine service aboardship and his pleasure in praising God for His goodness and mercy, despite the visitation of wrath. Adversity punctured his life only to reveal faith! Unfortunate circumstances surface what lies within us. We must not blame the circumstance if the sight doesn't please us. We should use it as an opportunity to grow beyond disappointment. For, when tough times pass, God expects His people to be on the far, not the near side of the Slough of Despond. When suffering comes to us, as come it shall, what will it reveal about us that we have kept hidden till its visitation?

⌘　⌘　⌘　⌘　⌘　⌘

Subject Idea:	Testing
Scripture:	I Peter 1:7
Visual Item:	Butane gas lighter; nail; rock; candle; tongs
Truth Stressed:	Adversity will weaken or destroy us unless we remain close to God.
Procedure:	Test the nail and rock with the lighter while holding them with tongs. Note that the fire scorches without endangering them. Hold the candle horizontally in the tongs while you heat the middle. In seconds the candle bends on itself.

Applications:

1. Each element can be melted, given enough heat—the candle before the nail, the nail before the rock—but each is capable of destruction. Our mental, emotional and spiritual constitution determines how deep, long and intense adversity must be to impact us. A smaller adversity can wreck one person while a bigger one leaves another unmoved. We can discuss whether it's character or religious faith or genes that make different people, even in the same family, respond differently to the same adversity. Indeed, some people are like the candle, others the nail and some the rock.

2. What we know for certain is that adversity reveals what we are. Like the mistral wind of Provence, France, adversity's cold, hard blows wreck some lives and leave others virtually untouched. Yet, niggling problems may undo those the mistral leaves quite unaffected. In some lives adversity rouses the equanimity and humility that success destroys. Some people see disaster in every setback while others see opportunity in the starkest disaster! Millions of soldiers fought in World War II. Some of them, gentle and agreeable before the fighting, returned as abusive, violent husbands and fathers. Yet others returned prepared to be missionaries to the very people who brutalized them.

3. The secret in overcoming stress is the tensile, spiritual strength God gives. When we decide to confront, not flee the crisis, our will burgeons, our soul assumes the strength

of tempered steel, and we conquer! No brokenness can break the spirit given to God.

4. God gives each Christian a faith that enlarges as it's stressed; that develops as it's bludgeoned; that retains joy as it struggles and inner wealth while deprived of outward gain. If we remain intimate with God, what afflicts us may incinerate the outer but leaves life's inner core untouched. Or, having reached it, burn to refinement its potential glory.

5. We can build our lives strong enough to withstand the heat adversity applies. Jesus doesn't want us melting under trials; he wants us to emerge scorched and charred but intact!

⌘   ⌘   ⌘   ⌘   ⌘   ⌘

Subject Idea: Trust

Scripture: Proverbs 24:10

Visual Item: Pillow; raw egg; glass bowl; Handi-wipe

Truth Stressed: Even the fragile has strength when thrown on God's mercy.

Procedure: Show all three items separately; show that the raw egg, vulnerable to any abuse, can safely be dropped to the pillow. If you want, crack the egg into the bowl to prove it's raw.

Applications:

1. While the egg is a nearly perfect shape, it's also perfectly vulnerable. "Walking on eggshells" is a description of the care taken not to crush something or someone fragile.

2. Christians need to understand their faith's vulnerability to adversity. In fact, no people are more potentially fragile than Christians, simply because of the risks we take. If we didn't claim so much for Jesus, we wouldn't be called bigots by our diversified culture. If we didn't so strongly demand purity in society, our personal sins wouldn't be so embarrassing. Indeed, if we don't want to be criticized,

we should trade our spiritual convictions for opinions! No one will be offended then. It's as we affirm faith in a great God that we risk! "God is able," we say; "God answers prayer," we affirm; "We can always trust God to provide and care," we promise. And how easily and often those claims and affirmations are tested, delayed and denied, both personally and in those to whom we witness! When that happens, all we've affirmed can turn to doubt. We can't iron out of life the dangers that unanswered prayer, sickness, family problems, job loss, etc. pose to our confidence in a compassionate, prayer-hearing God.

3. Jeremiah preached God's sovereignty that threatened wholesale destruction of Israel, but God wouldn't keep him from being thrown into a cistern. Paul exorcized a python spirit from a girl in Philippi, but the Christ exorcizing the demon wouldn't keep his preachers from a savage beating and more brutal mistreatment in a jail cell. How did they reconcile their victorious preaching with their personal disasters? Simply by separating the message from the adversity. Their personal sorrow didn't weaken God or the cause they served. What will it be for us when what we affirm as general truth isn't specifically expressed in our lives? Will we struggle with a perpetual "why," or will we trust God, regardless, knowing that His word, not our experiences, verifies His word? Trusting is always the harder lesson to learn, but the more productive, once mastered.

4. In that sense, trials offer the advantage of validating our message even as we personally fail to profit by or suffer from them! Then adversity exalts, not debases us. If, in obedience to the Master's integrity, we *attest Him*, suffering perfects our witness, even as it personally harms us. And, if after the struggle we reap victory, after obedience we reap reward.

5. To remain safe in danger, we need the security of God's protective care. We need the certainty of succor, security, rest, repose. We know we're going to get hurt in proclaiming such lofty grace to a perverted world, and sometimes we'll think we're mortally wounded, but grace

is there to cushion our fall, to keep us from hitting hard and splattering all over life.

6. Any adversity can prove our fragility. And that certainty can intimidate us from being so sure of God and from repeating Christ's ultimatums. Knowing it's possible for failure to impede renewed effort, God comes to our rescue. By falling into God's arms we'll not only be cushioned from breaking, but we'll be kept useful and willing to try again! We'll never know how strong even fragility can be till we submit it to God. Then we'll learn how mighty our raw Christian witness can be!

⌘   ⌘   ⌘   ⌘   ⌘   ⌘

Subject Idea: Endurance
Scripture: Luke 22:39
Visual Item: Large jigsaw puzzle — 1,000+ pieces
Truth Stressed: We get through adversity by a persevering discipleship.
Procedure: Show the puzzle; note that anyone can get from the first to the completed picture by fitting piece to piece.

Applications:

1. The secret to completing the puzzle is to persevere through mental blocks, delays and the inability to find the pieces we need at a particular time. Sometimes we pick individual pieces, not immediately useful, and put them on the table approximately where they'll be needed. Sometimes we work laboriously piece by piece wherever we've started. Whatever, we continue doing what we started in order to go where we want: we keep putting pieces to the puzzle! Jesus knew what awaited him in Gethsemane; nevertheless, he went there, as usual! He kept putting the pieces of his life together!

2. Satan's intention in adversity is to distract, divert and confuse us; to lure us from the potential in discipleship by

focusing on its problems. To escape his power, we purely and simply hang on at certain periods. By our fingernails, if need be; by the "skin of our teeth", if necessary. We hang on because we can't do more! That's victory for the Christian and defeat for Satan. He wants to discourage us into letting go, so any discouragement that ultimately remains faithful destroys Satan. In those times we can rest assured life *will* get better, then we can counter-attack. In those circumstances we hang on for another day, another hour or another minute, whatever time frame we need to break the day into merely to survive till we can eventually overcome.

3. Resilient obstinacy in discipleship is necessary when adversity visits because nothing seems to last so long as hard times; never does God seem farther away or less interested in us. Delaying improvement in our condition or letting adversity just hang around, Satan uses difficulties to encourage disaffection. On those occasions we need to remind ourselves that God may have made us only a candle, but we're inextinguishable if fueled from His word!

4. We need to be familiar enough with failure that it won't break us, but not so accustomed to it that we consider it our fixed destiny. Success is our fixed destiny; failure is an existing, but not an eternal fixture in us. And neither is adversity. Given that certainty, when beaten by life, come back for more. When whipped, present ourselves ready to fight again. Hurt by our last assault, let's hurl ourselves anew at the obstacle or task.

5. Hindsight always puts adversity in its rightful place—as a testing, not a disaster. By seeing the end while we suffer, we learn the lessons God wants to teach us while in the experience. It takes courage to ask for adversity's continuance until we've learned its lessons, but it's the only sure way to make it a positive learning experience; that we're better for having endured it; and that we won't have to endure it or something like it again for having failed to learn what God wanted taught!

⌘   ⌘   ⌘   ⌘   ⌘   ⌘

Subject Idea:	Creativity
Scripture:	Philippians 1:12-14
Visual Item:	A too-large hat
Truth Stressed:	Adversities can keep us from experiencing God.
Procedure:	Find a hat big enough to cover your eyes. Before you don it, ask the people if they've ever sat behind someone big enough to block their view or behind someone wearing a hat that blocked their view? What was their response?

Applications:

1. Sometimes the obstacle can't be eliminated. Poor health may be irreversible; physical limitation may render goals impossible. The Christian knows that, even in limitations, God is at work. We live as fully as possible within whatever we suffer.

2. We may not see the movie or see the pastor preaching by sitting behind a large person, but the movie's unfolding anyway; the message is proclaimed anyway. Just so, even when we can't see God for the adversity, God is still THERE! He doesn't move. That we can't see or feel or experience Him doesn't eliminate the God who's always THERE!

3. In the theater or church, we can move to a different location so we can see better. In life, we have the option to move and get a better *perspective* on the obstacle. Not always possible physically, it's necessary spiritually, mentally and emotionally; sometimes it's the only way to survive and overcome adversity. This is a two-edged sword. One, it's a very great promise; two, we have to exercise the power to maneuver there! We often find it easier to sit behind the obstacle and complain that it's there! Indeed, even when we have nothing to complain about, we do it anyway just to keep in practice! That's called self-pity, and we all occasionally court and embrace it.

4. We never know when our trouble-free, unobstructed view of life will be interrupted. At any time the strong can

suddenly become weak; the healthy ill; the prosperous penurious; the benefactors supplicants. Suddenly, instead of consecutive successes, blow after adverse blow falls, one obstacle after another appears, looming, lethal!

5. Whatever we face, discipleship continues. We must determine that, as Christ suffered to perfection, we can suffer to maturity. We must determine that, by his grace, we'll become an overcomer, not a victim of life. We must determine that we'll serve now, immediately, where we are, with what we have, not waiting till the obstacles are removed and the adversity's passed. Obstacles may not be fun, but they're great teachers. And while they can blind us to God's abiding presence, they can also reveal spiritual graces we never before experienced.

6. What changes an obstacle into an opportunity is seizing it for a good purpose, making something of it that it didn't originally intend or portend. Otherwise, what *could* be an obstacle *is*—even the things meant to be opportunities.

⌘   ⌘   ⌘   ⌘   ⌘   ⌘

Subject Idea: Attitude

Scripture: Philippians 1:15-18

Visual Item: Glass half-filled with water

Truth Stressed: The way we look at adversity determines its ultimate impact on us and our ultimate response to it.

Procedure: Show glass; ask for the two ways to look at it: half full, half empty.

Applications:

1. It may not matter how we view the glass, but very often the way we view adversity determines its ultimate expense to our energy, faith and optimism.

2. Given our distinct personalities and life experiences, two people can look at the same occurrence and draw different conclusions. That won't necessarily change. Nor is it

necessary to respond favorably initially in order to overcome a problem ultimately. True: the sooner we see it as a chance to grow, the quicker we'll mature. But since people respond to different stimuli at distinct speeds, the ultimate is always more important than the initial reaction.

3. The one reaction Christians must avoid when facing adversity, especially when it comes unexpectedly and inescapably, is to blame God. Often our first response, blame must be chained as a mad dog, or it will ravage our faith. However we struggle to achieve it, believers have no choice but to ask God to help them through the trial to a more mature faith. That sees the glass half-full! It matures as it experiences! The other way only "limps" along, rousing self-pity, not self-confidence. No one else can determine our response; we do that intentionally. We can do it wrongly by beginning wrongly, then correcting it later. We can begin correctly and let the trial exhaust us. But we determine its ultimate impact on us.

4. To have the knack of thinking our glass is half-full and ready to sip, we need to unlearn negative thinking and reinforce positive thinking, even under trials. This can be achieved by taking chances and succeeding. That encourages optimism; that sees the glass half-full; that sees the brighter, not the darker side of life. Optimism can also be gained by trying again *after* failing or by continuing to try after each failure. Nothing builds esteem like the practiced determination not to surrender.

5. In addition to our own better mental and physical health, seeing the glass half-full makes us superior company! People will be impressed when we have every reason to be sad, but are happy; they'll only reluctantly be guests of the pity-parties we throw ourselves. Do we want to make a positive impact or be a negative influence? We need to learn that our personal happiness or misery depends on our response to adversity, not on the adversity itself!

BIBLE

The Bible freely details the failures, wickedness and mistakes of all, even of its heroes. It also unfailingly stresses God's perfection, which is why it freely describes humanity's sinfulness. The Bible's purpose is to draw our attention to God, not to the fallen instruments He uses. In these illustrations, the humanity Jesus created in Adam and perfected in himself and the amazing clarity of God's word, matched by the invariable integrity of its immutable Author, explain the permanence of His instructions to all generations.

Subject Idea: Literacy

Scripture: II Timothy 2:15

Visual Item: VCR booklet

Truth Stressed: Our relationship with God demands a maturing knowledge of His word.

Procedure: Flip through booklet; ask how many feel they comprehend what they read in it.

Applications:

1. The VCR booklet is an apparently simple explanation of the VCR that becomes increasingly difficult to comprehend. While merely running the VCR may be easy, try following directions on how to tape a TV show you can't watch live. Or how to set the VCR's clock, eliminating all those goose eggs. Unlike the VCR, the Bible is an apparently obscure, difficult book that becomes disarmingly simple as it's read. It's one book that invites investigation from people who fear to crack it.

2. The VCR tells time, tapes TV shows, makes the remote control possible and plays videos. But only as we learn the system does it fulfill its potential. The Bible is great literature, incipient science, exact history, ancient culture, the life of sinners and saints, and especially, the story of God's activity in making humanity in His image and saving us from sin through Jesus Christ. But only as we become familiar with God's word does it achieve its

greatest success with us. For only as we come to know God through Christ do we find the eternal life revealed in Him.

3. People fear the Bible through unfamiliarity with its terms, culture and subject content. Actually, the terms used by the Bible are easy enough to understand. It's the terms we've adapted about the Bible that confuse. A Bible dictionary is helpful in explaining cultural usage that may bewilder us; a commentary can help clarify questions from difficult passages. But nearly anyone, even with a modest education, can profitably read God's word by itself, unadorned. It's the one historical book that grows increasingly clear the more it's read.

4. Every church should provide programmed opportunities for new members to become acquainted with basic Bible facts, and for all members to study it in whatever detail they're pleased to pursue.

5. We might read this booklet a dozen times and achieve a modest increase in our knowledge of the VCR. A dozen times through the Gospel of John or the book of Genesis will measurably enlarge our mind, soul and spirit. Our knowledge of electronics will determine how fast we master the VCR booklet. But if we bring *only* an open mind to God's word, whatever we know of the spiritual life, we'll vastly increase our store of knowledge and enlarge our soul each time we read! We may read the VCR booklet and wonder why we took the time. But if we read God's word with an open, inquiring mind, we'll know why we did and thank God for it.

⌘　⌘　⌘　⌘　⌘　⌘

Subject Idea:	Truth
Scripture:	Psalm 119:105
Visual Item:	Compass
Truth Stressed:	Only the Bible tells us the truth about God and ourselves.

Procedure: Show the compass. Explain that it's an irre-
placeable instrument for a hiker or explorer
because it keeps people from getting lost.

Applications:

1.   The Bible fully and flawlessly describes God's will and
demands. Like a compass needle pointing northward,
drawn by the magnetic pole, God's word points to God,
drawn by His irresistible presence in it.

2.   Our vote to legalize a sin won't override God's vote that
condemns it. We say we can't legislate morality, but we
go to great extremes to stem immorality by penal legis-
lation: if a person robs a bank despite laws against it, he's
punished. Our determination to change moral values
won't deter God's greater determination to uphold them.
If we want to know what behavior harms us, and is thus
denounced by God; improves us, and is thus advocated by
God, we need look no further than the Bible. It alone
points straight to God's truth; of all religious writings, it
alone can, will and does every time, without fail; it is
constant, never changing!

3.   If we're in the woods and think we're going east, but
check the compass heading and find ourselves going west,
who do we believe? Will we persist in what we *feel* is
east, or depend on the instrument that unerringly points
north and which, therefore, always lets us know all directions? Would we put our experience above the
compass' instinctive pull to north? What would our
friends say if they knew we decided to ignore the compass
to follow our "instincts"? Mankind has an unerring sense
of following the wrong way, example and model, all the
while swearing our competitiveness with the Bible. Why
should it surprise us that God calls us fools for following
self when His word says that acknowledging Him is the
beginning of wisdom?

4.   Life is a spiritual wilderness—a basic fact Christians need
to understand. Many of the unsaved don't believe that.
They think that any model of behavior and belief is acceptable because so many have lived previously and
gotten through successfully. God denies that. Since no
one ever gets through life without dying, the only suc-

cessful way is the way that offers life beyond the grave, where people live again forever! The believer knows that life is a wilderness that easily swallows us if we don't know the way through it. We also know that Jesus mastered the wilderness and all the temptations it offered.

5. The Bible is invariable, therefore, unchanging. Like the compass, we can always trust its heading. If we happen to stray from the compass' heading, we can get back to the right path by consulting it. It always points north, just as the Bible invariably points to God. Christians, let's never be without the Bible in our spiritual pack, and let's always follow its directions.

⌘   ⌘   ⌘   ⌘   ⌘   ⌘

Subject Idea:	Construction
Scripture:	Ephesians 2:10
Visual Item:	Set of blueprints
Truth Stressed:	The Bible reveals the life that God accepts.
Procedure:	Show the blueprints, perhaps having someone help you turn the pages. Each page details the instructions that meet and surpass building code requirements for the structure being built.

Applications:

1. Unlike any building constructed in our city, which has to meet strict codes appropriate to the area, no rule demands that every life meet certain requirements. We're individually free to build life as we deem sufficient. Since God made us free agents, not automatons, we can reject all established moral patterns to break whatever new ground we desire. In this category are the tyrants, thieves, swindlers and immoral who demand the right to make their own rules. Of course, they ultimately find themselves punished by the old rules that never abandoned their throne just because sinners wanted to sit there. Just so, we'll suffer if we insist on blazing our own

trail. Since we're each building our life, we may as well build it to last and to endure with the least trouble.

2. As an architect knows the geography and geology of his location, God knows the inner workings of the human heart. As the architect's knowledge enables him to determine foundations, walls, floors and roofs to specifications that withstand stress and continue to survive, God's knowledge enables Him to outline behaviors and attitudes that help us survive and thrive, even in circumstances that intend to harm and disestablish us.

3. The architect builds to last, knowing his reputation's at stake. He won't skimp to get the job done faster or easier. He knows there are always contractors willing to do it cheaper and quicker, but he rejects their deceit. Innocent people will pay when greed rules the building process. God knows how to build a life that lasts, not only for the present but into the unimaginably distant future. His reputation's at stake in the lives He constructs, so He demands close-order supervision in building His workmanship in us. He has no intention of putting up a structure that will make Him a laughingstock. All too often His people *settle* for a Christian life that makes God a laughingstock, but that's our fault, not His. We're to blame for settling for something less than He wants, not Him for demanding more.

4. An architect sees potential in any given situation, where his clients see only limitations. That's why he's the architect, and they are the clients. In the same way, God sees potential in our lives and the circumstances we face. If we submit to Him the way dissatisfied home owners invite an architect to view their house, God not only sees what we are, but what we could become if we let Him turn our reality into His dream!

5. Architects can begin from scratch or remodel an existing structure. They may have their preference, but they'll accept either challenge. God prefers to build us right from the start, having our commitment from childhood. That saves us from making mistakes we later have to correct. But most of us, even when accepting Jesus early in life, make enough mistakes as we mature that we often need

reconstruction by the Holy Spirit. Obviously, those who have grown to adulthood without structuring to God's specifications face an especially daunting challenge. Like people already living in houses that need expansion or re-modeling, they know how much poor workmanship clutters their life. God doesn't care how He finds us, as a youth with a few or as an adult with many misconstrued ideals, attitudes and habits. God specializes in renewing the spiritual life of everyone who trusts His spiritual archi-tectural skill. Having built in Christ the life God seeks for all, He knows how to construct Christ's image in each person.

⌘　⌘　⌘　⌘　⌘　⌘

Subject Idea:	Purpose
Scripture:	Matthew 28:19-20
Visual Item:	Watering can; box of grass fertilizer
Truth Stressed:	The word of God produces mature spiritual life in its listeners.
Procedure:	Show can and box. Point out that, everything else being equal, the combination of water and fertilizer produces mature grass from the seeds.

Applications:
1. Fertilizer without water burns the seed; water without fer-tilizer drowns the seed. Only in combination do they produce a grass carpet. Combining fertilizer and water brings to uniform maturity the seed that might otherwise grow unevenly. Having applied both water and fertilizer, we expect a uniform stand of grass.
2. God nourishes us with His word so we can produce the fruit of the Holy Spirit. Too often, we teach non-Christians too much and are disappointed when they're overwhelmed by God's demands. We as often teach Christians too little and are disappointed by their failure to rise to God's expectations.

3. Christians need to learn that we haven't done our duty to God by merely *listening* to the Gospel. As if, by hearing, we complete our responsibility. Jesus taught us to *observe* what we learn, to put into action what we hear until our knowledge produces results.

4. How little we would be impressed by Jesus if he had said he wanted to be the Savior, but didn't want to die; or to be the Lord, but didn't want to rule; or to be the rabbi, but didn't want to teach! How then can we expect him to be impressed when we say we want to be Christians, but don't want to practice self-denial; or believers, but don't want to believe his commands; or trees, but don't want to produce the Spirit's fruit? Only in the combination of learning and *observing* does the Christ-life grow in us.

⌘ ⌘ ⌘ ⌘ ⌘ ⌘

Subject Idea:	Repetition
Scripture:	John 3:16; Ephesians 2:6-7
Visual Item:	Paper and cloth tablecloths
Truth Stressed:	The Bible can best be understood by repeated usage.
Procedure:	Have a couple people hold the paper tablecloth. Since it's good for one occasion, you would feel free to scribble on it, poke holes in it and when finished, wad it into a ball for discarding. Then have them hold up the cloth one. Would any man who valued his neck harm this tablecloth? Many hostesses put placemats over this cloth to maintain its appearance. Such care is taken because of its reuse value.

Applications:

1. God's word is at its best when re-used. Only as we repeat its applications do we mature, learning new truths as we build on previous knowledge. Initial understanding may

lead us to appreciate Bible passages; only repeated endeavors will lead us to comprehending them. Since we often *know* much more than we *comprehend*, repeated Bible readings are essential to spiritual growth. In this way books that once were difficult become delightful; ideas that once overpowered are dextrously handled. Insights come as we repeat our reading; for as we're getting deeper into the word, more of it gets into our minds and lives. The Bible is too comprehensive to be read at one sitting and too complex to be understood instantly. But both knowledge and illumination accrue through persistence.

2.   In reuse we find how the books correlate to each other, from one Testament to the next, one explaining the other, another acquiring deeper meaning from the other. Only through repeatedly practicing its message do we find why it's true that the Bible is its own best interpreter.

3.   Unlike even this beautiful tablecloth, which will eventually show its age when used enough, the Bible remains fresh and fadeless, through multiplied usage over the centuries, while exposed to every difficult and impossible circumstance. In fact, some antique tablecloths exist by being stored and unused—or used sparingly. The Bible, on the other hand, grows stronger in us the more it's handled. It isn't that it reinvents itself in order to be useful. It's simply that its timeless relevance is rediscovered in every age.

4.   The Bible is the book that we can taste, or masticate, or swallow; and any way we take it, it enlightens, uplifts and encourages. We can read portions of it or whole chapters and books. We can be scholars of the Old or the New Testament, or of both. But only those who devour it gain maximum value. For while we'll eventually discard this cloth, having worn it out, the Bible continues to uncover new dimensions that will never be sounded, scaled or encircled in this life.

5.   Simply reading the Bible will answer most of our questions about the spiritual life. Studying it will answer more. But no reading or studying will ever answer all our questions about God, Christ, the spiritual life and eternity.

The Bible is that kind of book: so new, in fact, that it alone, of all the world's literature, tells of incomprehensible things yet to be!

⌘   ⌘   ⌘   ⌘   ⌘   ⌘

Subject Idea: Instructions
Scripture: I Timothy 4:13; II Timothy 3:14-17
Visual Item: Prescription bottle
Truth Stressed: God's word cures humanity's spiritual disease.
Procedure: Show the bottle; tell the medication and purpose it serves; read the directions.

Applications:

1. Failure to follow the doctor's instructions for prescribed antibiotics has led to the growth of resistant bacteria and viruses. At the very least, if we read the directions on this bottle, then change them to suit our schedule, the doctor will criticize our complaint of non- or slow recovery. Since he's the doctor, and we're the patient, follow his instructions! Our willingness to change the directions on a doctor's prescription is nothing compared to humanity's inbred determination to change God's word to suit themselves. There are many religious writings outside the Bible, but beware: if they add to the Bible, they're lethal to our souls; if they add nothing to the Bible, they're irrelevant. There are religious writings that have served their cultures for centuries, but none approaches the ameliorating value of God's Holy Bible. And there are multitudes of crude imitations of the Bible that religious practitioners want to substitute for the Bible. But nothing is the Bible but the Bible; therefore, while other writings may be like or unlike the Bible, no writing compares or competes with or surpasses the Bible!

2. God knows what has caused the numerous wars, disease, famine, earthquakes, volcanic eruptions, racism, greed,

etc. in humanity. It's a truth many refuse to hear because they reject sin as a spiritual problem. Responsibility for misbehavior isn't a strong suit in American life. But, then, it hasn't been since Adam gracelessly blamed Eve for his sin. We want our way, but without criticism if it turns out badly or harmful. Others say we can't be blamed since we're still struggling to escape our animal ancestry. God has left no doubt: human sin has caused all the afflictions we despise and want removed, but we refuse to confess so they can be! Until we accept *that* basic Bible teaching, we won't even go to God for forgiveness, let alone take the prescription He dispenses. As no one knows us better than our Creator, we must accept His explanation of our tragedy and follow His instructions in escaping it!

3.   To excuse their refusal to accept and follow God, many plead inability to reconcile human accountability with God's foreknowledge. If He knew our parents would disobey, they ask, why did He make them liable to disobey? And if He knew we were to be this way, how can He condemn us for the inevitable—that He caused in the first place? The Bible won't haggle with hagglers. It won't explain God's foreknowledge vis-`a-vis our personal responsibility. If it won't, we can't. Since it demands both, Bible Christianity unapologetically teaches both!

4.   A major difference exists between a doctor's prescription and our sin. Each prescription is tailor-made for that individual and his level of illness. The indiscriminate use of the medication by others is both foolish and dangerous. We can't say to someone else with symptoms "like" ours, "Here, take this; it helped me; it'll help you." Only a doctor can diagnose and dispense! But the common Bible cure cures everyone's sin problem, in whatever age we're born, whatever our gender or race or culture. One message cures all because all sins are multiples of a single sin: disobedience to God's word, in whatever way He revealed it. It's that disobedience which is sin, not the particular way we express it! And that's why obedience to God's single prescription cures all who receive and ingest it as revealed!

⌘   ⌘   ⌘   ⌘   ⌘   ⌘

Subject Idea:	Directions
Scripture:	Jeremiah 6:16
Visual Item:	Road map
Truth Stressed:	God's word leads us successfully to life in Heaven.
Procedure:	Unfold a map of the United States and detail a few places we could visit and the best roads to them.

Applications:

1. How many know how to read a map? That those co-ordinates around the page really mean something? That there really is a north, south, east and west, and not just left, right or straight ahead? Biblical illiteracy is staggering. Here is the single historical volume with which we need to be conversant because it recalls the past, describes the present and foretells the future. Yet it remains the best-sold, least-read book on earth.

2. How many of us would begin a trip to an entirely new location without consulting a map? Maybe having been there once we can go without outside guidance, but would we try it the first time? God's word warns us that we're only going through life once—we're not being recycled until we get it right. Furthermore, God's word reminds us that we're not just going through life—to die and be no more, ever again. No, we're each alive now and forever and ever. We're heading through life to somewhere else. Since we've never been here or there before, we should consult God's spiritual guide without delay since many of us are well-advanced on our journey. And those who are only beginning can't be guaranteed they will be well-advanced in the future, for their future can be canceled any time!

3. How many of us admit to being lost, even if we are, and everyone knows it, including us? How many of us so hate admitting we're lost that we'll waste gallons in gasoline and exhaust everyone's patience driving around hoping to find our way? American society is so evil that people want, not only to sin, but to justify it; to make it not a wrong at all, but a commendable alternative lifestyle—

whether it's homosexuality or deceit or greed or immorality. We want to sin as we please and then find ways to assure ourselves that sinning's okay since we already are.

4.   How many times have we read the map, then found ourselves in the wrong place? And, wondering why, looked again and discovered we misread the directions by holding the map upside down or crossways? If, while we're alive, we take all the roads that lead *from* Heaven because we mistakenly read God's word, how can we expect to arrive *at* Heaven? Yet, every survey taken proves that while people may not be sure their neighbors will be in Heaven, they're sure of a personal reservation! Even though they don't follow God's guidebook! Amazing self-deception!

5.   How many times have we found the map wrong and ourselves right? As if cartographers don't spend millions of dollars and make exhaustive accuracy checks on their work. Yet, though God's spiritual guide guarantees that we can get from problems to solutions, sin to forgiveness and death to eternal life by following its directions, we arrogantly follow other roads to reach our goals. It shouldn't surprise us that God remains faithful to His guide, however faithless we are to it; or that He won't change His mind just because we can't make up ours!

⌘   ⌘   ⌘   ⌘   ⌘   ⌘

Subject Idea:	Revelation
Scripture:	James 1:22-25
Visual Item:	Hand-held or full-length mirror
Truth Stressed:	God reveals our true nature by comparing it with His word.
Procedure:	Ask how many use a mirror every single day; what do they look at first when they view themselves?—get a few ideas from the

congregation. Note that the purpose of a mirror is to reveal what is, not what we'd like to see there.

Applications:

1. When we consult the Bible, it mirrors what we are. It never lies about us. It honestly and daringly reflects reality about us, to us. That's why many people won't read the Bible; they don't want to face themselves. So they decide to find something less judgmental and more tolerant as the basis of their behavior. And there are plenty of authorities to assure us that we're really all right.

2. If we looked in a mirror and saw a cowlick in our hair, we'd eliminate it. If we saw food between our teeth, we'd reach for the dental floss. We know that the mirror doesn't lie; it shows what is, what others see when they look—whether our clothes match or clash or if we have lipstick on our cheek. Yet, when we read in God's word that lust is wrong, many critique Jesus for being a prude; or that we should forgive, many say Jesus never had the attacks against him they have to endure; or that he is the only way to God, many call him judgmental and narrow. Amazing that we can take the mirror's revelation of our face and body so seriously, but give short shrift to the Bible's description of our lost soul!

3. The Bible doesn't offer a fun-house mirror, enlarging small and shrinking big things, burlesquing reality. When it calls certain behavior sinful, our calling it commendable won't change God's judgment on it.

4. We owe our souls the same respect we give our body when the mirror shows imperfections we can correct. And while we can wear a mask to hide our real face, no mask hides us when we come before God's word. Our only wise recourse is to accept the Bible's evaluation of ourselves and repent of any spiritual imperfection. God forgives any sin that's accepted and confessed as sin!

5. Our mirror remains the final authority before we leave the house. We may consult it a dozen times between the time we start preparing to meet the day and when we leave for work. And almost the last thing we do before leaving the

bathroom—or house if we have a hall mirror—is to take one last look: are we ready to go? The Bible offers us the opportunity to check our lives constantly by looking into its truth. It never fails to reveal whether or not we're ready to meet the world as God's people.

6. The Bible knows us as we are, not as we like to think we are. Easily able to deceive ourselves, we find it impossible to fool God. Like looking in a mirror and ignoring everything it shows about our personal appearance, we can look in the Bible and ignore everything it says about our spiritual life. The difference: ignoring the mirror's revelation may raise a few titters or belly laughs from others. Ignoring the Bible's revelation will certainly, definitely and absolutely damn our souls. We should certainly not be so simple as to care what a mirror tells about our body but unconcerned what the Bible declares about our soul!

⌘   ⌘   ⌘   ⌘   ⌘   ⌘

Subject Idea: Warnings

Scripture: Genesis 2:16-17; Deuteronomy 30:16, 19

Visual Item: Empty bottle with poison label on it (get one large enough to see)

Truth Stressed: The Bible warns us to avoid dangers to our soul.

Procedure: Show the bottle; the purpose of the skull and crossbones is to identify the danger in the bottle.

Applications:

1. No sane person will intentionally ingest poison. We intentionally keep such potions out of harm's way if we have small children because they don't know the difference. It doesn't occur to us that we're being intolerant or judgmental when we refuse to let our loved ones or ourselves drink or eat anything poisonous. It just makes

good sense; we don't want them or ourselves deathly ill or dead! Yet, when God warns us that certain behaviors weaken or destroy our spiritual life, many think Him unfairly intolerant or judgmental.

2. Manufacturers know that poisons can be useful in eliminating parasites and predators, but only when used according to specifications. Any other use nullifies the poison's positives and increases its negatives. Sin is different: it has no positive value. It's always destructive, harmful, debilitating and damning. There never was such a thing as a "positive" sin. We deceive ourselves into thinking there might be, or we say that our sin isn't as bad as someone else's. But God says nothing good about any sin and condemns all sin!

3. Little sympathy would be shown the adult who knowingly swallowed poison. In fact, we'd consider him out of his mind. Should a child swallow or eat something fatal, we consider the parents out of their minds to make the child so vulnerable. Yet, how often parents refuse to distance themselves personally from behavior the Bible calls sinful and damnable. Then, adding to their guilt, they encourage their children's involvement in the same sinful behavior! Bad habits and sinful lifestyle patterns are *absorbed* by children, caught by merely seeing them in the parents.

4. While few parents are ever guilty of endangering their children's bodies with poisons, multiplied numbers inadvertently expose them to Satan's lies. The parents say they won't make any religious decisions for the child; he can make his own decisions when he's responsible! Would they leave rat poison on the kitchen table? Would they leave Liquid-Plummer on the kitchen counter, open and ready to pour? Yet they'll offer no religious instruction to their child, trusting him to know the difference between true and false religious teaching, though he doesn't know the difference between acceptable foodstuffs and deadly toxins?

CHURCH

From the Father's eternal fellowship with His Son we derive our instinctive longing for fellowship with other humans. From the time He called the Hebrews from Egypt, God's sacred assembly became the expression of Himself to a world longing for belonging! The following illustrations show examples of Christians committing themselves first to Jesus, then to the church He established, proving that we're adopted into God's ongoing family when we're born again.

Subject Idea: Service

Scripture: I Corinthians 12:12-27

Visual Item: Puzzle completed minus several pieces

Truth Stressed: Nonfunctioning Christians create holes in the church's life.

Procedure: Show the incomplete puzzle. Can they identify the puzzle without the missing pieces? Even though they can, is the puzzle complete?

Applications:

1. The church, like the puzzle, is complete only with all the pieces in place. True, we see the picture without the missing pieces, as people can tell what the church is without all the members sharing in its ministry, but neither the puzzle nor the church is complete until every piece/member fits.

2. Note that the removal of any piece, not just an "essential" piece, renders the puzzle incomplete. We could understand the loss if such "skill" people as the church pastor, youth director or choir director left, but we're tempted to consider the loss of other workers irrelevant. Yet, visitors see the facilities and grounds—the church's public persona—long before the personnel. How essential, then, is the church custodian? Visitors immediately notice sights the habitual attender no longer "sees"—peeling or faded paint, worn carpet, frayed chairs

and pews. How essential to the church's witness, then, is the building and grounds committee? So manicured lawns and dust-free furniture are as "essential" in getting a visitor's attention as the worship service or youth program in keeping it.

3. Christian service exalts utility, not vanity; reciprocity, not competition. And it's often the "irrelevant" thing that's well or poorly done that impresses or alienates the visitor.

4. Any member responsible for a ministry is an essential piece of the church's puzzle. If it isn't done in a timely, attractive, positive way, to that extent the church is incomplete. Any non-participating member leaves a hole in the church's profile that shouts its absence to the viewer. Count on it, that *hole*, to which most in the membership have grown habituated, is the very lack the visitor sees first, whether it's a non-existent youth program or unfriendly greeters.

⌘   ⌘   ⌘   ⌘   ⌘   ⌘

Subject Idea:	Fellowship
Scripture:	Ecclesiastes 4:12
Visual Item:	A number of popsicle sticks
Truth Stressed:	Christians are strong when united.
Procedure:	Have someone come to the pulpit. Hand him a popsicle stick and ask him to break it. Then put three to four sticks together and ask the same.

Applications:

1. Where the lone Christian, like a single popsicle stick, is liable to break under stress, Christians united in a cause resist breakage—the greater the number united, the more resistant to fracture. The reason is that individual Christians, like each stick, naturally borrow strength from the next, leaning on and against it, defying the outside force.

2. Though spiritual intimacy is feared by many Christians, the more involved with other believers we are, the better our chances of thriving in Christ. We need to lean on each other, retaining contact with the power base that consists of the total number of individuals involved in a combined effort. The intimacy necessary cannot and need not be forced. By sharing general knowledge, information and experiences, people grow into sharing private details. Intimacy that occurs naturally and gradually develops its own life in the body.

3. Christians need to make a practice of associating with those who strengthen their convictions, enlighten their understanding, deepen their faith and reinforce Christ's likeness. As weak as we are individually, as a *church* we're spiritually potent.

4. Value those occasions of fellowship as desert travelers prize oases, as Arctic explorers a fire. And always delight in reaching upward, above ourselves, to a brother or sister who's better informed or more mature. From such encounters we emerge better disciples.

5. The Christian who removes himself from the fellowship of believers—through pique, indifference or sin—soon finds himself like a single popsicle stick and as soon broken spiritually. Together we're practically invulnerable. Separate we're absolutely helpless. God designed it this way, knowing that making each person a kingdom to himself would ultimately be fatal to the whole body.

⌘   ⌘   ⌘   ⌘   ⌘   ⌘

Subject Idea: Support

Scripture: Galatians 6:2

Visual Item: Car jack

Truth Stressed: Christians need to lift each other in time of need.

Procedure: Show the jack. As you turn it, explain that hydraulics allow it to lift a car many times its weight.

Applications:

1. Every believer experiences difficulties that threaten to flatten spiritual resolve or convictions. In those difficult times, other Christians need to get under and lift their fallen compatriot, offering encouragement, actions, prayers, etc.

2. This can occasionally become financially expensive and time-intensive. Nevertheless, God expects His people to react quickly, generously and, if necessary, sacrificially to help a brother or sister temporarily threatened by misfortune. "I'm here for you" is a theme every church needs to advertise, rehearse and perseveringly perfect. No Christian or church is weaker for helping another be stronger; or lesser for helping another be greater.

3. This implies that each Christian carries his own burdens as far as possible: that's personal responsibility. He then seeks assistance when he can go no further: that's corporate opportunity. Further, this mutual borrowing implies a common equality: all who now loan will eventually need strength, encouragement, resolution, money, etc.

4. Only pride keeps the presently weak Christian from admitting need; only self-centeredness will keep the presently strong Christian from offering help. Neither pride nor egotism belongs in the church where human need is always so obvious and Christ's mercy so plentiful.

5. The symbiosis of the body of Christ leads to spiritual synergism. Dissimilar personalities as we are, we live together for the good of Christ and find our combined efforts significantly greater than all of us could achieve working alone.

⌘ ⌘ ⌘ ⌘ ⌘ ⌘

Subject Idea:	Teamwork
Scripture:	Romans 16:1-2, 12-13
Visual Item:	A length of rope
Truth Stressed:	Uniting their energies gives Christians almost invincible strength.
Procedure:	Bring up a young person you can beat and play Tug-O-War with him. Then ask five to seven men, women and older youth to come forward. Ask the audience if you could win the tug against so many.

Applications:

1. Satan loves to separate individual Christians from the body of believers. That gives him a premiere opportunity to overcome us. Sadly, many Christians, through another believer's offense or difference of opinion, stop attending services and Bible studies. All they see is the offense caused by another, not the spiritual danger to which they expose themselves by separating from the body.

2. If, despite differences in dispositions, age and spiritual growth, we remain united, even our distinctions strengthen the church's witness. It proves that, different as we are, we're nevertheless together in a cause greater than all our personal goals.

3. Since wolves thrive only as active members of the pack in killing prey large enough to survive, the lone wolf is soon the dead wolf. Spiritually, the lone wolf, who declares his independence of the body of believers, unknowingly advertises his weakness to Satan, who finds him small enough to snatch and swallow.

⌘　⌘　⌘　⌘　⌘　⌘

Subject Idea:	Health
Scripture:	Galatians 5:19-23
Visual Item:	A variety of fruit, some from tropical climates

Truth Stressed: Spiritual growth occurs only in a spiritual environment.

Procedure: Show an apple, a pineapple, a banana, an orange and an apricot. Ask what environment is necessary to significant growth. Ask what would happen to an orange tree in Boston or an apple tree in Phoenix.

Applications:

1. Church leadership often plans and works for growth but forgets to create an environment where spiritual and numerical growth occurs.

2. We can manufacture an artificial environment to grow fruits and vegetables: an orange might grow in the Arctic, but only in an expensive hothouse. Even then, the resulting fruit would be unimpressive. Church leaders can't create an artificial environment for growth. If it doesn't occur naturally by the work of the Holy Spirit in the body, no lasting spiritual fruit develops there.

3. If the growth projected by leaders doesn't occur, they need to determine what in church life prevents it; since spiritual growth naturally occurs where the Holy Spirit rules, what work of the flesh has interfered? This demands painful, honest introspection and a willingness to remove whatever obstacle stands in the way. This is often so difficult that leaders make excuses instead of taking action, since some well-liked, generous, powerful person will be offended. So the church body withers as a spiritual garden because the church's husbandmen choose to tolerate instead of uprooting the fleshy plants.

4. Growth occurs in any declining or plateauing church if certain attitudes, procedures, traditions, etc. are altered or removed. But by making a decision not to act against the restraining factors, leaders let the church fail by inaction; in essence, by default!

5. Put grapes in the Arctic and apples in the Mojave Desert if you want work without reward and effort frustrated by failure. In many churches where pastors preach good sermons, consistently visit the sick and shut-ins, make evangelistic and pastoral calls and counsel and teach, little

growth occurs because they haven't changed the environment that limits growth. It's never easy to remove those barricades, but it's that or perish.

6.   Unity, love, faith, holiness, joy, etc. always produce spiritual results, even without fantastic campaigns. But the most powerfully financed, meticulously planned campaigns won't produce spiritual growth where envy, strife, deceit, immorality, etc. grow uncontrolled.

Subject Idea:	Resources
Scripture:	Matthew 14:16
Visual Item:	Loaf of bread, preferably French
Truth Stressed:	God meets human needs through His people.
Procedure:	Show loaf; explain that the loaves Jesus used were much smaller, yet he fed 8,000-15,000 people on at least two occasions. Ask if anyone in the service would try to feed the congregation with that loaf. Why not?

Applications:

1.   We can hold this loaf and give only a bite to a few, not their fill to all because the loaf is the creation of the baker, and we have no power to extend it. We can share what exists here, but we can't increase what's here.

2.   The loaves in Jesus' hands, however, were extensions of himself, whose resources excelled need with a superfluity of excess. Because he possessed the power to multiply any commodity from within his unsearchable reserves, the demand exhausted itself while the supply continued to grow. After the feedings, and everyone ate all he could, the disciples gathered twelve and seven basketfuls *left over*, unused, uneaten, ready to serve others!

3.   Spiritually, the church as a body of believers can feed any number of people who come to us looking for God. As Jesus told the disciples, the people don't need to go away from us with their spiritual needs unmet, shortchanged or disappointed.

4.   As God's Christ, Jesus fed the multitudes. As servants of
     God's Christ, we can continue to feed them spiritually—
     which was the real meaning of the miracle—and never
     suffer diminution in our personal or corporate spiritual
     provisions.

5.   Can the church meet all the demands placed on it? All the
     human needs clamoring for help? All the exhausting
     labors demanded by ever-increasing causes? Yes, if as in-
     dividuals and congregations we access God's limitless
     spiritual supply. The Christ who gave bread to the crowds
     lives in his people to feed the spiritually hungry until
     they're full. And, by way of extension, to minister to
     many other needs. If we offer him our small spiritual
     store, he multiplies it by his infinite ingenuity into an
     unimaginable hoard. Our successes will completely
     eclipse our failures; our assets will vastly outweigh our li-
     abilities.

DISCIPLESHIP

Forgiveness of sin involves two procedures: self-denial and discipleship. Self-denial is the radical surgery that eliminates our metastasized spiritual cancer. Discipleship is the spiritual nourishment afterwards. Without the surgery, we'll die; without the nourishment, we'll not recover. May the following illustrations enlarge our appreciation of life in God's Son.

Subject Idea: Faithfulness

Scripture: John 15:5

Visual Item: A living plant with developed branches and leaves

Truth Stressed: Obedient faith is essential to continued spiritual life.

Procedure: Show the living plant. Pinch off an assortment of branches, leaves and/or flowers. Stress that, while life continues in the plant, the severed branches, leaves and flowers have already died, even as they show apparent life.

Applications:

1. As the severed branches have lost the ability to reproduce the fruit of the plant, disobedience destroys ability to reproduce the Christ-life. Still, Jesus, the church and the Christian faith continue if we remove ourselves from them.

2. A leaf lately broken off retains the appearance of life, but that's deceptive, for all life has been withdrawn from it. It's really dead on the spot because only as life continually flows from the plant do the branches live. Sooner or later, in this case much sooner, it will be obvious that these branches died with their severance from the plant.

3. People can sometimes retain the appearance of spiritual life—worship attendance, tithing, teaching—long after they've died inside through disobedience. A crisis in their life will occur, and they'll stop attending, stop giving, stop

praying, etc. And people will wonder why they suddenly stopped? They didn't "suddenly." They've been spiritually dead awhile or a long time, and it took only the crisis to prove it.

4. Remaining actively obedient to Jesus isn't just one of the options Christians have, a convenient alternative *we* choose to exercise. It's essential to our continued discipleship, the only way to remain alive in Christ.

⌘　⌘　⌘　⌘　⌘　⌘

Subject Idea:	Grace
Scripture:	Romans 1:7; 3:24
Visual Item:	Foot pump; Shop-Vac; two twin- or full-sized air mattresses
Truth Stressed:	Grace alone offers the peace with God that so many seek.
Procedure:	Have two people with you, one to begin pumping the mattress with the foot pump, the other using the Shop-Vac on the second mattress. When Shop-Vac mattress is finished, have the other stop.

Applications:

1. The foot pump represents human efforts to find peace with God. The Shop-Vac represents the grace Christ gives each Christian—with this caveat: we can't use human efforts and do it at all.

2. In one sense, while we can eventually pump up an air mattress using a foot pump, we can't pump up the Christian life by any method we use. That comes only through the Holy Spirit.

3. We can spend our life seeking forgiveness of sin and peace with God and never find it. Or we can at the outset accept Christ's offer of forgiveness through grace, then spend the rest of life exhausting ourselves in his service. In the end, the former way leaves us prostrate, without

fulfillment. The latter way leaves us constantly refreshed, whatever energy we expend in Christ's service.

⌘   ⌘   ⌘   ⌘   ⌘   ⌘

Subject Idea:	Genuineness
Scripture:	Isaiah 40:25-26
Visual Item:	Doll and real baby
Truth Stressed:	The cost of knowing the true God is repaid by belonging to Him.
Procedure:	Show both doll and baby to the audience. Point out that the doll looks like the baby in every visible way, but the doll is only virtual reality, manufactured to be a possession.

Applications:

1. While no responsible person fails to distinguish the real baby from the doll, many people have little ability to distinguish the apparent from the real God. Bible illiteracy always begets that inability. Therefore, Bible literacy can eliminate it.

2. Only a baby would choose a doll over another baby to hold and enjoy—because the baby can handle the doll. Many people want a god they can handle—something to be a pet, not a threat; something less so they can be boss.

3. As only the living child can respond to our affection and care, only the living God can meet our needs and exceed our expectations. We may wait a few months to feel a real baby's love, but the first time he hugs our neck and says, "I wuv you," ecstasy will eclipse all the effort. But how long will it take the doll to wrap its arms around us and say those words? The many gods to which people give themselves will fail them in crises; count on it. And we'll rue our foolishness in following a god who didn't cost us much. But the real God will be there, just when

we need Him most, and we'll know He's been worth the price we paid to believe in and follow Him!

⌘   ⌘   ⌘   ⌘   ⌘   ⌘

Subject Idea: Influence
Scripture: Matthew 5:13
Visual Item: Full salt shaker
Truth Stressed: Christians must share themselves with the unsaved to influence them.
Procedure: Show salt shaker. What is it? The looks indicate a salt shaker. The only way to know for sure is to shake some out and have a taste of it.

Applications:

1. Since Christianity works only when activated, Christians must share their faith. We instinctively keep the influence of faith inside the body of believers when it fulfills its purpose only by getting into the lives of unbelievers. We spend significant amounts of time declaring to each other that we *can* preserve and flavor life, but too little time proving it. Only when distributed does salt work; only when shared with others will Christianity influence them.

2. As salt loses its flavor only by being diluted, not used, Christian faith can be weakened only by diluting it with the world, never by sharing its full strength with the lost.

3. Sprinkle a little salt: encourage Christians to do the same with their faith wherever they can. Emphasize that the effort to share faith, not success in doing it, is the essence of our task. We can't always do all we want with people. Their resistance or shortcomings may limit the amount of witness we shake into their lives. Shake what we can, when we can.

⌘   ⌘   ⌘   ⌘   ⌘   ⌘

Subject Idea: Reproduction

Scripture: Galatians 5:22-23

Visual Item: Apple seeds and apple

Truth Stressed: Christianity has the native ability to reproduce itself in each generation.

Procedure: Show a seed: see how small. Show an apple: see that seed's small fruit.

Applications:

1. It's inherently possible for Christianity to thrive, not just survive, in every generation. As a single seed produces an apple tree full of apples, all of which have many seeds to produce more apples, each Christian potentially can reproduce himself in many other lives. If our spiritual family tree were drawn, how large a Christian family would we have produced?

2. As fruit proves the seed's identity, Christians have particular traits that characterize them. Anyone can tell if we're really Christians by examining our fruit. Do we produce the Spirit's fruit?

3. If the seed boasts of being an apple seed, it better produce apples; if we boast of a personal relationship with Jesus, we better be Christ-like.

4. It's impossible for an apple seed to produce a peach; nature works in endless harmony with God's principle: after its own kind. To make the point, let's say that an apple seed produces a peach. We would say either the seed lied about its real identity or was confused about its real identity.

5. Sometimes Christians advertise, but can't deliver their faith. One of three problems has occurred. Either they don't know exactly what Christianity is to be; or they want to please Christ but find the flesh intruding; or they know very well and don't care.

6. Confusion can be corrected by education and experience. Inconsistency can be overcome by persistent effort and prayer. Unconcern can be cured only by repentance and, if necessary, re-conversion to Christ.

⌘　⌘　⌘　⌘　⌘　⌘

Subject Idea: Renewal

Scripture: II Corinthians 12:5

Visual Item: Plastic gallon milk jug

Truth Stressed: God can use and re-use any person whatever his condition, problem or limitation.

Procedure: As you crush the milk jug, talk about the factors in life that can harm and render us apparently useless to self, others and God. Then blow forcefully into the jug and see it resume most of its former shape.

Applications:

1. Like breath blown into the collapsed jug, God's grace renews human life. We can't keep life from battering us out of shape; whether we collapse or return to normal depends on our response. God gives victory over life if we let His grace influence setbacks, difficulties and obstacles.

2. The jar filled up gradually as I blew into it, representing our recovery from adversity. But not to worry: much good work and many great successes can be done in bits and pieces. The key is to maintain our spiritual momentum.

3. Note that the jar isn't quite as perfect as before the crushing. It has lines and dents from its ordeal. Nevertheless, it still holds milk. It isn't unexpected that we suffer lasting effects from our run-in with life. But we must not be defeated by the effects since they are only effects, not the presence of the confrontation. Scarred and wrinkled we may be, but we shall carry on for Christ!

4. The last excuse we want to make for not recovering is that we won't be as perfect as we were before the affliction. We can't subscribe to the excuse, "since I can't give my best, I won't give anything: since I'm not perfect, I'm not usable." Christ's grace majors in victories using previously defeated, hurt, demeaned people!

⌘   ⌘   ⌘   ⌘   ⌘   ⌘

Subject Idea: Maturity
Scripture: Philippians 3: 12; II Peter 1:5-7
Visual Item: Puzzle
Truth Stressed: Growing into a mature disciple takes time,
                effort and energy.
Procedure: Spread puzzle pieces in view of the people
                (perhaps a communion table if it wouldn't
                offend anyone). Stress that the puzzle goes
                in place one piece at a time. Even if several
                work on it, the procedure is the same.

Applications:

1. As maturity is the goal of discipleship, persistence is the process of attaining it. Only through the process is the goal achieved.

2. Maturity takes time and planning as puzzles take time and planning. As we don't get a puzzle together by throwing the pieces on a table, we don't become mature without working a plan.

3. Prayer, Bible study, fellowship, worship, tithing and witnessing, *et al.,* are all essentials of the process. Christians anxious for maturity without the effort necessary to achieve it are invariably disappointed with Jesus. The trouble isn't in the expectation, but in the timing. Satisfaction with Christ always occurs if we perseveringly pursue his teachings; if we understand that contentment and progress come in stages.

4. The puzzle manufacturer knows what the finished project looks like. God knows exactly what He wants from each of us and what we can become if we take the time to "put it all together."

5. We should never discard any piece God asks us to put into life, thinking that without it we can make quicker, greater "progress." Take whatever step God requires; put into place whatever virtue He requires; abolish whatever vice; patiently accept any divine refusal; quickly follow any divine leading. We never know how *that* particular step, or piece, or reaction will interpret and decipher the next

step or how it may make the next step possible and activate other steps beyond it.

⌘   ⌘   ⌘   ⌘   ⌘   ⌘

Subject Idea: Perseverance
Scripture: Matthew 13:8, 23
Visual Item: Badminton racquet and shuttlecock
Truth Stressed: Following through is as necessary as initial commitment to discipleship.
Procedure: Hit shuttlecock from waist, using wrist action. Hit from shoulder, using wrist action. Throw shuttlecock into the air and swing with complete follow-through.

Applications:

1. As accuracy in badminton depends on placement of the birdie and follow-through with the racquet, persevering in discipleship eliminates many errors in judgment, mistakes, failures and sins.

2. In fact, though we often begin our Christian walk with inferior understanding and impure motives, perseveringly learning of Christ helps us finish strongly.

3. The disciple has to be an investor, not a speculator in the Christian life: to stay in when times are bad; to retain spiritual values when they're out of favor in society; to remain faithful though zeal decreases and grace diminishes; to be confident though no return seems possible.

4. As a marathon soon exhausts the sprinter, the life-long nature of discipleship discourages the religious profiteer. Sometimes only by concentrating on ultimate profits can we absorb present losses associated with the Christ-life.

⌘   ⌘   ⌘   ⌘   ⌘   ⌘

Subject Idea:	Originality
Scripture:	John 9:25
Visual Item:	Box of instant potatoes; box of Minute Rice; Whole potato; cup of ucooked wild brown rice
Truth Stressed:	A quality, in-depth personal relationship with Christ takes times to develop.
Procedure:	Ask the audience what it would rather eat, given the time to enjoy a meal: the real item or the real item reduced to convenience?

Applications:

1. As a restaurant that starts from scratch in preparing will take longer to serve your meal than one that begins with pre-cooked foods—even a hamburger freshly flame-broiled will taste better than one lifted from the steamer tray in which pre-cooked ones are stashed—developing a quality Christ-likeness takes more time than a superficial faith.

2. There's a distinctive excellence to Christ-likeness that only time can produce. While we may get something comparable to Christ-likeness without that time investment, the "taste test" proves the difference.

3. There may be some products on the market, but I haven't found instant *anything* that retains all the flavors and freshness of the original, for a simple reason: the instant removes from the original the ingredients that demand time to develop. In oatmeal, the husk; in wheat, the germ; in rice, the polishing. Blandness results in the pre-chewed, pre-digested variety.

4. Christian faith must be a real, personal experience between us and Christ. All that we learn from others must be filtered through our own life's experiences before we can truly say, "I know." Otherwise it's often, "I know because someone told me"—always an essential to Christian life since we need teachers. But being able to say, "I know because what someone told me I've discovered in my personal walk" is ultimately necessary.

5. Understand that what another person says can be wrong. And what we experience, based on what he says, can be wrong. Nonetheless, real Christianity demands an original encounter with Jesus in each life.

⌘   ⌘   ⌘   ⌘   ⌘   ⌘

Subject Idea: Excellence

Scripture: Acts 1:8

Visual Item: New Nike/Reebok, etc. sneakers; Levi's, etc. jeans; Rave hair spray

Truth Stressed: Being imprinted with Christ's name should motivate our growth towards the perfection he demonstrated.

Procedure: Mention a brand name and ask audience to identify mentally each with a product. Then show the product most often associated with the name.

Applications:

1. Manufacturers each want us to wear their product since it's their greatest advertisement. Jesus wants his people to be his best advertisement.

2. Manufacturers have a major advantage over Christ. Before we buy their product, it's already gone through strict testing and quality control checks. Any incomplete, flawed product is withdrawn and discarded—or sold as advertised seconds. Only the manufacturers' best gets to retail store shelves. They know the value of selling only the perfected product.

3. Jesus, however, sees his name worn and symbols of faith in him paraded before a watching public by hopelessly inadequate examples. His perfection, filtered through flawed human instruments, hardly ever resembles his true nature! Sometimes it's a base caricature of him. At best Christ's product—spiritual renewal in human life—is constantly in the process of being improved, and only improved, never perfected!

4. Since church leaders exercise little spiritual quality control, almost any behavior is tolerated in the members, even gross immorality, a misbehavior the apostle Paul warned must not be tolerated in the body of Christ. And that says nothing of "lesser" sins he says must be disciplined: greed, divisiveness, laziness. Without supervision from those responsible for church quality control, almost any activity or behavior similar to or purporting to be Christian is allowed in church fellowship and in public under church sponsorship.

5. To assure membership *development* in Christ-likeness, church leaders must be in personal contact with the members, inquiring into their spiritual walk, offering assistance when they fail, despite trying to succeed and imposing discipline when they're impenitent.

6. Jesus offers a grace no secular company can afford: where flawed products are discarded, flawed Christians are merely rebuked and encouraged to grow. God doesn't discard people: He changes them. Only if we refuse to be changed will He discard us.

⌘   ⌘   ⌘   ⌘   ⌘   ⌘

Subject Idea: Lordship

Scripture: Mark 1:16-20

Visual Item: TV remote control

Truth Stressed: We determine Christ's lordship of life.

Procedure: Show the remote. Ask whether the husband or the wife generally controls it while you're watching TV together. Ask how many women surf the channels during breaks; why not? How many men do it; why?

Applications:

1. The remote represents our will, our ego, our ambition, our morals, our future plans, etc. Who has control of our will, ego, ambition, morals, plans, etc.? Do we, or does Christ?

2. God has given each person free will; while theoretically dying to self-will before baptism, Christians necessarily retain the right to free will after baptism. The danger of free will is that we'll exercise it in self-willed ways, an awesome, God-given privilege and responsibility.

3. As independent humans, Christians *can* exercise free will in self-willed ways. But, remembering that baptism marked the difference between our old and new self, we refuse the theory of independence for the reality of obedience.

4. Have we? If Jesus wants us elsewhere than where we are, will we go? If he demands behavioral changes, will we comply? Who holds the remote in our Christian life?

5. We can rest assured if Jesus does. He'll never click us unless it's necessary and in our best interest.

EVANGELISM

More than once, after hearing a particular sermon or lesson, we've said, "I wish so and so had been here. It would have spoken to his need." Must the message perish because so and so didn't attend? Weren't we in attendance? Didn't we hear? Can't the message live on in us to reach that person? Isn't that our responsibility as Christians? The following illustrations offer a challenge to be individual Christians sharing their faith in Christ.

Subject Idea:	Communication
Scripture:	Acts 1:8; Philemon 6
Visual Item:	Hand-held or wheeled seed spreader
Truth Stressed:	Christians must broadcast Christ's good news.
Procedure:	Demonstrate the models; note that all models generously spread the seed, some under more, some under less control.

Applications:

1. Since Christianity extends God's one and only offering of forgiveness, the Bible takes evangelism for granted. The nature of faith offers no apologies for communicating it. The participles of Matthew 28:18-20, which, as Professor Mark Scott has said, have the force of a command, comprise our marching orders.

2. Unlike the one spreading seed, Christians don't always know when someone sees or hears our witness. Knowing that Paul and Silas witnessed to an unseen crowd in the unrelieved black of an inner prison challenges us to be vigilant in our lifestyle.

3. As a seed spreader can't do its work hanging on a toolshed wall, Christians can't witness by isolating themselves from their lost associates, keeping faith as a private domain. The worth of the Christian faith is seen as much in its public applications as in its private ecstasy.

4. We can still witness when we can't actually evangelize. Both concepts are necessary. As Paul and Silas proved in the Philippian cell, witnessing can be any act or attitude

that exalts Christ—the natural behavior of faith, whatever the circumstances; all that God requires, but the least that God asks. Evangelism is verbalized witnessing—the reason behind the example; the motivation behind the behavior. While evangelism can occur only when the subject is ready to receive it, witnessing can be offered to anyone listening and watching, whether favorable or hostile to Christ and whatever the spiritual disposition.

5. Sowing is the farmer's or gardener's last task. A lot of previous work prepares the soil. Christians need to be wise spiritual husbandmen, cultivating the people we hope our witness can open to evangelism.

6. The amount of seed sown determines the size of the harvest. The number of Christians involved in active witnessing and evangelism determines the number of unsaved people reached.

7. Both witnessing and evangelism are pro- , not re-active. They're inoculants against the initial presence of sin rather than antibiotics curing the infection. Churches that emphasize the *recovery* of sinners are more proactive in witnessing and evangelism than those majoring in children's homes, housing for the homeless, jail ministries, etc. Both are necessary because most churches aren't majoring in witnessing and evangelism. The latter would be less necessary if the former were assiduously practiced.

⌘ ⌘ ⌘ ⌘ ⌘ ⌘

Subject Idea:	Effects
Scripture:	John 4:28-30
Visual Item:	Candles with splatter guard; matches
Truth Stressed:	Our combined witness turns a small into a blazing light.
Procedure:	Previously contact the person who controls the lights. Also give every person a candle and a match to one at the end of each row.

>At your word have all lights in the assembly darkened.

Applications:

1. Light your candle. Note the amazing amount of light it casts. The one candle diminishes the darkness enough for us to evacuate the sanctuary by its light alone. We wouldn't be stumbling over objects on the floor or bumping into each other as we left.

2. Have the person at the end of each row light his candle, then have that candle light the next, each person lighting the one next until every candle in the sanctuary is aflame. (Be sure to use splash guards to keep wax off the pews and floor. You also may need to extinguish all the candles before proceeding.)

3. The light from one candle spread like a wave across the sanctuary, growing brighter with each lighting until a strong illumination occurred. A person would necessarily be blind not to see in this light.

4. Our personal influence may be limited, but it isn't non-existent. That's why we need to offer a positive model of our faith. True: our personal experience isn't all Jesus has to prove his reality. If that were so, only as we proved Christianity would it be true. The Christian faith is based on Christ's victorious life, not on any individual's belief or rejection. Since Christ works with individuals, however, what happens to us is important to others. Our personal experience may not amount to much, but it's the fact of the change, not its magnitude, that matters.

5. The distinctive nature of light means that darkness yields to it, not vice-versa. Only by having a light dim or extinguished can darkness reign; otherwise darkness diminishes, however gradually, before the light. Christians need to express their light wherever possible. Spiritual darkness is scary, dangerous and contrary to God's will. When Jesus came, his personality shined a light that *banished* the darkness in people's lives. If darkness had been acceptable, Jesus wouldn't have had to shine his light. If any previous light had been sufficient to banish the darkness, Jesus wouldn't have had to shine his light. If living without God had been acceptable, Jesus

wouldn't have had to shine his light. He died as a necessity, not as a convenience. Therefore, Christians, let's shine our light for Jesus! Wherever we do, life ameliorates, relationships improve, terrors flee.

6.   As darkness is dangerous to any sighted person, spiritual darkness is dangerous to all persons. Blind people can survive in a world of light because those who see minimize and eliminate obstacles that otherwise endanger them. Just so, many who want to be spiritually blind retain moral lives because the spiritually-sighted make it possible. The presence of believers keeps skeptics and atheists from paying the penalty their spiritual darkness would inevitably impose on them.

7.   As it's the nature of a candle to shine, it's the nature of the Christian life to illuminate both the believer and anyone he influences. We need to be very sure that we *do* illuminate, not further darken life. That what we cast before others is a reason to see, not an excuse to deny God. As living our faith always enlightens, failing our faith invariably destroys any light we try to create.

8.   Jesus didn't say we needed to be a majority before we shine for him. Each Christian assumes the role of lamplighter; he shines his light—his experience—in every possible way. However, Jesus didn't leave us alone to shine for him. As our united lighting of the candles proved, we're together in the endeavor. We're one person, yet we're only one of many and never alone in carrying Christ's torch. Our united effort has great value and can't be denied, it's so strong. And that offers a provocative reason we need to be consistent in our shining. Not only does our small victory make a difference, it may make another person's victory possible. That's why we must never refuse to shine when commanded or fail to shine, given the opportunity. We never know what unsaved person might be looking for a light, and we never know how our light can give another Christian courage to shine his. And, wonder of wonders, we can never know how our witness, though rejected, can make another Christian's successful with the same person!

More than one Christian has reaped the benefit of another Christian's efforts!

⌘   ⌘   ⌘   ⌘   ⌘   ⌘

Subject Idea: Invitation

Scripture: John 1:45-46

Visual Item: Luminary bag (a fireproof paper bag, used often at Halloween and Christmas, decorated with the season's motif, with slits or hole into which sand or rocks are put to provide stability and to hold a lighted candle; often placed along sidewalks to offer a sprightly invitation to guests approaching the house from garage or street.)

Truth Stressed: The Christian life invites the lost to Jesus.

Procedure: Set the candle inside the bag, anchored by sand. Light it. (Dim the sanctuary lights if possible.)

Applications:

1.   "Come and see Jesus" should be the motto of the Christian life. That's the least we have to offer. Our example should be an invitation for people to accept him personally. In fact, we should make it practically impossible for people not to accept Jesus. As nothing in any literature, sacred or secular, says so emphatically and so well what the Bible says about God in Christ, nothing in life suggests anything comparable to the life Jesus saves from sin and for righteousness.

2.   The candle doesn't offer much light; really, it offers a festive welcome more than illumination. And our personal light, while only a dim reflection of Christ's blinding light, nevertheless must offer a joy that hints of ecstasy!

3.   Sometimes the only invitation we can offer people is to "come and see" by attending church services or a small

group meeting or a special program. Not open to evangelism, our friends might be open to a non-threatening, no-obligation special occasion. We need to enter whatever opening people offer, rather than break down their closed doors!

4.   The sand or stones offer a symbol of the reason we *can* invite people to Christ. We possess an attractive stability, maturity and direction. We can personally be light-hearted and pleasant, while being deadly earnest about our faith. While we laugh, joke and enjoy life, our purpose is serious, and our confidence is contagious. We believe strongly what God teaches; we refuse to be carried away by every new teaching heard. Our society isn't any different from Athenian life: people still want to hear the latest teaching, to see if it's superior to the old. People who don't want God manage never to find Him; to avoid Him, they *seek* Him as an excuse never to *find*! We're not deceived; nothing is superior to God in Christ. Having found Them, we'll never surrender Them.

5.   God puts the best of Himself in us so we can show the best of ourselves to the unsaved, a living illustration of Christ's life—visible, inviting investigation, welcoming seekers, and so incomparably winsome the unsaved want Jesus, too. By living inside God's will and outside accepted societal patterns, we express an attractive, optimistic eccentricity that appeals! That's the Christian life: the life of Christ in his people. Right here. Right now. In us. Exposing his grace to the unsaved. And, like the United States Constitution, despite its flaws, the world has never seen any life better than the Christian life. Nothing, anywhere!

6.   If we don't learn about Jesus, we'll lose our soul. If we learn about Jesus, but don't transmit his message, others will lose theirs. And what a waste either way when Jesus Christ can save everyone absolutely and completely, all sins forgiven, none retained; all grace extended, none withheld!

7.   Jesus had but twelve Apostles and no more. But at the foot of the cross he has room for all his disciples, and to

each disciple he gives the same overpowering grace he gave each Apostle: in the Name of Jesus Christ, conquer!

⌘　⌘　⌘　⌘　⌘　⌘

Subject Idea:	Safety
Scripture:	I John 2:17
Visual Item:	Exit signs mounted on wall in building (or bring an exit sign to the pulpit)
Truth Stressed:	Jesus offers the only escape from sin with all it portends, to forgiveness with all it promises.
Procedure:	Show your sign or have everyone look at an exit sign over each doorway into the sanctuary. Ask what one word comes to mind when they think of the sign: ESCAPE.

Applications:

1. The sign serves our interests by offering the quickest possible egress from the building in emergencies. If we don't know how to exit the building, look above any doorway here, and that's the way out. Fire department regulations demand their presence in all public buildings. They may never be used, but in case they're needed, they're essential because people can become disoriented and distracted in a crisis.

2. The Bible declares this world's thought inimical to the spiritual life and destructive of Christian values. It despises God and exalts humanity; it demeans prayer and exalts knowledge; it denies Heaven and affirms earthly existence as an end in itself. If we don't escape this world's system, we'll perish forever in Hell. This teaching is basic to Bible revelation, yet overlooked, even by many Christians. So much preaching completely overlooks this most basic of all revelation: this world is under the sentence of death, and the only escape from it is through Jesus Christ!

3. His presence is essential to our escape. It isn't enough to recognize the danger this life poses to our spiritual life; we need both to recognize the exit from it and how to access that escape. Many religions have been founded on man's desire to flee the terrors imposed by life. In consequence, they've inflicted terror in the cures they've devised: heartless executions, self-flagellations, complex rituals—all self-defeating measures that merely perpetuate the problem. The other side of the exit sign has to be safety, not equal or greater danger; security, not more uncertainty. We don't want to escape the lion only to confront the bear! We need what Jesus Christ alone provides: escape to life from death, to forgiveness from punishment, to fellowship from isolation, to meaning from absurdity. He leads us from bad to better, from better to best, from best to perfection!

4. We may never need the exit sign above our doors, but we'll need an escape from the world's values if we want to live again. Most of us go a lifetime and never seek an exit sign in a crisis, but how many escape death?

5. The light inside the sign must be on. It's against the law to have it out. In the same way, Christians can't afford not to advertise escape from the world. God demands we publicize it every possible way, keeping the unsaved alert to God's exit, should they look for it. The more ways the church can serve the community, the more ways it advertises escape from the world. God's regulations demand our active involvement in helping people understand their need to escape, not from life, but from the world system that suborns life to ungodly purposes.

⌘   ⌘   ⌘   ⌘   ⌘   ⌘

Subject Idea: Influence
Scripture: Mark 1:16-17
Visual Item: A fisherman with a tackle box
Truth Stressed: Christians need to use different methods in reaching the lost.

Procedure: Have an avid fisherman from the congregation show the different lures from his tackle box; have him explain why he uses multiple lures merely to fish.

Applications:

1.   We might wonder why fishermen invest money in different lures when fish are the only prey. Being such simple creatures that they leap at bait or a plastic lure, we might think just any worm or lure will do. Thinking that way quickly creates non-fishermen from potential recruits. Even fish have to be *attracted.*

2.   Like a fisherman failing to catch fish because he's used the wrong bait, churches often fail to attract visitors and new members because they insist on using programs and methods that please only them. Having an ownership mindset about the local church, they expect outsiders to first subscribe to their understanding of acceptable church life. Many churches seem determined to fish where *they* want to catch fish, not where the fish swim! They want the fish to come where they are, instead of going where the fish are in school. But how many fish leap into the boat?   We should give no one an excuse to refuse Jesus because we won't abandon a program we like; or intrude our frail opinions into Christ's eternal message.

3.   As no one lure works for all fish, it takes different programs to reach new people. A church needs many entry points into its fellowship: Bible studies, small groups, hosting blood banks, boy scouts, special services, musical groups, etc. While this approach will stretch our perceptions of acceptability, it can all be done without sacrificing doctrine. This means taking surveys to determine where peoples' interests lie, then designing programs to match. We may have to pay attention to their personal interests to gain their interest in Jesus—but isn't that part of being "fishers" of men? Dealing with different personalities, temperaments and interests never posed a threat to the Christ who intends to reach everybody in creation; why should it threaten us?

4.   Using different methods, interests, approaches, goals, education and careers, we can teach a singular gospel about

our Singular Lord. Knowing the people we want to reach and employing the baits and lures to which they respond, people will be caught for Jesus.

5.   Since people of similar background, education and career have vocabularies, interests and incomes, use the similarities to bridge the spiritual differences between the saved and lost. This sense of homogeneity is essential in building a diverse church; in essence, it becomes a grouping of small churches meeting in special interest groups throughout the week, then assembling in combined fellowship on Sundays.

6.   There are often enough different personalities, education and income levels in the church to reach every person in a community. Our problem isn't a lack of people, but an oversight of responsibility. If we're concerned about reaching multitudes of people, we have to know Jesus reached individuals first. That approach considers our church as an educational institution, with us as students — and we want to increase matriculation in our school!

⌘   ⌘   ⌘   ⌘   ⌘   ⌘

Subject Idea: Bible
Scripture: John 15:3
Visual Item: Can of WD-40; rusty bolt and nut
Truth Stressed: The Bible works when used in evangelism.
Procedure: From the label read some uses of WD-40. Spray the bolt and nut. In time, the oil loosens the rust so the nut can be removed.

Applications:
1.   Since the purpose of evangelism is conversion, not baptism or church membership, the tool that elicits conversion should be used. The Bible is that tool.
2.   This immediately limits the content of evangelism. We're not to answer every question people have or teach deep doctrine. We're to stress humanity's creation in God's

image; our conscious, intentional sinfulness; Christ's sacrifice to forgive; and our need to obey his summons to discipleship. Other sins find their solution in forgiveness; other questions their answers in obedience.

3. That makes God's absolutes, not our speculations, the basis of faith. Pre-Christians need to be awakened, not only to the debasement of their spirit, but to God's cure. Reading the headlines can stress the debasement. Only God's Spirit, working through the word, saves us. The word of God both convicts the sinner of his sin—like WD-40 loosening the rust—and removes it so the human spirit can once again work within God's will. No other existing force or procedure serves both purposes.

4. Since rehabilitation of the sinner begins by breaking the sinner, many settle for self-esteem—which can be built in more acceptable, less demanding ways. To quiet God's demands, they assure themselves that recapturing personal self-esteem is the holy grail of existence. People learn to confront life confidently that way, but not how to be at peace with God. The Bible teaches that salvation alone offers the forgiveness that awakens our true self-worth—a worth based on God's working on our behalf at Calvary. That many people settle for self-esteem so they don't have to pay the price of being forgiven, doesn't lessen or eliminate their need of forgiveness. Sooner or later we have to confront, not our problems, but our sinfulness before God—a liability discharged for us only by the Master's death. Only the Bible dares to tell the truth about us and to assure us of God's grace despite it.

5. If we want character, not just conformity, in our converts, expose them to Jesus Christ. See what they make of him; challenge them, if they're brave enough, to see what he will make of them. Jesus always referred interrogations to the word of God. If he thought so highly of the Old Testament, can we think less highly of the New? We can get people merely to believe a creed by teaching ritual; we get Christ-like converts only by exposing them to the Christ in his word.

⌘ ⌘ ⌘ ⌘ ⌘ ⌘

Subject Idea: Influence

Scripture: Luke 4:42-44

Visual Item: Baked potato; salt shaker

Truth Stressed: Only as Christians affiliate with the lost can we win them to Christ.

Procedure: Ask people to volunteer some food items to which they add salt. Show the potato and shaker. Put shaker beside the plate: does that add salt? Put shaker on the plate: does that? Put shaker on top of the potato: does that? Obviously, only when shaken out of the cellar does the salt function.

Applications:

1. Christians live in two environments, but not with bifurcated purposes and personalities. We have a Heaven-anchored, earth-based life, living here by the code derived from God. That calling imposes burdens non-believers don't bear and enriches us in ways they can't share.

2. We lift life wherever we share ourselves. The problem Christians have isn't in knowing their worth, but in knowing where it's to be shown. Jesus said *we* were the salt of the earth; he never said *he* was. We are, because wherever we are, we offer a testimony about Christ's life that cannot be ignored or denied. It can be rejected and brutalized, but that's a problem the unsaved, not we, have to resolve.

3. Where, then, is this influence to be felt? Not among believers in worship, study and fellowship, but in the everyday world. The salt that accumulates when believers gather is to be shaken out in all our daily relationships. Worship and study should energize our witness, not just satisfy our expectations. They equip us to serve, not just be contented with faith. Worship is what a supply depot is to an army—the place to get equipped for successful warfare.

4. A powerful and positive witness attracts and demands attention. Jesus puts his disciples across the path of skeptics and procrastinators to encourage their faith and

obedience. People can't easily ignore our witness if they see God living in us. They can't disrespect church attendance if they see us attending. He has reclaimed all that we lost, and He uses Christians to file the papers. If we can't bring ourselves to verbalize our witness, we can invite people to church services or special meetings. If we're consistent in lifestyle and excited about our church, people won't grow tired of our example or our invitations.

5.   While witnessing to the unsaved, we feel the pull of our anchor. We live in a power-hungry, pleasure-mad, possession-driven world, but we're witnesses to it, not mimics of or participants in it. We offer negatives and positives: we won't worship Caesar, but we'll pray for him; we won't accept immorality, but we'll honor marriage; we won't lust for possessions, but we'll keep less so we can give more to others. Above all, we won't insult the Christian faith by caressing it as an ancient, attenuated heirloom meant only to be collected and admired, not lived and tested — something for only Christians to appreciate and understand. Christianity fears no association with unsaved people so long as Christians keep themselves from unsaved behaviors! In that way we practice Biblical mass evangelism: being masses of believers reaching individuals.

⌘   ⌘   ⌘   ⌘   ⌘   ⌘

Subject Idea:	Representation
Scripture:	Mark 2:23-24
Visual Item:	College or professional starter jacket, jersey or cap
Truth Stressed:	Our life must positively reinforce our claims.
Procedure:	While you don the apparel, note that it symbolizes your interest in or allegiance to the team advertised.

Applications:

1. Being a fan of college or pro sports doesn't demand a particular lifestyle. Wearing the name of Jesus does. God holds us accountable for our endowment. In a larger sense, whether we don sportswear that visibly declares support for a team, Christians can't opt out of competing for Christ by saying no one needs to know we're his follower. Christianity is visible, and any attempt to seclude it diminishes the thoroughly aggressive nature of the Christian faith.

2. "Witness" tee shirts and jerseys are an agreeable way to make a statement, but they can make a negative impact if our life betrays the slogan. Any public statement in support of Jesus needs to be backed by unassailable integrity. If we wear a cross or necklace, or affix fish or slogans to our car bumper, we better discipline our lifestyle: watch our language, the way we drive, our work habits. We're never playing to empty stands. And Jesus is held accountable, innocent as he is of our wrongdoing!

3. We don't constantly wear the clothes that declare our allegiance to a team, but Jesus can't be put on and off like a jacket. He's in us and with us, as Lord of everyday life, and wants to affect all we are and do. Since Christianity offers a distinct faith, it empowers a distinctly Christ-like life. Because we wear his name, we intend to live with him and be like him. We intend to identify with him and align ourselves with anything he's taught. We'll stand with him on any stance he's taken on any subject.

4. Since we're just saved sinners but want to live again, we trust him who rose from the grave instead of anyone still dead. Since we want forgiveness, we trust him who died to save, not anyone still in sin. We know that people who don't claim to be Christians and who don't intend to become Christians, still expect those professing godliness to be holy and to express a Christ-righteousness that draws, not a Pharisaic-righteousness that alienates people.

5. We're proud to claim the NAME, we intend to possess what we advertise and to deliver what we promote. The one who gives the vessel he saves the privilege of being a

sacrifice *without* destroying the vessel deserves unreserved commitment.

⌘ ⌘ ⌘ ⌘ ⌘ ⌘

Subject Idea:	Value
Scripture:	James 5:19-20
Visual Item:	Five or six items of various worth to us: a penny, watch, ring, Bible, book, picture of pet, family pictures, pictures of son or daughter, etc.
Truth Stressed:	The value we place on people determines our effort to find them when they're lost.
Procedure:	Show whatever items you have, starting with the least to the greatest in value; conclude with the one you would go to great lengths and expense to recover.

Applications:

1. If all we owned was lost, what part of it would we go to any lengths to retrieve? From another perspective, if we had to evacuate our house within ten minutes, what would we spend time gathering? We value possessions and people by their importance to us, from particular relationship or memories shared with them. An heirloom from a grandparent can mean more than a recently purchased dress or suit. God values humanity by His distinctive relationship as Creator forming us in His image. That part of Himself in us fuels God's love for us. His nature in us made our rescue from spiritual death worth any price, even when it demanded His own Son.

2. What is the priority of our church? A building program? The budget? The youth? The music program? Worship services, etc.? Where we place our interest we invest our emphasis, time and treasure. Can any church be faithful to Christ's sacrifice that doesn't first appreciate the rescue of human beings from Hell? God cared enough to search

for us, though many of us didn't know we were lost—and some of us may still think we aren't! What interest do we have in reaching other lost people?

3. Churches substitute other activities for evangelism for various reasons: it's costly, frightening, unnecessary (There are many believers who have all the Christian friends they need and want. It isn't that more aren't lost, or God doesn't want more saved, but we're satisfied with the people in our interest group) and unrewarding—why bother when so many people are expert in evading the issue when Christ is introduced?

4. There are three reasons we need to be involved in finding the lost. First, every responsible adult needs salvation. None of the Twelve could be righteous without Jesus: not Saul of Tarsus; not Paul the Apostle; not Cornelius the Just. No one can. Second, nothing gives satisfaction to Christians like seeing friends, neighbors and relatives saved through our personal effort! Third, the person we're helping most of all is self. If only from self-interest, what could be more important than finding the lost? The very person we baptize won't have to be arrested later for killing us or our loved ones while DUI. If personal interest should motivate any action in Christians, it should be evangelism. We now see an accumulation of societal problems traceable to the lack of evangelism among people in the entertainment industry, who now influence morals and values. We have an obligation to both God and to society. We fulfill the latter by being faithful to the former. We can never fulfill the former by being faithful to the latter. We can't ever make earthly life better by neglecting Heaven's demands. But making an active Christian out of a sinner makes him a beneficial citizen who obeys the laws, cares for his neighbor and looks for ways to help others.

FAITH

God's being God is something changeless, never diminishing or growing. He contains and possesses, at any time, past, present or future, everything being God could possibly be. It's our understanding of God that changes, develops, shrinks, balloons or disappears. In these illustrations, the iron-clad conviction that God's sovereignty explains whatever we *must* know and leaves the rest to faith. Where He sees the need to explain, we accept; where He doesn't, we trust.

Subject Idea:	Trusting
Scripture:	Deuteronomy 33:27
Visual Item:	Four strong-armed male volunteers; chair
Truth Stressed:	To trust God means we rely on Him completely.
Procedure:	Put the chair in view of all; have the volunteers stand behind you, two on each side, their arms interlocked at the wrist with the person across. Mount the chair, align your body so you'll fall into the arms of the volunteers, then face the audience with your back to the volunteers. Tell them that at the count of three you'll cross your arms and free-fall backwards into their arms. Lock your knees, don't look back...then fall. After you're caught, let your supporters lower you to the floor. (Rehearsing this will be necessary.)

Applications:

1. This was a "trust drop," a perfect example of trust. First, I had confidence that, when I fell, the brothers would be there to catch me. Second, I risked harm to myself by falling helplessly into their arms. Third, I never would have taken the chance if I harbored any doubt about their ability or intention to catch me. And fourth, I'm on my feet telling you that my trust in these brothers was well-placed. Let's see how each point relates to trusting God.

2.   Bible teaching declares that God is there when we need
     Him. That's an unpopular affirmation today, but it
     remains foundational to believers. We trust the Bible's
     promise. Faith may be a leap, but not into the dark, where
     we hope someone waits. Faith is falling from darkness to
     light and from weakness into strong, everlasting arms!
     God has given countless examples of both His existence
     and His concern for all creation, particularly humanity.
     He's the God who first originated everything and has,
     ever since, sustained it by constant, flawless oversight.

3.   Since we can't test-tube prove God, it's true that we risk
     our life, our health, our plans and our future on the propo-
     sition that, when we commit ourselves to Him, God will
     be there, waiting, arms outstretched! But human beings
     have to trust something or someone; our transience, mor-
     tality and limitations naturally create that dependence.
     Indeed, our transience and mortality demand that we find
     something we consider lasting and immortal to be the re-
     ceptacle of all we cherish but can't attain, desire but never
     achieve. Our decision is merely to determine the object of
     that trust—what or whom! We can't say we won't trust,
     we'll just depend on ourselves. That's merely perverted
     faith—the oldest idolatry on the planet. How could we
     ever trust self, of all created things, when we had no
     control over our birth, and we're so sure to die! Why not
     trust the Christ who made us, went to the cross to save us
     and rose from the dead to justify faith in him? God won't
     eliminate the risk factor involved in faith. And sometimes
     the risk seems so strong that people trust God, but not
     completely; enough to make them confident, but too little
     to make them fearless; enough to encourage them to fall
     into God's arms, but not so confidently they'll do it
     without a safety net below.

4.   Since Christians haven't a single spiritually suicidal
     thought, and the strongest possible intention of living
     fully now and perfectly later, we've learned to trust God
     in Christ, who alone proves willing and able to save!
     We're the ultimate survivalists. We aim to overcome, not
     surrender; to live, not perish. But we're also the realists
     among survivalists because we know the key is in per-

ceptions, not geography; in a spiritual, not military warfare. It's possible that these brothers, despite their best intentions, wouldn't have broken my fall, and I would have hurt myself by their failure. My weight might have broken the arms locked to catch me.

5. But what burden can we cast on Jesus that overcomes his strength to bear? Christians confidently ask, "If it's a scary thing to fall into God's arms, whose arms would render it fearless?" He promises that He'll be there when we need Him most; that He'll hold us up and carry us when we can't walk alone. And if the thought of letting go and falling into His everlasting arms won't motivate us, into whose arms would we possibly be willing to fall?

6. Those who have lived with God long enough to have proved Him at all know that they can prove Him "o'er and o'er," for He'll always be as faithful as He's always been. Our willingness to trust God can be based on a few or on the many experiences where we've tried Him. For whether by few or by many, we've always found Him a present help in trouble, listening when we call; helping us resist or survive or believe or forgive, or whatever it takes to overcome the world!

⌘　⌘　⌘　⌘　⌘　⌘

Subject Idea:	Trusting
Scripture:	John 10:11
Visual Item:	Several volunteers; blindfolds for their eyes
Truth Stressed:	Faith means following wherever Jesus leads.
Procedure:	After explaining that you're going to blindfold them, turn them around a few times to disorient them, then have them follow where you lead, ask for 3 or 4 volunteers. Spend a few minutes guiding them around obstacles they can't see. Remove

the blindfolds and have the people return to their seats.

Applications:

1. This "trust walk" demonstrates faith in God's leading. Not being able to see, but trusting me, the brothers and sisters followed me. They didn't know where we were going, but trusted me to get them safely there and back.

2. Jesus called himself the Good Shepherd, and his people sheep, because he's God's Leader, and we're those needing guidance. Confessing Christ as the Son of God means that we trust whatever he says and acknowledge his lordship over every matter of faith and behavior. Because he affirmed the account of Jonah's being swallowed by a big fish, we affirm miracles. Because he affirmed the Genesis account of a man and a woman as the genesis of the nuclear home, we affirm marriage. He said it; that settles it, whatever any others say.

3. However, belief merely gives substance to *our* life, not to Christ's teaching, ministry or purpose. We don't deceive ourselves by thinking that our affirmation substantiates as our denial would invalidate him. He himself is the proof of all he said and did. This confidence, however unpopular it makes us, always bolsters us. For while we love others, work with others, value others, we trust only Jesus Christ for our life! No one else could extract from us the allegiance we freely offer him!

4. It wasn't hard to see that some of the volunteers followed more, some less readily. Some needed more, some less encouragement. But none showed a reluctance to *be* led. This means that, while we're all pilgrims on a common spiritual journey, we don't all progress to the same level of faith at the same rate. Indeed, Christian brotherhood compels us to admit both our inferiority to Christ and our need to show patience with other people's perceived inferiority to us. We shouldn't be surprised when others fail us or mistreat us or desert us, etc.; we've personally done all those things to Jesus, and he doesn't abandon us. His example demands that we tolerate each other's weaknesses as he forgives our sins and that we preserve

fellowship when disagreements arise since he retains in his sheepfold even those whose misbehavior offends his oversight. Occasions of discrepancy among Christians challenge us to return to our common source of trust and to remember: while we love each other, we trust only Jesus!

5.   If a volunteer had refused to follow, I wouldn't have felt offended. (Sometimes I wouldn't follow me!) But if a believer in Jesus refuses to follow him, he cannot be Christ's sheep. His sheep follow him, perhaps cautiously at first, then with more confidence as they discover their own strength in his faithfulness. But wherever he leads, his sheep go!

6.   Like other leaders, Jesus leads us through everything we experience by having endured it first. But he alone can lead us beyond our experience, knowledge and wisdom to where he alone has gone, is and remains! Like other leaders, Jesus said he would lead his sheep; that we could trust him; that we would never be ashamed if we did; that he knew the obstacles we faced and would teach us to avoid them.   What credentials do other teachers have, and where are they now? If we follow a leader who can only help us to a better life without overcoming the grave, aren't we following a corpse, not a shepherd? If all he can lead us to is the cemetery and a tomb where he himself lies, what *eternal* good is he? None but Jesus offers God's ideal personality for behavior. Nothing but his word offers God's standard of truth.

⌘   ⌘   ⌘   ⌘   ⌘   ⌘

Subject Idea:	Obedience
Scripture:	Psalm 119:14, 18
Visual Item:	Book of origami (Oriental paper folding) available from the local library; partially folded origami project
Truth Stressed:	Faith means following God's directions for life.

Procedure: The books offer easily followed steps for
                    folding paper into a variety of realistic
                    animals and shapes. Complete one of the
                    shapes prior to the presentation until you're
                    familiar with it. Offer the people the par-
                    tially finished project; let them guess its
                    identify. Finish folding it until the shape or
                    animal is revealed. Show the book that
                    offered step by step instructions.

Applications:

1. I've never had any experience with origami until
    preparing this project. By following the directions I made
    a fair representation of a (show animal or shape made).
    God's directions in His word guarantee that the least-ex-
    perienced, least-informed believer can become a
    proficient Christian by following Bible directions. Each
    disciple makes his choice of a self-willed or God-directed
    life. Faith urges us to let God lead, to resist the powerful
    temptation to build life according to our specifications.

2. God knows what He wants from us and provides the
    means to achieve it. Without specific directions from
    God, we don't know either one! The process begins with
    single steps that lead to the initial successes that en-
    courage continual steps. The result is a concatenation of
    procedures that develops a lifestyle of spiritual conquest.
    Like the origami (shape or animal), the Christian life
    begins with the simple step of committing ourselves to
    God's direction.

3. It's possible that we could become so skilled in origami
    that we create shapes in our own mind. Then we can
    write the book. Until we achieve that skill-level, we dis-
    regard the instructions to our disconcertion. While
    learning, whatever we produce won't be what the book
    describes. There never comes a time when Christians get
    strong enough or wise enough or confident enough to start
    living apart from God's will. We'll create a life, yes, and
    perhaps one that pleases and contents us, but not the
    single model that God reveals and honors. Obeying
    God's instruction rather than our inclinations may be
    vexing, especially as we become more skilled in the

spiritual life. We may want to take a more independent role, thinking for ourselves instead of seeking God's word, making decisions apart from His will. Failure has a way of humbling that arrogance. (And, if we're fortunate, failure will occur before we've ventured too far from reliance on God and have fewer mistakes to correct.) Since God wrote the book on the spiritual life, no one knows the subject but He.

4. Our first efforts with origami fail to produce the journeyman look that practice produces. Just so, God won't demand maturity from beginners who follow His will, though maturity remains His goal for us. He'll be patient while we grow, but He expects us to make the effort!

⌘   ⌘   ⌘   ⌘   ⌘   ⌘

Subject Idea:	Trust
Scripture:	Psalm 119:152
Visual Item:	Addressed letter; stamp; cereal box; container of butterscotch pudding; spoon
Truth Stressed:	Living by faith in God shouldn't be difficult since we live every day by faith in humanity.
Procedure:	Use the stamp first; show the other items during the applications. Show the envelope without a stamp. Have you shown any trust in the Post Office? No. Put a stamp on the letter. Have you shown any faith in the Post Office? No. Ask what it takes to show your faith in the Post Office — mail the letter. Trust is putting the letter in a mail box.

Applications:

1. We live every day by faith, not by sight. Billions of dollars move through the mails daily, paying bills, receiving dividends, pensions, rent checks, *et al*. That takes

faith—sometimes more faith than the Post Office proves it deserves. And we think living by faith in God is difficult?

2. Here's a box of Kelloggs' Raisin Bran. (Read the label.) We don't know that the company put in the box what the label says. We *assume* it did because it's a reputable company and, besides, if it gets caught lying, it will be fined. Of course, we can say, "Well, neither the Post Office nor Kelloggs is perfect, but both have proven track records." And God doesn't? They've done for corporate profits what He hasn't to protect Christ's name? We accord respect to flawed human organizations because they're *mainly* competent and truthful, but doubt the perfect Being who's *always* faithful?   We really have to live by faith if we ascribe more credibility to human companies than to God's integrity!

3. We may say, "Well, there are rules controlling these companies and government bureaucrats galore making sure they're enforced." And there aren't spiritual rules controlling the universe? We really have to live by faith if we feel that legislators in (your state capital or) Washington, D.C. have more integrity enforcing their rules than the Supreme Ruler in enforcing His! Or that those legislators have more concern for our welfare than He who created us!

4. Take a taste of the pudding. Mmm...tastes just like butterscotch—because it is! A very important point because when Jesus lived among us, he acted exactly like God in every situation he faced: miracles flourished, teachings soared, love multiplied, etc. As the pudding tastes exactly as we've defined butterscotch to taste, God acts just as He's defined Himself. The problem is, He doesn't always act as *we* define Him. When He doesn't, we decide He's a fraud; how dare He not oblige our expectations! Who is at fault at such contretemps?

5. We activate faith almost every moment of the day, and always in humanity's good name or better intentions. When we live by faith with far less reason and far weaker evidence, why should we find it difficult to trust the Greatest Being of all engaged in the greatest cause of all?

6.   People who dislike each other, intrigue against each other and seek the advantage of each other, daily sign contracts declaring faith in each other's integrity. Then these same people criticize the Christian for utterly trusting God because God has, time after time, circumstance after circumstance, proven faithful, true, trustworthy, loving, concerned and forgiving. If, against the evidence, sinners sign papers to gain a temporary advantage that will certainly be a long term loss, how can they blame us for signing our life over to the God who gives a full life now and a perfect life later? THINK!

7.   We live by faith, not by sight. And we decide to live by sight only because experience proves faith right! World history and Christian experience both declare the sufficiency of God in every way He promised to be! And no one who trusts Him will ever be ashamed of that trust. God will not fail the faith we put in Him!

8.   Indeed, we live by faith every day and don't give it a second thought. And when we do think about it, we convince ourselves that good reasons exist for living by faith and not by sight. Then, in the same breath, we pretend there aren't infallible reasons to trust God! What a depraved race!

⌘   ⌘   ⌘   ⌘   ⌘   ⌘

Subject Idea:	Trusting
Scripture:	I Corinthians 10:13
Visual Item:	A 25-foot rope; enough 2 to 3 foot lengths of rope for each person in the audience, including young people
Truth Stressed:	God's presence enables us to always have hope.
Procedure:	Show the wound rope. As you tell the people that life is like a rope, hold one end and let the rest fall to the floor. Continue to feed the rope through your hands as you

talk about passing through circumstances that test our faith in God's love and concern. While they come to us at different times and in various ways, we all encounter difficulties, young and older people alike. No one is exempt. Then there are times that aren't just difficult, but seemingly impossible, when we've "reached the end of our rope"—be sure you *have* as you say it — So there we are, strength gone, hope vanished, all alone. What are we to do?—as you hold the end up. Perhaps someone will say aloud, "tie a knot." If not, you say it and do so.

Applications:

1. How does this knot apply to us? There's always something to grasp, whatever experience badgers or blasts our life! Each person experiences what could break him, kill the desire to live, rouse the desire to give up and drop out of life: a loved one's death, job loss, divorce, problems with our children, extended illness, etc., but just when we reach the end of our rope, we find a knot that God tied so we can hold on!

2. Some experiences have no effect on us; some affect us hardly at all; some moderately; some severely; some catastrophically. Whatever it is, we shall each come to a time of decision: "Shall I go on or give up?" Faith teaches us that, while life is hard, faith is tougher and can re-make, re-work and re-fashion any circumstance we face!

3. What's in faith that gives it such assurance isn't *something*, but Someone as the object—God Himself! When sure of nothing else, not even of our ability to go on, we can be sure of God. (Though He's what many surrender first of all when life goes wrong—and it's easy to do, even for mature Christians! But that surrender is counterproductive because it implies God's unmasked insufficiency, and it's deadly because it means He can't reach through our humanity to embolden the soul made in His image!)

4. God is: we can hold to that. Grab that certainty and don't
    let go. Seize and embrace it. And when, after you've
    hung on as long as possible and still feel your grip
    loosening, cry out for Jesus to hang on to you if you let go
    of him—and he shall! No one, who has confessed his in-
    ability to hang on after trying, will fail to find Jesus
    hanging on to him, regardless! Grace is more than suf-
    ficient to save us from sin and from our humanity.

5. God is at the beginning, so we can know our origin; at the
    end so we can know our destiny, and He's with us today
    so we can experience hope and fearlessness! When
    there's no one else, there is God, and there God is, so we
    won't be alone or feel abandoned! Darkness may hide
    Him, but He's as surely in the shadows protecting as in
    the light guiding us. It takes faith to believe that, but faith
    believes what God has taught, even when personal expe-
    rience denies it, doubts it, refuses it. When we have to
    face what we dread, He's there to help. When we face
    what we dare, He's there to sustain; and when we face
    what we dare not, He's there to embolden! *There*, when
    we don't think we need Him; when we're sure we don't;
    when we think we do; when we know we must have Him
    or we'll die! There all the time!

6. As you leave today, you'll receive a 2 to 3 foot rope with
    a knot tied at one end. Please take it with you as a re-
    minder: when you come to the end of your rope, God has
    it knotted for you. Hang on to the knot: GOD IS! We'll
    live day by day this week, in mostly private struggles, no
    one seeing or knowing—but here and now, in this
    promise, is power to overcome our world: GOD IS! He
    may be all we have left, but He's more than we'll ever
    need!

⌘   ⌘   ⌘   ⌘   ⌘   ⌘

Subject Idea: Guidance
Scripture: Galatians 5:17; Revelation 1:18

Visual Item:	Enlarged picture or overhead transparency of an airplane instrument panel
Truth Stressed:	We must always trust God's word.
Procedure:	Have someone familiar with the instrument panel identify the gauges and why pilots learn to trust them above their own judgment.

Applications:

1.   The instruments provide guidance for the pilot when he's not sure where to go and when he's sure but wants to go safely. The pilot learns to trust his instruments even when he "feels" another way. God's wisdom, revealed in the Bible, His spiritual instrument, can always be trusted to guide us through life as we prepare for eternity.

2.   Our fleshly nature constantly battles our spiritual nature over this issue. Our flesh assures us that we can find our own way without God; denouncing that humanism, our spiritual nature demands that we seek God. Our personal success or failure depends on who wins the argument: the flesh deluded by specious arguments or the spirit learned in God's truth!

3.   This is also a struggle within the committed Christian. When a contest between the emotions and God's plain teaching occurs, which wins? When our think-so collides with God's say-so, *who says so*? Pilots are trained to trust their instruments because pilots can get confused, thinking they're vertical when they're really horizontal, which is always dangerous; and horizontal when they're really vertical, which can be lethal!

4.   Why should we trust our religious *instincts* when God's word so clearly warns against it? Satan plundered Eve's religious instincts in the Garden, and we've never mastered them since. That's why God painstakingly wrote the Bible. He wouldn't have spent the time, energy, creativity, blood, patience and perseverance of His people to produce and preserve the Bible if it were irrelevant or an alternative to our instincts!

5.   Instruments are put in planes because space is a strange, foreign, hostile world to humanity. It's the principality of

the birds and winds, of electrical impulses and interstellar planetary bodies—but not of human bodies. We're strangers there and need the guidance of instruments to get us up, keep us up, keep us safe and get us back down to our natural dimension. We're as spiritually helpless in life as we are physically in space. Spiritually, understand. Not mentally or physically or socially, though all these are negatively or positively impacted by our response to spiritual ignorance.

6. We can't trust our instincts to know God. Our pride will invariably lead us from God to arrogance. Pride can take us to the mountains; to the desert; to the moon, but pride will never take us to the Cross at all, where Jesus leads us first of all, and God demands we go. Pride will lead to adamant self-justification before God; to exalting self before God, but pride will never lead us to fall humbly before God.

7. Let's trust the spiritual instruments God gave us: His word, the Holy Spirit, Christian friends, our pastors. They care about saving us, not deceiving us; about sharing with us what God taught them, not overload us with religious nonsense; about telling us like it is whether or not we like it like it is!

⌘   ⌘   ⌘   ⌘   ⌘   ⌘

Subject Idea:	Directions
Scripture:	Galatians 4:8-11
Visual Item:	Prescription bottle of medicine or antibiotics
Truth Stressed:	God knows exactly what he wants from us and has clearly instructed us how to achieve it.
Procedure:	Show the bottle; read the instructions for the medication's use: dosage, length of time; daily schedule. If you have the accompanying pamphlet, read some of its directions and warnings.

Applications:

1. The doctor prescribes what he feels we need to correct a problem. He may be wrong. He can over-prescribe by giving medication that's too strong. That brings a re-action, not a cure. He can under-prescribe, either in the type of medicine, its dosage or the length of time taken. That brings an extension of the problem, not a cure.

2. God makes neither mistake. He infallibly knows exactly what works to cure our sin problem and prescribes exactly what works. We should take God's prescription exactly as He orders it filled.

3. Many once-controlled illnesses and diseases are making raging comebacks because people take their medicine till they "feel better" or borrow medicine prescribed for a friend or relative, as if each person can make his own di-agnosis and prescribe the cure. Spiritual problems develop and remain resistant because we've convinced ourselves that we know exactly what we need to be cured—whatever God says. We're not only the patient, but the doctor as well, diagnosing and prescribing for our ills with equal skill and felicity. But if a person who serves as his own lawyer has a fool for a client, what is a sinner who serves as his own savior?

4. Invariably, when we turn from the Living Physician to quacks, we always pick one who tells us what we want to hear and prescribes the medication we're willing to take at an agreeable rate and schedule. We choose religious doctrine because it *suits* us, our inclinations, our edu-cation. We seek until we find someone who supports conclusions we've already drawn, who outlines principles we've already established and convictions we've already formed.

5. God is unimpressed by our instincts, convictions, prin-ciples and wishes. He makes the rules and enforces them; we live by them or take the consequences. He would save every person ever to live if He had His way. But He doesn't have His way if we insist on ours. And if we want to talk about something God can't do, it's save us our way! He can't because He won't. Not from the start. Not now. Not ever!

FORGIVENESS

Horses being led from burning stables have been known to bolt their rescuers and return to the fire, thinking the inferno represents security. Far too many believers, once well on the way out of their past, have broken from Christ and drifted back to what they thought represented something better. It isn't hard to see why. While the Christian life is starkly tough, demanding and uncompromising, the old is life so permissive and forgiving. Forgiveness—in this context don't confuse it with forgiving—can't be altered or diminished. It demands a price paid to remove sin, and accountability of the rescued to the rescuer. Being forgiving means we freely accept our humanity and tolerate its idiosyncrasies. In these illustrations, reasons Christians can rejoice, both in the privileges forgiveness grants and in the obligations it imposes.

Subject Idea: Forgiving

Scripture: Matthew 18:23-25, 28

Visual Item: A hundred $1 bills

Truth Stressed: God forgives our worse as we forgive other people's lesser sins.

Procedure: Put a single dollar bill in one place: beside it the 99 one-dollar bills. Multiply the 99 by a million—imagine a stack of bills three thousand feet high.

Applications:

1. However wronged by another, the single dollar bill remains the size of their offense while the stack three thousand feet high—and climbing— remains our offense against God. Nothing is more natural, or more contrary to Bible truth, than to concentrate on someone else's offense against us instead of ours against God, perhaps hoping that maximizing their faults minimizes ours. God eliminates that mistake by overloading scripture with our guilt in betraying Him, with little in comparison about other people's wrongdoing against us.

2. Like the wolf deserves the hatred of the shepherd, we deserve God's wrath; execution, not pity. We've torn ourselves apart fighting His will; we've broken ourselves to pieces flinging ourselves against His truth. We've harmed virtue and glorified evil, made righteousness feel ashamed of expressing itself and emboldened deceit and pride. We've made every mistake possible, and we'll make more, given the time!

3. The awareness of our *unfitness* to be forgiven lies at the heart of our acceptability to God. Only as we accept our unfitness do we qualify for forgiveness. If we can accept God's forgiveness, despite our personal unworthiness to receive it, why can't we forgive others despite theirs? Would we let our pride exceed God's humility; our self-love to outreach His self-sacrificing love; our passion for revenge to eclipse His desire for mercy?

4. Why does God insist that we practice the forgiveness we receive? First, He knows that forgiving others frees us from the mental, emotional and physical problems that exacting revenge imposes. It enlarges as revenge limits, shrinks and desiccates our spirit. Second, while we must forgive for our own welfare, whether the offender seeks it or wants it or asks for it or thinks we're crazy for even suggesting it, Jesus insists we forgive to prove both our forgiveness and the presence of God that prompts it. By having God hide His face from our sins, not from us, we learn to accept others, despite their faults. Third, God conditions our continued forgiveness on our continual willingness to forgive.

5. What legacy do we want to leave? That we're good haters? That we never forget a wrong done us? That we'll find a way to get even? Or, since God has extended to us a forgiveness we didn't deserve, we'll extend it to others? And since we're now God's friends, we refuse to be another person's enemy, however truculent he is to us? For while we can't keep him from hating us, he can't reduce us to hating him!

6. For every negative impact revenge exacts, forgiveness registers a positive. Where revenge abridges, forgiveness expands our soul; where revenge inflicts cruelty, for-

giveness exudes mercy; where revenge is ugly, forgiveness is winsome. Both prove much about us; more
importantly, both do much to us!

⌘   ⌘   ⌘   ⌘   ⌘   ⌘

Subject Idea:	Reconciliation
Scripture:	John 15:4-5; I John 1:9
Visual Item:	Clear container filled with unmixed oil and water
Truth Stressed:	The unrighteous can be one with the righteous by being purified.
Procedure:	Note the natural separation of the two elements; that while water naturally mixes with other fluids, it can only be forced to combine with oil. For the purpose of the illustration, the oil symbolizes God, the water human nature. Shake the container, and the two elements combine.

Applications:

1. Fallen humanity cannot live in peace with the perfect
    God. We're the ones separated from Him since He's
    never changed, moved, advanced or retreated from what
    He eternally is. There's no need for unforgiven sinners to
    claim friendship with God so long as their carnal lives
    declare war against Him. And there's no need to assure
    people they're found until we convince them they're lost.
    We spend useless time and effort urging church mem-
    bership on sinners who need forgiveness, but who don't
    recognize it. They'll see the church as essential only
    when they see their sinfulness as notorious! They won't
    be won from a lifestyle they see no hazard in embracing.
    God pours it on us—we're sinners deserving condem-
    nation. Until we accept that definition of ourselves, we'll
    never seek rescue, and we'll balk like overloaded mules at
    the self-denial Christ places at the heart and soul of con-
    version—the basic terms He'll never alter! To be

amenable to His radical solution we have to be conscious-stricken about our guilt before God!

2.   God took the initiative in bringing us together, something we could never effect. We'd either get it all wrong, with the religions that emphasize human sacrifice to effect forgiveness, or we'd deny that any problem existed, declaring it the fiction of a priestly class intent on maintaining dominance. God effected the merging of our impurity with His holiness as Jesus died; he released God's love to us and absorbed God's wrath against sin. Blood had to be shed, and only the perfect sacrifice of an unsullied blood could achieve the merger. That's how God mixes our water with His oil; He subsumes our water to His oil. He will be one with us, but only as we unconditionally surrender to Him. Having Jesus facilitate the oneness, God accepts no other claimant as the unifier!

3.   The death that potentially saves the entire human race actually saves only individuals who personally appropriate it. When Jesus said, "It is finished," it was; all that God wanted done to achieve perfect reunion with us had been done, nothing excepted! But how shall it save us if we deny we need it, or if we admit we need it but don't personally accept it? Given freely to all, God's forgiveness must be accepted by each convert!

4.   As only continuous shaking retains this mixture, only persevering discipleship retains oneness with God. Set this container and let both elements settle, they'll invariably separate. And while it's the responsibility of neither the oil nor the water to retain the mixture—they're just different components—it's our responsibility to stay in the Son. If we remain in him, he remains in us. We take that initiative, pursuing that purpose. If we stop being a faithful believer, we'll settle into the old life as surely as oil and water separate, given time. And that will be a disaster, for God will allow to be one with His perfection only those His Son's sacrifice declares perfect! Individual sins won't remove that oneness; only our settled, determined sinfulness will cause that removal. But let us be forewarned: let no single sin remain unrepented lest it join

with others to expedite the inevitable separation from God!

⌘　⌘　⌘　⌘　⌘　⌘

Subject Idea:	Reality
Scripture:	Philippians 3:13
Visual Item:	Few jars of cosmetics
Truth Stressed:	Forgiveness changes us from the inside out.
Procedure:	Perhaps you could let your wife or another woman explain the purpose of each cosmetic, extolling its worth or regretting its inadequacy.

Applications:

1. Women have the advantage over men in our culture; they can cover blemishes and imperfections with significant success due to advanced creations of the beauty industry. With most men, women see exactly what they're getting. With many women, only the morning mirror knows for sure. Still, as one woman discovered, she fell in love with a generously coiffured man, only to discover he wore a hairpiece. By that time, too much in love, she didn't care.

2. If we're talking of friendship, courtship or marriage between mortals, who cares if the hair has a stubborn cow-lick or the face a mole or the head a billiard ball shine? It's the person inside the body that matters. But we're not talking about mortals responding to mortals, but about mortals actually being in God's presence, beholding His awesome, terrifying grandeur. How can *we* do that? Every Old Testament example of such encounters terrifies us — on their knees, face to the ground they flew, trembling. And there's John, like a dead man before the Christ with whom he had once felt so familiar he lay head to chest. How can we hope to look on God without stark raving terror consuming and incinerating us? Indeed, if it's a matter of what's *inside us*, how shall we dare

consider it? When nothing is hidden, and all revealed; when all masks are off, and only the forgiven access God, what will it be for us? When only heart-changing conversion suffices, what value will formal church membership have? When only Christ's blood covers, what influence will fame, riches and human goodness have?

3. God enables us to let our past go, every sin of it, so we don't have to keep going back, piling them up and clucking our despair! They're gone; let them go! God doesn't gunnysack our past; why should we? He removes it; let's be free of it. All that our past can ever do is teach, encourage and create spiritual conviction in us; it can't ever again haunt us!

4. But shall we expect God to welcome us if we intentionally substitute surface for marrow faith? When it cost Christ his blood, can ephemeral religion impress God? When He's said only soul-rattling conversion admits us, will we still try to force our way into His presence? Will we dare anchor our soul to unrepented sin when He's expressly forbidden imperfection in His presence?

5. If we want to cleanse the instruments of worship, offer the blood of animals, as the Old Testament demands. If you want to cleanse the human heart, plead for the blood of Jesus. Each sacrifice will suffice for its purpose. But never expect the blood of bulls and goats to cleanse our spirit and renew our mind!

⌘   ⌘   ⌘   ⌘   ⌘   ⌘

Subject Idea:	Purification
Scripture:	Ephesians 1:19b-22
Visual Item:	Clean chalk board and eraser
Truth Stressed:	The sinless Christ removes all our sins.
Procedure:	Note the pristine condition of the board— representing our life at birth. Make marks,

figures, drawings, squiggles all over the board—representing the sins of life as we enter accountability; we never accumulate less, but more sinfulness as life continues.

Applications:

1. Theologians have for centuries debated the dichotomous or trichotomous nature of humanity. Are we body and soul or body, soul and spirit? I believe we're all three, for the following reason: the soul is the "living being" revealed in every baby's cry for food, love, diaper change and attention. Only as the infant develops, understanding parental permission or denial, does the Spirit of God within begin either to awaken or wither, depending on parental response. Allowed to behave without accountability and to misbehave without correction, only the toddler's "living-being soul" develops, not the "Image-of-God spirit" within him. Because children will make wrong decisions, however correct the parental advice, discipline and punishment may be, by the age of accountability they've marred their life like I've marred this board.

2. Infant baptism not only unnecessarily imposes a burden on a naturally-pure child, but denies clear New Testament teaching about believer's baptism. Only by performing mental gymnastics can defenders of infant baptism justify it to themselves, but they can never objectively defend it. However, when accountability comes—and that occurs at different ages—purification has to occur. God won't admit us to His presence as if we hadn't been away; to Paradise as if we hadn't stalked out in Eden! Immersion for the forgiveness of sin effects our original purification. Repentance and confession effect our continued purification afterward.

3. Here we are, then, sinners everyone, and sure to be condemned. We can't fight our way out of sin because that's like struggling to remove ourselves from quicksand—the more we struggle, the quicker and deeper we sink. How are we going to have our sins removed? (Here take the eraser and wipe the board clean.) What happened to the

marks? They're gone! Where did they go? On the eraser! The eraser cleaned the board and became dirty in the process. It might clean the board a few more times, but eventually I'll have to pound out the accumulated dust. In the same way God eradicated our sins by stroking Christ's sacrificial blood across them. Before he died, there they all were, glaring and glowing. After he passed over, the slate was clean! But in the process of taking on himself our sins, he became unclean — he became SIN, pure as he was before wiping himself across our board! God put him on the cross, not only to forgive innumerable sins, but to destroy the principle of SIN, epitomized in Satan. As a result, Jesus can now forgive our sins and guarantee Satan's and SIN's eventual eradication.

4. Christ's resurrection from the dead is absolutely essential to the forgiveness his death provides. Without his bodily resurrection, our sins might be forgiven, but a resurrected life would be impossible. If Jesus forgave us by dying, then took sin to the grave with him and kept it there, what is it but more of the same Old Testament sacrifices of bulls and goats? Their blood sufficed to purify, but not to resurrect! Jesus Christ's resurrection offered a removal of our old and a reinforcement of our new life; a proactive, not a reactive faith!

5. We may become a church member for as many reasons as there are people, but we better become a Christian for one and only one reason—because that's the only way we'll ever delight in seeing God; delight in being at Judgment; delight in seeing the books opened because we'll know our sins won't be there; delight in seeing the Book of Life opened because we'll know our name will be!

⌘   ⌘   ⌘   ⌘   ⌘   ⌘

Subject Idea: Reconciliation
Scripture: Luke 6:15 (Matthew and Simon...Zealot);
Acts 1:13 (same men still together)

Visual Item: Zippered jacket or sweater

Truth Stressed: Jesus specializes in uniting opposing personalities.

Procedure: Put the jacket/sweater on; leave unzipped.

Applications:

1. What we have here are two parts belonging to a whole cloth. If left apart, I'm only partly protected. That might serve if it isn't too cold or windy, but not otherwise. In the same way, when disciples get into disagreements with their Christian brothers and sisters, we can't escape belonging to the same body; we're together in Christ. We may not be personally united, but we both claim the same Lord and Savior.

2. Draw the jacket halves together and put the zipper pin in the zipper box, without zipping up. The jacket doesn't offer full coverage. It's still functioning at less than manufactured capacity. Just so, Christians may be in close physical proximity with each other, but that isn't unity. To be honest, however, a civilized proximity may be all that's possible at first, especially when people have had serious differences. Maintaining fellowship under such conditions is desirable, if difficult. It won't be a peace treaty, but if each protagonist can simply agree to remain mentally disarmed, at least we won't be "shooting on sight," and reconciliation is still possible—and a conclusive peace! Maybe at this point we can't be friends, but we can be civilized acquaintances. (There are some who mock this half-way measure. "Let's just get along," they demand, "Jesus won't accept anything less." Which is true long-term, but Jesus knows us well enough to distinguish between what's ideal and real, and he settles for what can now be done and built on later.) Thus, while forgetting the differences is possible only with the passing of time, *willing* forgiveness is the ultimate key to forgetting!

3. (Zip all the way to the top.) Now the jacket/sweater offers full protection. Both sides of the whole are reconciled, tied together by the common zipper. In the same way, God reconciles us to each other *as* He reconciles us to

Himself. True, it's easier to get away from the persons we don't like, but that doesn't automatically make them less a part of the whole cloth—or ourselves the totality of it! In such a circumstance, forgiving is always tougher, but better, while anger and revenge are always easier, but destructive. As forgiveness lightens, revenge burdens life. Praying for the person will improve our attitude towards him, even if it offers no immediate change in him. Forgiving eliminates our instinctive need to keep acting out the violence that disagreements build, oftentimes in silly, petty ways that shame us even as we express them. Those unsatisfactory ways assure long-term guilt even as they offer short-term satisfaction!

4.   Perhaps we'll need a mediator to help resolve the differences. (Every church should have in place a conflict resolution group to handle such emergencies.) But it's up to Christians to demonstrate what Jesus proved: discordant personalities can stay together by agreeing on him, and enemies can become friends by each associating with him. Zippers don't zip on their own, and people *learn* to forgive by being reminded of their spiritual enfranchisement.

⌘   ⌘   ⌘   ⌘   ⌘   ⌘

Subject Idea:	Removal
Scripture:	Galatians 5:19-21a
Visual Item:	Piece of paper; book of matches; container for burning paper
Truth Stressed:	Forgiveness means the removal of sins.
Procedure:	Show the blank paper. As someone reads Galatians 5:19-21a, write the sins written there. (Use Colossians 3:5, 8 as an alternative listing.) The paper represents our personal life. While we may not commit every sin condemned, one is enough to lose

our soul. Hold the paper up; how many would want to appear before God with even one of the sins unforgiven? How are we helpless sinners ever going to enter God's presence? Light a match and touch it to the paper. Hold it as long as possible before dropping it into the container. After it's consumed, show them the ashes.

Applications:

1. God obliterates our sins when we accept Jesus as Savior and Lord. When He's finished applying Christ's grace to our sins, they're annihilated by grace! Our past is removed, do we understand? Our brokenness is now whole; our war is now peace; our emptiness is now complete. God eliminates the sin! It's permanently gone, not filed for future reference. It's incinerated, like this paper. God has proclaimed amnesty for all who trust Christ; we're forgiven, one and all; we're forgiven of each and every sin!

2. Some people have trouble believing this. We don't know all their sins, or we wouldn't be so generous with grace, they demur. Well...we may not know all the sins each commits, but we know the perfection of Christ's sacrifice. He died for the sins of the *whole world.* Bad a sinner as we are, has anyone committed all possible sins that exist? So we don't need to recount every sin each commits if we know Christ's death covers them all! Satan can't possibly deliver more accusations than Christ has offered for- giveness!

3. Think what this means! If we're forgiven any sin, we can boldly accept personal responsibility for our failure. And we may as well because, while God offers forgiveness of, He makes no excuses for our sins. But since Christ has paid the price to remove them, we don't have to blame parents, environment or government for our failures! We can live with the personal responsibility once we're sure that guilt is gone! Not only do we not have to blame anyone else, we don't have to abuse ourselves for our mistakes — drinking, shooting or smoking some foreign

substance to forget, to escape ourselves. Since Jesus set us free, we have nothing from which we seek escape.

4. However, we often experience a resurrection of behavior we thought gone for good. "I agreed to forget that," we say, " and here it is again, beckoning!" Not to worry over our visits to those past behaviors so long as we don't establish residence there again! Ghosts from our past may return to haunt. Nightmares might occasionally afflict us. We might curse the stupidity of those reactionary decisions. But persevering in righteousness guarantees that there'll come a time when we can think of them without pain while always remembering the lesson they taught.

5. Forgiveness goes directly to our core, where thoughts originate, values arise and decisions are made. And once we agree that we want it, we are re-created in Christ's image, he snatches us from condemnation to affirmation, from disgraces removed to graces retained, from every vestige of evil to an embryonic holiness in his image!

GOD

There's a remarkable absence of the fear of God in the world because there's a remarkably feeble fear of God in the church. Our songs and sermons, our Bible school lessons and small groups can't say enough about God's unconditional love, but say little about God's wrath on the disobedient.

Monotheism is at once a relief and a warning to humanity. It offers relief from the multiplicity of gods that confuse and enslave, but it also imposes the autocracy of the One God. If polytheism were true, humanity could choose from any of the alternative religions now demanding equality with Christianity. Since monotheism is true, His being the only God eliminates any competing view. We must come to terms with God's will and sovereignty. May the following illustrations impress on us the need to listen as God dictates and to obey as He commands.

Subject Idea: Sovereignty

Scripture: Deuteronomy 4:1-2

Visual Item: Coffee can with slit in top; half sheet of paper; alligator clip; short section of 2 x 4 lumber

Truth Stressed: Show the slit. Insert the sheet of paper; try to conform the alligator clip to enter the aperture; then fruitlessly force the 2 x 4 against it.

Applications:

1. An ancient spiritual curse afflicts the human race. Only God knows how to remove it and restore humanity to an infinite blessedness. Only He, with the answer, not we with the problem. Like the can slit, which accepts a piece of paper, but not the clip or 2 x 4, God accepts only who He determines fits His requirements for forgiveness and eternal life.

2. However long we push, the clip and 2 x 4 won't be forced through this slit. We might eventually collapse the top of the coffee can, but only because we insist on fitting dis-

similar objects and apertures. However, we can never *force* our way into God's presence. His will won't collapse before us, surrendering to our sheer audacity and persistence. We can enter God's presence, indeed, praise God. But only as He determines that we fit in, not as we decide to coerce Him.

3.   Under whatever covenant humanity has lived, acceptance of God's word has accessed His presence. Jesus reduced that slit to self-denial. Whoever denies himself, and accepts Christ's lordship, enters God's presence. Let us be warned: since self-denial gains that entrance, anything other leaves us outside. Nothing enters this coffee can as configured except a slip of paper. And nothing enters into God's presence except a crucified self-will.

⌘   ⌘   ⌘   ⌘   ⌘   ⌘

Subject Idea:	Sovereignty
Scripture:	Exodus 25:40; Acts 7:44
Visual Item:	A disposable shirt or blouse pattern
Truth Stressed:	God has carefully outlined His will for human life.
Procedure:	Have individuals hold pieces of the pattern before the assembly. Explain that as constituted, the pattern produces the advertised object. Then, with scissors, cut off parts of the pattern until it's a shambles. How many feel that its altered state would produce the advertised object?

Applications:

1.   God revealed His person and will in the Bible, His only authentic revelation to humanity. While other religions claim equal access to God's will through their holy writings, the Old and New Testaments affirm themselves as the only original, God-given revelation of Himself. Make no mistake, both declare that no other book is as good as the original, let alone superior to it.

2. This pattern now seen is wildly different from its original
    design. If I had cut it more modestly, it would now be
    only slightly different—but still different and, therefore,
    not like the original. It takes the Bible to be like the
    Bible; only God's will in the Bible is as good as God's
    will in the Bible. However mildly or wildly different
    other representations of God's will are, they aren't the
    same as or equal to the original!

3. Perhaps even a beginner could make a blouse or shirt by
    explicitly following the original pattern. Only an expert
    seamstress could make sense of the revised pattern.
    Listen carefully now: none of us has the expertise to find
    our way into God's presence. We cannot devise a way
    using directions from separate sources. We cannot
    theorize a way as we proceed through life. God's
    presence can be accessed, but only as we take the Bible
    as His original pattern and follow its directions.
    Whatever else people create from other models, this
    pattern guarantees us forgiveness and eternal life.

4. It isn't as if we're familiar enough with the spiritual life to
    know our way to God without help. Indeed, the human
    race expresses a remarkable creativity in every area
    except the spiritual life, which comes only through God's
    strenuous struggle with our egotism. And, even those
    who surmount their ego and obey, admit inability in de-
    veloping their soul. No one will ever get so familiar with
    spiritual realities that we instinctively know how to fit
    ourselves into them. That is and remains a work of grace.

5. Many feel free to cut out of the Bible what they feel isn't
    true, as I cut from the pattern what I felt isn't relevant.
    Since I'm not a seamstress, such indiscriminate whacking
    shows my ignorance. Since all of us are on our one and
    only trip through life and have no genius whatever in the
    Christian life, what does it make us to whack out of the
    Scripture what we consider irrelevant?

⌘   ⌘   ⌘   ⌘   ⌘   ⌘

Subject Idea:	Grace
Scripture:	Matthew 18:1-4; Philippians 2:12-13
Visual Item:	Fairly heavy dumbbells
Truth Stressed:	God must lift the burdens of discipleship for us.
Procedure:	Have a younger child come forward; ask him to lift barbells that you know are too heavy. After he tries and fails, and while his hand is on the barbell, put your hand on his and help him do a curl.

Applications:

1. The spiritual life is possible only when we put our hands to the discipleship task, then let God give us the lift. God clearly understands that. We're the ones under the illusion that it's only necessary for God to tell us what He wants, turn us loose to do it and return later for His share of the increase.

2. God knows He needs to watch our every step, guide every thought, overcome every mistake and, to get his work done, ask the Holy Spirit to supply both the idea and the will to succeed. It's never been any different; it can't ever be.

3. If we think it unfair to ask a child to lift this barbell since we adults could, remember: the Bible everywhere calls us *children*, but never *adults* of God, taking for granted our personal helplessness before our spiritual task. Jesus had any number of adults in the room—including the Twelve Disciples—when someone asked him to identify the greatest in the kingdom, and he chose a child, not any adult.

4. Children of God we are and remain, no matter how old in years or experience or maturity. Indeed, the most spiritually mature person in the kingdom is the first to acknowledge that all he can do is put his hand to his task—then trust his Heavenly Father's power to fulfill it successfully.

⌘   ⌘   ⌘   ⌘   ⌘   ⌘

Subject Idea:	Power
Scripture:	Isaiah 40:12, 22
Visual Item:	Pitcher of water; straw; Shop-Vac
Truth Stressed:	God's unconditional power should humble us before Him.
Procedure:	Set the pitcher in full view. Sip a few swallows through the straw. Ask how long it will take you to drink it all. Put the nozzle of the Shop-Vac in the pitcher and flip the switch.

Applications:

1. At whatever level we care to compare, on whatever scale we care to weigh our comparative skills, that demonstrates the difference between God's power and ours. The stark distinction should humble us before God, bringing us to our knees in adoration and confession. It should shame the egotism that ceaselessly struts and the pride that as ceaselessly boasts before God.

2. Almost every instance of human success is neutralized by an equivalent failure. We build engines that develop millions of pounds of thrust to carry space vehicles into orbit around the earth—but think nothing of the 6^{21} ton earth (that's 6 plus 21 zeroes), around which it flies. We marvel at space vehicles that speed at 17,000 miles an hour, but think nothing of stars in the Milky Way that travel at 2 million miles per hour!

3. Incredibly, God's greater against our lesser power seems a threat instead of being a security for us. Where it should humble us before God, it turns us vehemently competitive towards Him—as if to prove that however powerful He may be, we're more envious still! And while we carelessly use God's pre-existent resources to build all our manufactured products, we exalt our skill in manufacture while ignoring His in creation. In fact, knowing that if we admitted the Creator's role in the universe we would *perforce* owe our debt to Him, we instead postulate the foolishness of evolution to account for order, intelligence, reason, uniformity and usefulness.

4. God won't force us to accept Him or His power. But
    He'll never deny Himself or minimize His arbitrary au-
    thority just to make us feel more secure. In fact, He
    insists that we accept His separation and distinction from
    us—He is God, we are mortals—as the primary means by
    which weak mortals can access His unlimited resources.

⌘   ⌘   ⌘   ⌘   ⌘   ⌘

Subject Idea: Protection
Scripture: Hebrews 13:5-6
Visual Item: Life jacket
Truth Stressed: We can confidently put our life in God's
                   care.
Procedure: Put on life jacket and relate its purpose. If
                   something unfortunate happens to our
                   vessel, we're safe, however deep or tur-
                   bulent the water.

Applications:

1. As every water-borne vessel has life jackets as mandated
    safety equipment, every person needs designated safety
    equipment in his life; something we can trust to save us
    from the consequences of spiritual failure; something that
    will keep us from falling out of sight and getting lost in
    the aftermath of failure, where so many dangers to our re-
    lationship with God lurk. God offers His love as that
    unchanged, unchanging something. Even when darkness
    hides God's lovely face, we can rely on His "unchanging
    grace" to be there for us.
2. Just as the life jacket allows us to continue swimming
    without fear of sinking once our vessel has capsized, trust
    in God's love keeps us going as Christians when we've
    been submerged in unfortunate circumstances.
3. More than likely, we'll never need the life jacket safety
    requirements demand we wear aboard watercraft. Only a
    few people experience such catastrophes. Life doesn't

treat us so gently, however. Sooner or later, life's rough, turbulent ways toss us out of our boat—our daily rhythm, our confidence in God, our assurance of sustaining grace. And we find ourselves flailing in the water, incensed to be so easily overturned and terrified that we'll despise God and loathe grace in reprisal. At such times, God's preserver wraps securely around us. Even when we don't know if we have hold of God, His love has hold of us.

4.   While we're *in* the drink, we're at peace. *While*...not merely *after* the experience, and we're safe at last, and we can take a breath and thank God. While it's happening, and it seems our life's imperilled, we can rest in the security of God's presence, wrapped around us like a life preserver.

⌘   ⌘   ⌘   ⌘   ⌘   ⌘

Subject Idea: Grace
Scripture: Romans 5:10
Visual Item: Five-gallon bucket
Truth Stressed: Only by grace are we saved.
Procedure: Call a tractable child forward. Ask him to step into the bucket. Then ask him to grab the handle and, when you count three, lift himself into the air. Then you grab the handle and lift both bucket and child.

Applications:
1.   Every saved human being will be carried by Christ's grace into God's presence. No one else! No adult, however intelligent, charming, wealthy, inventive, etc., can any more win, earn or merit his way to God than this child can lift himself by the bucket's handle.
2.   What we cannot do, God's grace can and does! When we were helpless, Christ died for us. When we were yet God's enemies, Christ died to make us His friends.
3.   We remain in the state of friendship with God by the same power of grace that lifted us there. What began by our

trusting Christ's sufficiency continues by our persevering trust in his constant sufficiency. Purchased by Christ's sacrifice, we remain in his name and under his blood.

⌘   ⌘   ⌘   ⌘   ⌘   ⌘

Subject Idea:	Security
Scripture:	Isaiah 55:1-7
Visual Item:	Car jack
Truth Stressed:	God's strength uplifts us in emergencies.
Procedure:	Show the jack and ask how many have had to use one in the past few months. Ask if anyone has gone through life without a flat or blowout. Although we hardly think of it while on the road, the first hint of a flat or blowout stresses the jack's importance.

Applications:

1. A sense of security is the strongest asset of the car jack. Because it's in the trunk, if needed, we casually set out on trips of hundreds and thousands of miles. Given all the road hazards, the state of our roads and, often, the worn state of our tires, we have remarkably few problems while driving.

2. If we don't keep good tires on the car, we're certain to give the jack extra work. And if we don't keep faith and holiness strong in our lives, we'll often find ourselves crisis-ridden and morally uncertain. We'll find that life seems a never-ending procession of moral and spiritual dilemmas. We can't seem to get our life solved once for all. Indeed, a strong Christian life prevents many of the problems plaguing weak or non-Christians.

3. However, as even the best tire can go flat or blow, the strongest Christian life will have problems, anxieties, sorrows and losses. We may never need the car jack; we will finally and ultimately need God's grace to uphold us in trouble.

4. The jack has to be in the car to be useful in an emergency.
    While we may carry it for years without using it, it must
    remain there or it can't help. Just so, God must be in our
    life on a daily basis before we can profitably access His
    emergency help. We need Him as our daily friend to call
    on Him in crisis. For what He offers in the crisis isn't just
    release or exemption from it, but a presence that enlivens,
    empowers and enriches our daily Christian experience.
    An emergency simply continues, however much accen-
    tuated, what has been an ongoing relationship with the
    kind, familiar, loving Father in Heaven, not just as the Big
    Guy in the Sky from whom we seek a favor—after which
    we each go our separate ways.

5. No...God's help in crisis should teach us what we're slow
    to learn and often don't want to know: He must be a daily
    presence. We make it successfully and victoriously
    through everyday experiences and indiscriminate adver-
    sities by His sustaining grace. Don't wait to invite God
    into life when an emergency comes—when we have to
    ask a total stranger for help. Invite Him into life now and
    live faithfully in His love. Then we'll know His prophy-
    lactic presence against life's anxieties and worries and His
    deliverance from life's disasters and crises.

⌘   ⌘   ⌘   ⌘   ⌘   ⌘

Subject Idea: Name
Scripture: Exodus 20:7
Visual Item: Paper and cloth napkins
Truth Stressed: God's name is to be accorded absolute, un-
                 qualified respect.
Procedure: Show both napkins.   As we're aware, one
                 is designed for everyday use, the other for
                 special occasions.   One is designed as a
                 throwaway, the other to be washed and re-
                 used. In even a matter of napkins, we honor
                 one kind above another.

Applications:

1.   Names have meaning and never fail to evoke emotional responses. Think of our response to the name Moses, Lincoln, Satan, Mother Teresa, Stalin. Each personifies values we admire or abhor, respect or despise. We accord each the honor he/she deserves. We would no sooner equate Stalin with goodness than Mother Teresa with tyranny. And we would consider a good person's name degraded if used in unworthy ways or to support unworthy causes.

2.   Think of the name GOD. What images does it form in our mind? What is our intellectual response? How do we feel emotionally? What is our spiritual reflection? Our throwaway society considers little worthwhile enough to preserve or admirable enough to exalt to a pedestal—relationships, morals, values. GOD hardly rates above dog with many people, especially those who remind us what God is, spelled backwards.

3.   God has no doubt about the value of His name. It contains His entire being. When we invoke God's name in any way, we involve His nature, personality, interests, goals— everything about God! Just as we use paper napkins for our lunch at home and cloth napkins when we want to show respect to someone we host for dinner, Christians must ... absolutely must...use God's name in only the most exalted ways to benefit only the most sacred causes.

4.   Furthermore, as we personally respect and honor Him, we bear impatiently anyone else's contempt of His name. If, when we consider God, we want to fall on our knees and cry "Holy," we're not going to tolerate others damning this and that in God's name.

5.   Indeed...Christians should blush...we think more of our own than of God's name. If someone questions our birthright, we're ready to fight. If someone drags God's name through the mud, we consider Him a paper napkin made to be thrown away! If a cloth napkin, by its manufacture, deserves better treatment than a paper napkin, by

its manufacture, what accord do we owe the Name of God, since it expresses the person of the Almighty?

⌘   ⌘   ⌘   ⌘   ⌘   ⌘

Subject Idea: Warnings
Scripture: Genesis 2:16-17
Visual Item: Smoke detector
Truth Stressed: God warns us to avoid spiritual danger.
Procedure: Show the detector. Press the button for testing. Ask what they would do if, in the middle of the night, they heard the smoke alarm.

Applications:

1.   When the detector sounds, we get up, flee to safety and avoid the threatened area. At the very least, we begin searching for the ignition point of the alarm.

2.   Are we as wise spiritually? When God condemns immorality, do we flee it? When He orders us to control our tongue, do we put a leash on it? When He demands a persevering discipleship, do we stay in the harness for the long pull?

3.   A smoke detector's warnings may go unheeded if we know their source: it may be reacting only to toaster smoke. When God rings a warning, we need to get clear of the danger and stay away. While we have no skill in determining the nature of danger, God does; if He says something's wrong, it is! And if we persist in behavior He declares wrong, we're going to die in our sins!

4.   It was God's love that limited Adam's access to the Tree of Life while prohibiting access to the Tree of the Knowledge of Good and Evil. It was God's love that banished Adam and Eve from accessing the Tree of Life once they sinned. And it's still God's love that warns us away from anything that jeopardizes our eternal soul.

Those who love their true selves obey God's warnings and prohibitions.

⌘   ⌘   ⌘   ⌘   ⌘   ⌘

Subject Idea:	Blessings
Scripture:	Matthew 10:8
Visual Item:	3 or 4 foot section of 3 to 4 inch sewer PVC pipe; gallon of water; rag big enough to clog pipe
Truth Stressed:	God wants us to be conduits of spiritual graces.
Procedure:	Pour some water through the unobstructed pipe into the bucket. Then stuff the pipe with the rag and pour as much as possible without overflowing.

Applications:

1. God's people must be both reservoirs and aqueducts. We must contain God's word and benefits in order to have something to share. To speak of what we don't possess would be treachery; to speak confidently of what we don't possess at all unconscionable hypocrisy. In some churches, this poses a significant problem since they believe little of substance and have few fundamental convictions about God, the Bible and the church.

2. Many other churches, however, possessing full reservoirs of gospel truth, reluctantly and, only as much as they think necessary, release it to others. What we abundantly receive into our lives and church must be poured as abundantly into other lives and churches. That's a challenge often unmet by us. We let trickles of blessings flow to others from the vast reservoir reserved for self, but the Master's instructions are clear: we're to be aqueducts of the benefactions poured into our life.

3. No reason exists to retain God's benefits as though they're limited or only grudgingly and periodically bestowed.

God renews His resources within us daily, and the supply is constant and endlessly renewable.

4. The issue resolves itself into a disturbing question for many Christians: should those hearing but not communicating the gospel have the privilege of continued hearing? Should a superfluity of grace exist in a few lives when a spectacular lack exists in most?

5. Notice: with the pipe unobstructed, torrents in, torrents out; with it plugged, torrents in, trickles out. What happens to the excess? It's in the pipeline waiting to be released. Spiritually speaking, the spiritual energies just lie around unused. Or they get used in self-centered efforts—Bible studies, potlucks and other make-work projects that we equate with Bible fellowship. It also becomes the source of problems—bickering, gossip and divisions. Unused spiritual energy backs up and soon reeks. Yet, many Christians remain content to receive torrents of blessings and let only trickles leak to others.

⌘　⌘　⌘　⌘　⌘　⌘

Subject Idea:	Association
Scripture:	Acts 11:26; Romans 12:1
Visual Item:	Several brand name articles
Truth Stressed:	Possessing God's name imposes a strict lifestyle on us.
Procedure:	Show the articles and briefly explain the value of a name brand in advertising and sales.

Applications:

1. Name brands proclaim quality, durability and value. Manufacturers dare to put their company's logo on the product because they invest immense sums in market research, product development, manufacture and advertising. They fearlessly attach the company name to guarantee buyer satisfaction.

2.   Further, to illustrate the value of the cereal, jeans, make-up, vehicle, etc., the company recruits celebrities to showcase their product. These people are carefully chosen to enlarge, not overshadow the product. The manufacturers' message is: this is the kind of person we want to reach; further, this kind of person allows his name to be used on our product because he knows and appreciates value. The manufacturers know that celebrity presence sells products.

3.   God shamelessly, confidently and boldly put Christ's life on display before the world. In every instance equal to the task, Jesus dramatized God's presence in human form. God's people now have the awesome privilege and responsibility of expressing Christ's life. Amazing as it seems, given all our frailties, failures and sinfulness, God does so boldly, confidently and shamelessly. He knows the world has nothing that compares with the Christ-honoring life; that even the poorest Christian example outshines the world's best example. But God won't settle for His product's being mutilated or tainted, impaired or inferior. He aims to build into His people the brilliance His Son expressed while in the flesh. This thrilling privilege of bearing in our daily walk the name of Jesus energizes, exercises and releases the spiritual potential within us.

⌘   ⌘   ⌘   ⌘   ⌘   ⌘

Subject Idea: Changelessness
Scripture: Malachi 3:6
Visual Item: A length of 2 x 4 lumber you have measured; tape measure
Truth Stressed: God has specifically determined the perimeters of truth.
Procedure: Show the wood and ask for several guesses on its length. Record the numbers and ask the people to vote their choice of the

guesses.   Measure the wood and give them
the exact length.

Applications:

1. A lot of religious people want truth to be as flexible as our
guesses at this 2 x 4's length. They feel, as one denomi-
national leader said, that there are many dimensions of
truth. That's wrong. There are many dimensions *in*, not
many dimensions *of* truth. The latter idea opens God's
truth to personal prejudices and misperceptions. The
former allows us the freedom to roam, investigate and
unearth previously unfathomed distances in God's word.

2. All truth resides within the perimeters God Himself has
established, whatever discipline of study, lifestyle or
belief the Bible addresses. Outside those perimeters no
truth exists, but only lies that Satan brazenly equates with
truth in order to deceive the world.

3. God's word specifically outlines the doctrine and lifestyle
of all who seek Him. All who avail themselves of that
word find themselves constantly refreshed and surprised
by joy. We cannot imagine why people want to step
outside those defined limits, thinking something superior
exists outside. Nothing does!

4. Everyone voted his feelings and convictions about this
board's length. But no opinion changed its exact length.
It didn't extend or recede to please us. Of course, it's a
dead piece of a once living tree. But the Living God is no
more *inclined* to change His truth than this dead wood
can. Our vote against God's word won't force Him to ab-
rogate those offending books and passages. Our vote for
certain doctrines won't encourage God to retain them.
God, the Sovereign of the world, determined to remain
GOD, despite our egotistical silliness, has written what
He wanted to say, said what He meant and made it clear.
He demands that we, to make ourselves acceptable to
Him, adjust our expectations of truth to the limitations He
imposed on it. Whether or not we do, He'll never adjust,
alter or delete His truth just to make us more comfortable
or His word more appealing.

⌘   ⌘   ⌘   ⌘   ⌘   ⌘

Subject Idea:	Changes
Scripture:	II Corinthians 3:7-18
Visual Item:	Four pictures of the same person's face: 1. Dark, 2. Lighter, 3. Bright, 4. Glowing. (You may need help from a photographer to achieve the desired effect. Choose someone with an unfailing sense of humor.)
Truth Stressed:	Worship anticipates our future glory.
Procedure:	Show the first three pictures, representing us as at certain stages of our day or week. Express gratitude to the person who served as your model. Use the fourth picture as directed.

Applications:

1.   The first picture represents many of us any given morning—or what we become through a week of career, family and church responsibilities. We become obsessed with negatives that darken our life. This isn't the real *me*, we know, but it's what I've allowed myself to become. (If it is the real me, we really have a problem and better get help.) Then along comes Sunday and, on any given Sunday morning, it's church time, and we don't want to go. In fact, we don't think we can make it today! We just don't feel like "church" today! We're either mad at someone or have had an argument with our spouse or child, and we'd rather not go someplace where we have to appear happy when we're irritated or pious when we feel profane! Indeed, if all who "almost didn't make it to church" hadn't, mark that as the lowest attendance ever! Sometimes even religious people find it possible to do what they'd rather not!

2.   The second picture represents what happens to us during the day. As we meet challenges, accomplish goals and expel inertia by activity, we begin to feel good about ourselves. Hasn't been so bad after all, we think; we think we can make it now. When Sunday comes, and we attend in spite of our inclinations to stay home, we sense a change occurring. The teaching, fellowship, singing, preaching and enthusiasm of worship eclipse our mor-

tality and bring God back into view. The celebration of Heaven brought to earth reminds us how glad we are that we obeyed our Master's commands instead of Satan's enticements — and being so happy we didn't miss this experience we'll be better prepared the next time Satan urges us to stay away.

3. The third picture should represent us after our day's activity — tired, maybe exhausted, but filled with a sense of achievement. After worship services, aglow with the Spirit, recharged spiritually, our emotional batteries overflowing with energy, we're ready to serve the Christ in home, career and in the world. If worship has its intended effect, we'll glow, and others will see and praise God. But be forewarned: if we *feel* we're glowing, we're really drawing attention to ourselves. Moses didn't know that his face glowed!

4. (Show the fourth picture.) This represents what each faithful Christian is to become when Christ returns and the Holy City comes down from Heaven. Notice the nimbus surrounding the person. You may not realize it, but it's the same person in picture number one — show the picture. Yes, the very same — but now, in this hopelessly inadequate representation of future joy, radiantly aglow! Think of that the next time we snub a fellow believer; or take revenge; or consider him our social inferior; or refuse to forgive him — that very person shall one day *glow this way*! And if he/she were to begin that process right now, we'd resist falling before him/her only by the strongest refusals! We've never met a Christian who was *common*! Everyone's potentially a miniature of Jesus Christ now and a certain replica of Jesus Christ eternally!

5. On any given Sunday, when we come to church, what face do we wear? What face represents our spiritual state this instant? If we've come sad, worn, exhausted, beaten, we should leave with another face entirely! If we don't, has worship failed us? Or have we failed to let God love us as He so desperately desires? Remember, as God's child, we'll one day and forever afterwards, glow with ethereal majesty. Why not let Jesus give us a presentiment of number four by turning us into number three (hold each up in turn)? We're destined to shine like the sun! Why not begin now to burst with that illumination?

HEAVEN AND HELL

Both Heaven and Hell exist as the ultimate destinies of particular choices, an unpopular idea today, with behavior without responsibility the mantra spouted everywhere. Even when found in the act of committing crimes, the guilty plead a poor home life or undue influence by even more wicked associates. Some people won't choose Heaven because they feel it's boring; a few choose Hell because they feel it isn't. In these illustrations, Heaven and Hell are the ultimate destiny of people's choices in life, with this caveat: no one in Heaven will ever regret the experience, and no one in Hell will ever cherish it!

Subject Idea:	Progress
Scripture:	Matthew 13:7, 22
Visual Item:	Plane ticket; itinerary copied on overhead transparency, if possible
Truth Stressed:	Jesus offers us Heaven, but Satan wants us to refuse the offer.
Procedure:	Show the ticket and give the destination; if you have the itinerary on the overhead, show the stops made; otherwise, verbally explain them.

Applications:

1. Christ's sacrifice has reserved our passage from earth to Heaven; from death to life; from condemnation to forgiveness. However, Satan's temptations, incursions and roadblocks threaten to cancel our reservation and have us sent to Hell instead.

2. As we prepare for any trip, we take what we feel is essential and leave what isn't. Often we leave whatever can be purchased later. However, only as we prepare now can we be assured of arriving in Heaven later. No one who waits till he "gets" there to buy the essentials for staying finds anything available. Preparation for the next world begins and continues in this world. We won't have after-

death opportunities to correct mistakes made here or supply deficiencies accrued here.

3. All airlines encourage passengers to arrive at least an hour before departure. Problems with parking may boost arrival time to two hours. That rule of departure applies to going to Heaven: accept Christ as early as is reasonable if a child, and immediately if an adult. Bearing the daily fruit of God's Spirit, not just waiting to die, is an ongoing privilege of belonging to Christ.

4. (If the flight isn't non-stop.) You'll notice that this itinerary has intermediate stops—an appropriate thought, since our Heaven-bound progress is never a non-stop flight. We can't just get on a spiritual high and float through life to God's presence. There are always stops along the way, and at each one Satan tries to void our progress. In an airport we can miss our flight by arriving late, by having too little time to get from one terminal to another or by suffering weather delays or mechanical problems. No fewer opportunities to be delayed exist in the spiritual life. Satan won't let us proceed without trying to divert or abort us. That's his aim, and he'll succeed if we're not alert to his deceit and guile. Disagreements with other Christians, feeling overlooked by the members or staff in a time of need, the multiplying demands of family and career, etc., can all be part of Satan's grand design of first interrupting our Heaven-bound course, then re-directing us to Hell. Let us be forewarned; let us beware!

⌘   ⌘   ⌘   ⌘   ⌘   ⌘

Subject Idea:	Choices
Scripture:	Revelation 21:7-8
Visual Item:	Two boxes of the same puzzle. Complete one puzzle and mount on a board for exhibition; uncover the other box for use at the appropriate time.

Truth Stressed: Present choices determine eternal destiny.

Procedure: Show the completed puzzle with interesting details highlighted. This represents Heaven. Make applications.

Applications:

1. Too many for counting, the following ecstasies suggest a few reasons we'll be glad when God welcomes us home. First, Heaven is in every way as real as the God who prepares it. Second, righteousness is its basis—the holiness that presently suffers persecution, debasement and ridicule in a world permeated with fleshly and intellectual ambition. Third, we'll *realize* all we personally want to be—spiritual, intelligent, charming, tactful, loving, etc. No, not just realize, but exceed all our expectations in these areas by eliminating anything incomplete, discordant, inconsistent and imperfect. Fourth, Heaven banishes all negatives, including all memory of judgment and condemnation! All that we'll remember about this life is that, once in Christ, we instantly began to live eternally with him. And all that we experienced—all—nothing exempted, was a pleasure, and nothing was a sorrow! Fifth, we'll have absolute *awareness*, a focused intensity of thought, being and perception, every fiber of our personality alive, radiant, sharpened, sensitized with joy! Sixth, each person will retain his distinctiveness, adding his own giftedness to the praise of God. Seventh, our spiritual metabolism will activate all our intellectual and spiritual capacity, enabling us to appreciate fully everything we see and understand deeply everything we hear. Eighth, everyone there will be co-heirs of God's glory; all will shine equally brightly, for all will reflect the Common Light! Ninth, everyone there will be just like us—as intensely focused, perfect, complete and free from limitations. What an infinite joy that is—reason enough by itself to be in Heaven—since nearly all our problems here are people-related. Heaven is exempt from people problems! (At this point, take the second puzzle box, hold it in front of you, and while holding the box, fling the pieces into the air. (It might be well to have a blanket below to catch the pieces.)

2. For every positive when thinking of Heaven, put a negative for Hell, for Hell has no positives. Like the pieces of the puzzle below, Hell is chaos; is regret; is disillusionment; is denial; is criticism; is bitterness; is accusation; is warfare; is distress; is harshness; is hatred. In Hell people have memories of what they previously called pleasures, only to find them miseries. They live with gnawing regret and with consuming frustration. Everyone there is like them, too, but always in each other's way, being pushed aside and, if refusing, being violently removed. Intrigue never ceases, and deceit is constant. There's no peace or singing or fellowship— only intense competition and rivalry and ambition! And they will never admit they were wrong and will always blame God for their fate.
3. With such menace so absolutely sure, why would we risk a forever-and-ever Hell? With such promise so absolutely sure, why wouldn't we want Heaven as our eternal home?

⌘   ⌘   ⌘   ⌘   ⌘   ⌘

Subject Idea:	Eternity
Scripture:	Revelation 21:27; 22:5
Visual Item:	A volunteer; a large ball of string, long enough to go the length of your sanctuary and beyond, each length of different colors (use food dye); strings for ties
Truth Stressed:	The decisions we presently make determine our eternal destiny.
Procedure:	Hold one end of the string and have the volunteer hold the ball. Tell the people that, believing God created everything 6,000-10,000 years ago, you're going to offer an illustration explaining the difference between time and eternity. Have the volunteer walk off six feet of the string. Have

this section colored with the different dyes, and tied at intervals, as it represents human history, while the ball represents eternity. Have the ball held high so the people can see the difference. Make applications, leaving the volunteer in place.

Applications:

1. I've tied different colored yarn at intervals along the string, representing the time frame of Bible events. The first tie, close to my hand is Adam and Eve, given the opportunity to obey God when confronted with the chance to disobey. They failed, and notice now, how that decision affected all succeeding history, represented by the colored string. The actions and decisions of leaders always impact beyond their personal lives. Every human since Adam and Eve has been negatively affected by their single mistake.

2. For the purpose of the illustration, on a scale of a foot per 1000 years, I've put the first string at 20 inches, representing God's punishment of the world in Noah's flood. Humanity took Adam and Eve's rebellion to its logical extreme: don't take God seriously, make your own decisions, live for the present. Approximately 300 years later (string at 24 inches), God called Abraham to reverse their rebellion into obedient trust. Nine hundred years more (string at 35 inches) brought David's birth as founder of the eternal monarchy. Over a thousand years later (put a scarlet string at 48 inches) Jesus came as heir of David's throne. And it's been approximately 2000 years since Jesus came, (string at 6 feet). (Also, add two colored strings an inch apart beyond the last string; explain them momentarily.)

3. This six foot section of string represents human history. But note: the ball represents eternity. (Have the volunteer unroll the ball as he walks away and outside the sanctuary, closing the door behind, with the string disappearing beyond the door.)

4. Note at the end of the colored string I've put two strings an inch apart. They represent the average lifespan of 70-80 years. None of us was born before 1900, while many

of us will live well into the next century. But note how close together the last two strings are: that's all the time we have to determine our eternal destiny. All who have lived, from the start to the finish of history, settle their eternal state by the decisions made in their generation! That's it, that small space in time, nothing more, no second chances after death! What we do in that inch space determines our *eternal* destiny! Beyond the last strips of yarn in this room, eternity is represented. Outside the sanctuary, disappearing before our eyes but continuing on, eternity lasts and lasts. Wherever we want to spend all that timeless dimension, we must prepare now!

5.   Remember I said that every human since Adam has been negatively affected by his mistake? Indeed, in addition to all the tragedies of history, Adam's failure inflicted a death sentence none escapes. Each person dies. However, *our* decisions now while we live, not Adam's sin in Eden, determine where we spend eternity—the rest of that ball of string! Blame him for our physical death, but blame only ourselves for eternal punishment because Jesus died to save us from that!

6.   Imagine if our volunteer were to walk that ball of string straight out of the building into the parking lot, through it and down/across the street, down the highway, out of town to the county line, the state line, etc.—on and on and on. And if he could keep going and never stop, that's an idea of eternity. Time is too short to live it for anyone but God, and eternity's too long to spend it anywhere but with God! Since eternity lasts forever, wherever we spend it, where are the beliefs and actions of our inch-in-time sending us?

⌘   ⌘   ⌘   ⌘   ⌘   ⌘

Subject Idea: Choices
Scripture: Deuteronomy 34:5-6; Matthew 17:3

Visual Item:	Three enlarged pictures of Berlin, Germany: one prior to World War II, one following WW II, one after reunification in 1990; volunteers to hold them; an enlarged picture of the New Jerusalem, kept hidden till the appropriate time.
Truth Stressed:	Our choices determine our life here and hereafter.
Procedure:	Explain that each picture illustrates how our choice of Satan or Jesus affects our eternal destiny.

Applications:

1. Show the pre-WW II Berlin. This represents us in our natural, unconverted state. Show the post-WW II Berlin. This represents what we become if we remain unconverted. Every time. Each person. Without fail.

2. Satan's single obsession is to smash us until we're reduced to spiritual ruins. And that's what happens if we refuse Christ's call to discipleship. By following our instinctive drive for self-preservation and by limiting our interest to this life, Satan achieves his goal. A focused commitment to everyday life offers Satan his most powerful and insidious weapon against the spiritual life. He knows that we long for fulfillment, crave satisfaction and seethe with ambition to achieve, so he perverts these perfectly normal drives into obsessions and has only to deceive us into self-will to serve his interests. That's all! Just be an ordinary, unconverted person! Something we do every day, answering the needs of the soul within us! Don't think about God or anybody else; think only of what contents self and our needs; what helps us to be fulfilled. The end of that pursuit is spiritual ruination!

3. Note that it may not be *moral* ruination in this life. Like atheists, we may decide that practicing the Golden Rule is beneficial in reaching our goal—and we'll practice it to serve our best interests. We may join fraternal clubs and service organizations because they do good works, and we want to return "something" to our community and society. We'll give to charities, serve on community boards and

help serve Thanksgiving and Christmas dinners to the homeless, bringing personal satisfaction. But this life is unaware of God and considers Him irrelevant to any practical purpose. Humanity tirelessly boasts its morality as a means of denying God's perfection! But while that nonsense doesn't even flutter with life, it ruins us.

4. A vast gulf exists between moral and spiritual — the word we now consider. (Show Berlin after reunification). Being spiritual means surrendering the egotism that dominated Adam. It substitutes God's word for our opinions. God, not self, becomes the focus of life.

5. That seems a small distinction. But the difference between Berlin after WW II and after reunification represents the distinction between a moral and a spiritual life. (Show both pictures.) Unsaved humanity, by adopting spiritual values, can be moral; only the redeemed human, possessed of the Holy Spirit, can be spiritual. If we let Jesus rule, he rebuilds any rubble in life; strengthens every weakness; sharpens every ability; increases our initial awareness of God into appreciation of God, dependence on God and thanksgiving to God. He builds a life that recognizes, welcomes and demonstrates God.

6. There's a sharp distinction between Berlin after reunification and Christ's work in us. There always will be, as in modern Germany, pockets of economic unrest, racism against minorities, difficulty in settling differences and feelings of disenfranchisement. In the life Jesus uses, only positive results occur. He enables every believer to reach his potential, each feeling himself the sole object of God's affection — who has so much love everyone feels the same way.

7. Jesus promises to go far beyond any good he presently provides to a new Heaven and earth. Like each new generation, every political party coming into office and every new chief executive officer, Jesus promises to make life better for everyone. Unlike them, he unfailingly reaches his goal. And Christ's perfection alone stands between our desire to be perfect and our inability to be, despite our efforts, surpassing God's unyielding demand for perfection in those accessing him!

8. (Show the picture of the New Jerusalem.) Berlin rebuilt after reunification represents humanity's ability to produce prosperity from adversity. But all that's consigned to dissolution, when only what Christ builds outlasts the fire of judgment to come. A rebuilt Berlin is an adequate capital for a reunited Germany, but not for the new world. That's reserved for God's city, coming down out of heaven as the eternal home of God's people. Satan can devastate life; he's ruined many. Only God can obliterate all that Satan's wrecked and renew it, with all signs of the former destruction eliminated in the renewal!

9. What life do we choose? (Show pre- and post-WW II Berlin.) An earthly lifestyle, committed to the five senses? If so, we're doomed to Hell. Mark it, and don't forget it: an unconverted life is a ruined life! (Show post-reunification Berlin.) A spiritually reconstructed life is alive with expectation and an incredible future, appealing to our sense of self-preservation. Which model guarantees eternal personal fulfillment? Berlin pre- and post-WW II or Berlin reunited?

10. More importantly to kingdom purposes, as present mistakes in choosing our model doom our future, investing now in God's future enriches everyday life! (Show New Jerusalem.) This is what each believer is destined to inherit. How can we act like picture number one when our destiny is number four? If we let it, our coming inheritance positively upgrades our present attitude, behavior and habits. Why would we ever want to act like picture one when we can presently live as a reflection of picture four?

⌘   ⌘   ⌘   ⌘   ⌘   ⌘

Subject Idea:	Renewal
Scripture:	John 14:1-2
Visual Item:	Gallon jar with objects hidden in sand: ring, coin, key, bracelet, candy in cellophane, etc.; volunteer

Truth Stressed: The present fallen life hides the glories of God's new world.

Procedure: Show the jar and tell the people you've hidden certain objects inside. Can they tell what? Ask the volunteer to come forward; give him a chance to look; can he tell what's inside? Then proceed in one of two ways: have the volunteer probe with his hands to uncover some of what's hidden there, or, using a window screen as a sifter, pour the entire jar into a larger container.

Applications:

1.   God's curse on Adam involved all creation since Adam was responsible for Eve's fall. The fact that he was *with* her when she ate the fruit rendered his acquiescence inexcusable. Suddenly subjected to vanity, creation failed to prolong Adam's life—its original purpose. Before their sin, they ate fruit and lived; after their sin, they ate but still died. However, though fallen, creation continually expresses beauties that enthrall us. Sunrises and sunsets, prairies abloom, hillsides of golden grain, purple mountain majesties and breakers lashing rocky shores all declare something of a greater, now depleted glory.

2.   (If you leave the sand in the jar). If we don't empty all the sand, we won't know what may still be hidden in the remainder. That's why death is necessary for the believer, however heartbreaking for the survivor. We must leave this body and this world because they presently hide the greater glories God has prepared. He can't show them here since sin buried them too deeply inside us for present exploration. That's why it's foolish for people to look to this world for satisfaction and fulfillment. It can't provide either. It can only provide what we need to survive here, not to live with God here or hereafter!

3.   Unlike humanity, creation anxiously awaits its death, though it's death by incineration, because it sees renovated life rising from the ashes! How strange that we, thought to be intelligent, refuse to die, while creation, thought to be inanimate—unfeeling, unhearing,

unmoved—can't wait for its change! It's in a state of constant excitement, anticipating renewal by fire. Obviously, creation accepts facts we ignore!

4.   (If you leave sand in the jar). When I said I had hidden objects in the sand, you believed, though you couldn't personally tell and see. You believed since you know I wouldn't lie. Letting you see some of them simply verified what you believed, based on the integrity I've built with you. How much more should we believe God's promise of incredible glories, strengths, insights, etc. to come when right now we experience their lesser manifestations! Not only should we believe because it's impossible for God to lie, but because we've experienced the evidence He's let us uncover! And we can believe utterly when He tells us that there's much more where that came from and much more of the same still inside!

5.   (If you empty whole jar.) Our entire Christian experience verifies the greater experience yet to come. Even now, spiritual qualities unleashed by our conversion convince us of infinitely greater qualities ahead. The forgiveness presently enjoyed thrills us, while it only hints of a perfected holiness. The righteousness that Christ confers only whets our appetite for the righteousness to be possessed without limit or obstacle in an unlimited body. Wherever the Holy Spirit abides, he invariably assures us of more of the same at an accelerated pace, at an exalted level. All our present victories, laid out before us like all the objects in this jar, convince us that present victory over the flesh guarantees future conquest of death, Satan, sin and Hell! For, as Christianity forgives our past and empowers our present, it beatifies our future!

⌘ ⌘ ⌘ ⌘ ⌘ ⌘

Subject Idea: Invitation
Scripture: Philippians 2:12; Hebrews 3:15-19
Visual Item: Wedding or birthday party invitation

Truth Stressed: We determine whether we accept God's invitation to Heaven.

Procedure: Show the invitation and, if agreeable to all and offensive to none, read it.

Applications:

1.   Note that it invites the addressee to a particular function at a specific place and time. Just so, in the love letter He's written to the world, God invites everyone to Heaven. Where this invitation went only to those chosen by the families involved, God's invitation extends to all. He sent Jesus to save everyone, no one exempted; each one, no one proscribed. God's desire is that each person ever to live would be saved. He has no favorites that He'll invite to the exclusion of others. That's our style, not God's.

2.   Those receiving the invitation decide whether to attend. Distance may prevent it or lack of acquaintance with one of the parties or lack of value placed on the relationship. There would be a reason for not attending. In conversing with the unsaved, Christians need to surface their reasons for rejecting God's invitation to Heaven. Why do they choose not to be saved? To let non-Christians go unchallenged when they refuse God's call means they never have to face the flaws in their thinking. There's no good reason to reject God's invitation to salvation, though humanity never stops creating exquisite excuses! Rejecting God in Christ not only disregards the evidence He's offered to encourage acceptance, but harms our best interests. To have our sins forgiven is in our best interest; to be reconciled to God is in our best interest; to possess a new attitude, a new perspective on life, is in our best interest! Christians, gently and graciously, but firmly and persuasively, inquire why the unsaved won't accept Jesus! Be ready to expose the fallacies in their position and to urge their submission to what can only be in their best interest!

3.   Those who don't answer this invitation and don't attend the ceremony or party may not suffer any consequences. But there will come a time when all who refuse God's invitation will wish they hadn't been so stupid; hadn't

allowed baseless excuses to keep them away; had stifled the pride that kept them away; had surrendered the ego that boasted its sufficiency! But then it'll be too late. To go to the wedding or the party a week after it's over may mean only a useless trip. To clamor for forgiveness when judgment has come means we've lost the chance to live and must go on dying eternally, without benefit of death to put us out of our misery! Answer God's invitation; attend the services; become a member of His body. Only those answering God's call and submitting to Christ's lordship will enter Heaven. For while we determine whether or not we'll accept God's invitation, He determines who enters His presence!

HOLY SPIRIT

From World War II battlefields in Tunisia, Anzio and over German cities, came stories of many—sometimes 60 percent—German long- and short-range shells penetrating planes, vehicles and battlefield positions without exploding. Even at the time, the Allied military attributed it to sabotage among munitions workers. One Flying Fortress returned to England with eleven shells inside the gas tanks. The crew found all of them empty, save one. In it was a note, written in Czech: "This is all we can do for you now."

In these illustrations are a few examples of the *no small thing* God does for us now through the Holy Spirit.

Subject Idea:	Openness
Scripture:	John 14:25; Acts 1:8
Visual Item:	Ball glove; softball; volunteer
Truth Stressed:	We need to make sure our lives are open to the Holy Spirit.
Procedure:	Have the volunteer take the ball and move about four feet away. Try to catch the ball while keeping the glove closed. Impossible!

Applications:

1. God wants a maturing spiritual relationship with us, but we determine its depth. We, not He, limit the extent of our discipleship, our usefulness to Him, our rate of progress as Christians. If we're less than overcomers in Christ, the problem isn't the absence of the Holy Spirit; he's present and ready to possess us. If we're open, God is sending him; if we're closed, God is still sending him because He knows how essential His Spirit is to a victorious life, but we're unable to receive because we aren't convinced! Like the glove, we can be closed, partly open or fully open to God's will. That choice is ours, and He'll respect it, whatever it is. We *receive* the Holy Spirit *if* we're open to him.

2. God sends the Holy Spirit on His terms, not ours; sometimes independent of, but always according to Bible teaching; within the different manifestations taught in Acts: (The gift of the Holy Spirit himself when we're baptized, Acts 2:38; the Baptism of the Holy Spirit, expressed only twice, Acts 2:4 and 10:44-46, to inaugurate Christianity and to extend it to the Gentiles; the special gifts of the Holy Spirit, granted only by the Apostles, Acts 8:18-19 and 19:6, to those they considered responsible enough to possess them.) Much confusion exists among God's people from a faulty understanding of these different manifestations. This leads Christians to diminish water baptism and to demand Holy Spirit baptism, though the former was commanded of every penitent and the latter given only to the Apostles and to Cornelius' household, and on both occasions to establish Christianity!

3. There are an unlimited number of ways we can close our lives to the Spirit, some of which occur so naturally we're guilty but unaware. Adversity can close us, as can unforgiven sin, ignorance of the Bible, materialism, interference from life (a recurring problem among Christians). Every time we do it, we miss what God throws us. We need to learn to live in the expectation of being surprised by joy!

⌘   ⌘   ⌘   ⌘   ⌘   ⌘

Subject Idea:	Dangers
Scripture:	Acts 2:3; I Thessalonians 5:19
Visual Item:	Fire extinguisher
Truth Stressed:	We need to eliminate factors that extinguish our spiritual life.
Procedure:	As you show the extinguisher, ask how many have one; where they store it; when it was last re-charged; why they keep it handy.

Applications:

1. The purpose of a fire extinguisher is to eliminate danger: to smother a potential threat to ourselves and our property. Since accidental fire poses a danger, the extinguisher represents a positive that removes a negative. All that is reversed spiritually. The Holy Spirit is a spark God thrusts into our heart at baptism that He wants to nourish into flame. He wants nothing to hinder, limit or smother that glowing, never-consuming incineration. He wants it encouraged, hastened and expanded.

2. We, however, often negate God's desire. In fact, thinking themselves spiritual extinguishers, some Christians consider it their responsibility to quench joy from the Christian life and replace it with gloom; to remove the successes enjoyed by a remembrance of failures experienced; to eradicate delight from a happy worship experience by misplaced criticism; to stop forward momentum by an untimely objection. Called "grace-builders" because they force others to exercise restraint and patience, these people almost always mean less harm than they cause and create more umbrage than they intend. Nevertheless, their spiritual foam freezes the Spirit's flame within Christ's body! Such people should painstakingly examine their motives, personalities and spiritual development to discover areas where they instinctively silence the Spirit. Removing their personal obstacles to God's grace will eliminate their almost instinctive need to restrain spiritual growth.

3. Not that we need outside interference to depress the Holy Spirit. Our own bad habits often do that; and our affiliation with companions who weaken our resolves; and our refusal to attend services and Bible studies; and our objection when Christian friends admonish us about harmful behavior patterns. We don't need help extinguishing the Spirit, but we always get it!

4. As fire in a furnace or fireplace exudes warmth, light and life, the Holy Spirit's presence creates a living, energetic, positive faith that appeals to and attracts others. We need to nourish the Spirit's fire within us. In some of us it may be yet a spark; not to fear, the spark will burst into flame

if we offer it spiritual fuel. In some it may be only a small blaze; not to fear, God will soon have it roaring if we refrain from thoughts and behaviors that choke, then stifle it.

⌘   ⌘   ⌘   ⌘   ⌘   ⌘

Subject Idea:	Guidance
Scripture:	John 14:16, 26; 15:26; 16:8, 13
Visual Item:	Medical encyclopedia
Truth Stressed:	The Holy Spirit powerfully convicts the world and guides the Christian.
Procedure:	Beforehand find a disease with fairly explicit symptoms. Without identifying it, read the symptoms and ask if it sounds familiar. Identify it. Have they had these symptoms but another disorder entirely? Will they trust their health to an encyclopedia or to a qualified physician?

Applications:

1. At its very best a medical encyclopedia can hint at our illness. More often, it doesn't give even a clue. It might make fascinating reading, but for diagnosis and cure we need a medical specialist. They make mistakes, too, but not as quickly as we when reading an encyclopedia.

2. God knows the scale of spiritual conflict we face and works actively to bring success in each person's life. The Holy Spirit has two functions: one for the unbeliever, the other for the Christian. The Holy Spirit convicts the world of guilt: about Jesus, because it doesn't believe he's God's Son; about righteousness, because Christ's resurrection and ascension proved he *was*; of judgment, because Jesus judges Satan by dying and overcoming death. Is the Spirit convicting anyone here in any of these areas? The Spirit will teach us where we're wrong about Jesus and ourselves and how we can correct our mistakes.

People are always more open to the comforting than to the difficult truth in the Bible. We can only appreciate the comforting truth about God if we accept the difficult truth about ourselves.

3.   As the Spirit of truth, the Holy Spirit guides the Christian. Like the Father and Son from whom he comes, the Holy Spirit is truth—not just true, as if he represents or teaches something—but is TRUTH, as he is God! He remains with us and in us; he purposefully brings glory to Jesus, not to himself; he speaks only what he's given to say; he reminds God's people of all the truth Jesus revealed; he expects us to testify to others as he has to us.

4.   The Spirit guides in practical ways also, all as a result of the theological education we receive from him: we understand Bible teaching, receive guidance in making decisions, choosing friends and careers; we remain free from false doctrines, corrupting influences and vile behavior. The presence of the Spirit always produces positive results in Christians and potentially positive results in the seeking, open-minded unsaved. All should listen carefully as the Holy Spirit speaks through the Bible. He knows exactly what he's saying, for he is the Perfect Professor of Ultimate Realities.

⌘   ⌘   ⌘   ⌘   ⌘   ⌘

Subject Idea:	Trust
Scripture:	John 11:25-26; John 14:18
Visual Item:	Road map
Truth Stressed:	We can trust the Holy Spirit's guidance.
Procedure:	Beforehand choose a destination. Open the map (you may need someone to help hold it) and show the route you expect to take. Question: Does anyone doubt that that road exists? (No). Could they be confident it exists if they had never been on it before? (Yes, because of the mapmaker's integrity.)

Applications:

1. God knows we need guidance to Heaven. He also knows that Heaven is too far distant to appeal to most people. To satisfy His requirements for our eventual entrance there, He offers proof of our present need of Him and of His present conquest of life. It's possible to miss the journey if we inordinately focus on the destination. Jesus clearly understood the need for both. Once we accept him, he promised, we begin eternal life. So all our succeeding years are spent enjoying our journey to Heaven even as we await our arrival there.

2. The Holy Spirit now empowers us to demonstrate that eternal life. If we think about it, the only proof we personally can offer for Heaven's existence is the ecstasy of our present life—to live so powerful a courage, holiness and love that people sense it, feel it and want it. After we're dead, we can't testify; after they're dead, they can't hear us. Now is the time the Spirit empowers us to offer that proof.

3. Christ's personal life and his conquest of death established his integrity. The Holy Spirit educates us in its depths! That integrity, the foundational inability of God to lie and His equal ability to tell the truth, establish the trustworthiness of Jesus Christ. The Holy Spirit guides us so we can presently conquer life and achieve resurrection. He knows where God wants us to go eventually and enables us to presently anticipate its life. Under orders from God to express personally the excellence of his presence, Christians focus on their future, yet find themselves presently joyous, fruitful and confident. While not possessing that future life, we participate in it by the Holy Spirit's presence in us. Whatever truth sins tells about our present frailty, Christ's perfection renders it a lie. However transient we now are, his eternal life proves it a lie. Our immorality and consequent mortality are annihilated by his immortality!

4. If we want to survive death, will we trust someone who died and rose again or those still dead? If we want eventual perfection, will we trust one who is Perfection or those still flummoxed by their flaws? Christ shows the

way through this life as proof of his mastery of the next. If Christians allow it, the Holy Spirit will so empower us with Christ's grace that the unsaved will be amazed and impressed. And they will say, "If Jesus can do that for them in a world that's going to end, what incredible majesties can he provide in a world that won't?"

⌘   ⌘   ⌘   ⌘   ⌘   ⌘

Subject Idea: Memories

Scripture: Ecclesiastes 7:10; Philippians 3:13

Visual Item: Family photo album

Truth Stressed: The Holy Spirit encourages our present faith by recalling his former faithfulness.

Procedure: Ask several people beforehand to bring a snapshot of some important event in their family. Have them show the picture and tell how the frozen-in-time picture has present meaning.

Applications:

1. As we've seen, showing the pictures and explaining their meaning have brought both tears and laughter. They rivet the event in our memory; the people in the picture, some now dead, for an instant live again. We hear their voices; see their smiles; relive an experience with them. Whether a wave of melancholia or delight washes over us, for that instant we're there with them, and they're here with us. While they can never return to us, something of what they were remains with us, helping make us what we've become.

2. While the past is fixed in stone and never changes, its lessons relate to us. The Holy Spirit, working through the word in our personal Christian experience, unveils the past to stimulate our discipleship. He reminds us of mistakes that have left the Christ-likeness within us undeveloped; of victories that have caused us to soar with

possibilities! Though we can only profitably learn from the past, never profitably live there, we disregard its lessons at the risk of repeating mistakes that it warns us to avoid, adding our own to make them worse.

3. By remembering our past, we can see how God led us when we felt all alone, loved us when we felt abandoned and protected us when we sensed only imminent danger. We can see how uncommonly wise were the refusals we thought heartless at the time and how prolifically productive the labor we then considered only vexatious.

4. By studying both the negative and positive in our past we build for the future. Sometimes past sights convulse us with a sudden ache of mistakes and failures we think better left unrecalled. They're too frightening to face because we continue to be trapped inside them—and the Holy Spirit whispers, "Why, when Jesus set you free?" We need to accept the bitter reality of their existence, for we can't alter past behavior that now embarrasses; or, like revisionist historians, reorganize it into something euphemistic, making ourselves better by making others worse. Use those occasions to be cleansed, repaired, renewed, released, not to justify or explain or deny!

5. In what one writer calls the luxury of nostalgia, we're all tempted to create an ideal past we want remembered to shield us from the person we've become and want to forget. That's destructive to us and a denial of the Master's sacrifice. He remakes us in His image precisely so we don't have to fashion a mythical saint we never were or despise the real sinner we've become. He saves, and saves all, and saves each one to the uttermost, to forgiveness we desperately seek, to ecstasy we passionately desire.

6. The Holy Spirit encourages us to study the past to learn acceptable behavior. God's moral principles remain undefiled by the national demand for situational ethics, and it remains unbowed before willful, individual disobedience. God reigns; evil perishes; righteousness continues forever and ever!

7. From the past, memories speak to Christians. As the Parthenon speaks of ancient Greece; as the Colosseum of

ancient Rome, the Lord's Supper speaks of a life given for all; baptism of a life committed to him who died; the temple mount of a youth clothed in peasant's clothing hiding the Divine Mystery; apostolic labors of an Ephesus, where Paul preached; of a Patmos, where John suffered. Like miners seeking a yellow metal, these memories are golden to us. We remember them; till the New Jerusalem comes down from heaven, we shall never forget. Only the Holy Spirit could use what many consider useless memories to such lofty spiritual remembrances.

JESUS

Richard Wurmbrand approached a female Russian officer on a Moscow street. Apologizing for the intrusion, he merely sought permission to witness about Christ.

Eyes suddenly beaming, she asked if Richard loved Christ. His affirmation triggered a storm of hugs and kisses from her. Bewildered, and hoping bystanders would think them long-lost relatives, he passionately returned the hugs and kisses.

Inviting her to his home, Richard and his wife listened astonished as it became clear she knew Jesus as a name and nothing else, yet a name she loved above everything else.

She explained the curiosity: she had been taught letters at home by seeing pictures—A for apple, B for bell, C for cat, etc. Through the years she noticed that her grandparents bowed before a picture of a person they called Cristos. That name, powerful enough to bring her grandparents to their knees before his picture, became her ideal of holiness.

And that was how she came to love the name by itself, knowing nothing but that just saying it delighted her. May the following illustrations about Jesus bring you at *least*, but much more *than* joy.

Subject Idea:	Access
Scripture:	John 10:7, 9
Visual Item:	Standing door frame
Truth Stressed:	We enter God's presence only through Jesus.
Procedure:	As everyone knows, the frame holds the door that gives entrance to and egress from a house. If we lock ourselves out, we have to try a window, but that's an emergency measure.

Applications:

1. By sequestering His name in the Holy of Holies, God defied casual access to Himself. Old Testament rituals

meticulously expressed God's remoteness because the Hebrews needed to understand His transcendence. No one could come into His presence casually, and the one permitted once a year followed strict guidelines.

2. Christ's repeated New Testament teaching expressed God's familiarity because we needed to understand His immanence. What Pastor Bill Steele calls the "touch me not" God of Moses revealed Himself as the "touch me lots" God in Christ. The God at a distance had become God up-close and personal. Even there, however, our delirium in approaching Him is sobered by clear and exact specifics of preparation.

3. Where it was once possible only for the High Priest, it's available to all now; where "impossible" has been replaced by "certainly," no one can *presume* when approaching God. Blood was shed in both instances to render access safe and secure. Under Law, a goat and bull died; under Grace, the Son of God died. At neither time were mortals allowed entry uncovered and alone, however exalted among their peers.

4. Since the tabernacle and temple served as symbols of Heaven and the mercy seat as the symbol of God, the blood of bulls and goats sufficed to exonerate the High Priest and people on the Day of Atonement. However, while things can cleanse symbols, sinful mortals need someone exactly like God to open Heaven's door as they approach. Jesus alone has that key.

5. Two kinds of people look for an alternate entrance to a house: an occupant who has locked himself out or a thief trying to break in. One belongs there but, by mistake, has temporarily lost entry; one with evil intent does not. God grants admission into His presence only through Jesus, who is the Door into Heaven. There is no emergency entrance in case we fail to possess Jesus. Only those with a reason will be in Heaven. No one without that reason will be found lurking for furtive entry. And Christ's Lordship is the single reason.

6. Let's not allow our sins to keep us out of Heaven; they didn't keep Jesus from dying to forgive us. Let's certainly not trust our self-worth to gain entrance there. Our ability

to face life here with equilibrium shouldn't be confused with our glaring inability to enter God's presence unattended!

⌘   ⌘   ⌘   ⌘   ⌘   ⌘

Subject Idea: Passover

Scripture: Exodus 12:7; Matthew 26:26-28

Visual Item: Standing door frame; thick ketchup in a bowl; one-inch brush

Truth Stressed: Jesus rescues from their sins those he empowers to serve his righteousness.

Procedure: As you apply the ketchup to all three surfaces of the frame, explain that the Lamb's blood protected the Hebrews from death when God killed the firstborn of Egypt's animals and humans.

Applications:

1. The Master's institution of the Lord's Supper anchors itself in and derives its meaning from Old Testament practice. No disciple misunderstood the origin of the cup that night. From childhood they had annually celebrated their nation's Passover as a liberation from Egyptian slavery.

2. While they viewed the Passover as a final, Jesus saw it as preparatory legacy. While they felt it spoke of past events, Jesus knew it alluded to future realities, particularly of his death on Calvary and his eventual return from Heaven. Thus, the practice instituted under Moses merely symbolized the reality Christ revealed.

3. The application of blood by the Israelites was for their education, not God's information. The death angel didn't have to check every house to find congealed blood on the doorposts. Something exquisitely and specifically spiritual was involved, a lesson all humanity needed to learn: we must be under blood to escape judgment—as

executed on Egypt then; as executed at the end against sin and sinners.

4. When he instituted his Table, Jesus offered both his body and blood as its essential elements: an interesting, but overlooked extension of the Passover meal, which stressed only the animal's splattered blood. Why in Exodus only the animal's blood and, at the Lord's Table, Christ's *body* and blood? Why didn't Jesus just say, "This is my blood," without referring to his body? Because, unlike the Lamb's blood that kept Israel from death that night but couldn't keep them alive in the desert afterwards, Jesus offers eternal life *beyond* forgiveness, in addition to *saving* from sin.

5. Where the lamb's blood referenced a single night's rescue from death, the New Testament brims with references to Christ's stately, prestigious, ongoing life after the rescue. His body relates to and enlarges our future as his blood relates to and removes our past. That's the reason for the absence of the animal's body in Exodus: its life, once taken, had no power but to cover sins. Christ's body, once taken, had re-creative, as his blood had redemptive powers because his resurrection revolutionized other bodies.

6. Christ's death canceled our sin-debt. He paid it off; we owe nothing. What we owe and will spend time and eternity repaying, is the holiness-debt that release from our sin-debt imposes. What a magnificent contrast: our sin-account versus our holiness account; the former's closed; the latter's open. Free from having to pay the former, we're obligated to the eternally delightful task of discharging the latter.

⌘ ⌘ ⌘ ⌘ ⌘ ⌘

Subject Idea:	Sufficiency
Scripture:	I John 1:9
Visual Item:	Red cellophane; posterboard; red marker

Truth Stressed: Christ's blood covers all sins.

Procedure: As you write with the marker, ask the audience to suggest sins of other people. (They'll feel free to do that.) Write down a goodly number.

Applications:

1. Acceptance of sin is essential to its removal. Refusing to acknowledge our unworthiness of God guarantees continual alienation from Him. He allows into His presence only those aware of the grace that guarantees their *right* of access.

2. In private, each of us should make a mental note of all our sins. If possible, write them out; brutally note all possible bad things about ourselves and abuse self over our inability to live as we desire and as God demands.

3. Then, over the page of acknowledged transgressions, inscribe in large letters FORGIVEN. (Do this over the sins written. Then put cellophane over the list.) That word is like this red cellophane: it brings reconciliation with God, for He forgives any confessed sin. That's the marvel of grace. God forgives, as is His delight; He forgives, as is our need.

4. Notice that the red cellophane covers the list of sins. We can't see through it to them because they're hidden under it. When we're in Christ, all that God sees is Christ's blood, not our sins. The one God called a Lamb for his gentleness and a Lion for his strength has overcome Satan, sin and death. He was tempted, so he can help, and he wants to. He was tempted but didn't fall, so he can save, and he has!

⌘   ⌘   ⌘   ⌘   ⌘   ⌘

Subject Idea: Pleasure

Scripture: Hebrews 10:31

Visual Item: Two inflated balloons, one inside a glass jar

Truth Stressed: God saves only those who hide themselves in Christ.

Procedure: Show the glass jar containing the balloon. Stress that there is no way to see the balloon without looking through the jar. Then show the other balloon. All we see is the balloon.

Applications:

1.   The jar represents Jesus and each balloon a type of humanity: saved and unsaved. If we're in Christ, as the balloon is inside the jar, God views us through Christ's grace. If we're outside Christ, we stand alone before a terrifying and paralyzing judgment. If we're in Christ, God sees only forgiveness enveloping us; if outside Christ, He sees all the imperfections, flaws, vices, sins, peccadilloes, etc. characterizing human nature.

2.   Scripture guarantees that everyone accepting Christ escapes judgment against sin and warns that anyone refusing Christ exposes every last frailty to a perfect God who tolerates no imperfection in His presence. Would we dare approach God on our own when He interdicts everything but Christ's intercession, when nothing but Christ's worthiness impresses or convinces or is acceptable to Him?

3.   At judgment, we'll stand either inside Christ and, therefore, invulnerable to God's wrath, or by ourselves and, therefore, exposed to it! No third alternative exists. Would we prefer to have God look at us through His Son, or to have no sanctuary from God's blazing wrath?

⌘   ⌘   ⌘   ⌘   ⌘   ⌘

Subject Idea: Voices

Scripture: John 10:4-5

Visual Item: Audiotape containing voices known by the congregation

Truth Stressed: Christians need to know Christ's voice so they can faithfully follow him.

Procedure: Play the tape of each voice and ask people to identify it. Stress that as each voice is heard people connect it with an individual they know very well.

Applications:

1. A stranger can as soon tell us the truth as a friend. But a friend's words have a built-in authenticity. Having explicit faith in the person, we develop explicit trust in his opinion. Just because we know Jesus is God's son, we accept, believe and obey whatever he says. He becomes the litmus against which we measure any other teaching, value or behavior.

2. Our first necessity is getting well acquainted with Jesus. Since he's our leader and the one we look to for forgiveness here and our life hereafter, we have no choice but to develop intimacy with him. If even stupid sheep unerringly know their shepherd's voice, Christians can't afford to be ignorant of Christ's. If sheep automatically flee the voice of a stranger, Christians can't afford to hearken to every voice in the religious world.

3. Today we tried to provide only the voices of those you love and respect. But even the most beloved and skilled Christians can make enemies. So maybe a voice incited unpleasant memories for you. And maybe it was that person's fault. Be assured, however, if the voice of Jesus excites any antipathy, disrespect or doubt about him, *we* need to repent. For our response to Jesus reveals the truth about us, not about him. If we're offended with him, we've made a mistake that demands correction.

4. Christ's voice absolutely warns and delights the obedient disciple. It warns and condemns only the disobedient— but, even then, as an act of his mercy so we won't die, not so he can express his rage. If an obedient disciple has learned anything about Jesus' voice, we've learned this for sure: whatever he says, he means!

⌘   ⌘   ⌘   ⌘   ⌘   ⌘

Subject Idea: Authority

Scripture: Psalm 23:4

Visual Item: Shepherd's staff with crook, made from spray-painted electrical conduit

Truth Stressed: The Master exercises complete authority over his people.

Procedure: Show the crook and explain its many uses to the shepherd: directing, controlling, counting, rescuing, protecting the sheep.

Applications:

1. The shepherd's crook is an extension of his personal control and authority. He's in charge of the sheep, not they of him. He knows what he wants from and for the sheep without seeking their opinions or asking their approval. He knows what his goals are, and he's willing to impose his authority on sheep and predator alike to achieve them.

2. The crook enforces the shepherd's will. What the shepherd intends as a protection of and discipline for his sheep, becomes corrective punishment to straying, rebellious sheep. They suffer if not compliant with the shepherd's leading. What he meant as a promise becomes a threat if they refuse his guidance. He knows that sheep can't be trusted to obey; in fact, they instinctively stray, mill, get confused, get in trouble, fail to find safety, etc. Without him, sheep are helpless. Therefore, when he offers help, any sheep insistent on its own way suffers. It's intolerable to the shepherd that an animal helpless as a sheep would refuse direction from the only person able to lead and protect it.

3. Many people, not a few of them Christians, can't overcome the inborn pride that assures them they can take care of themselves, that they know what's best for them. They resent Bible teaching that declares them spiritually and morally impotent and, therefore, absolutely reliant on God for all their views, beliefs and values. Further, they're insulted that the Bible would so unfairly mock their claims to spiritual integrity.

4. Like the shepherd with his sheep, Jesus remains unimpressed. He knows our lostness without him. And he determines his actions by what he knows is right, not what we think is—or want to be. He never consulted anyone when he made the rules at creation, and he's never sought anyone's counsel since. All humanity—all, his own sheep included—know the shepherd's mind only when he speaks it; know the shepherd's will only when he reveals it; experience the shepherd's guidance only when he leads. They don't know anything he doesn't tell!

⌘   ⌘   ⌘   ⌘   ⌘   ⌘

Subject Idea: Authority

Scripture: John 3:13; Revelation 5:5-7

Visual Item: An authoritative volume on any subject (example—a computer manual)

Truth Stressed: Jesus possesses complete authority over Heaven and earth.

Procedure: This how-to book offers definitive guidance on setting up the computer described, getting the greatest possible use from it and solving problems when it fails.

Applications:

1. Nothing is more hostile to America's religious diversity than Jesus Christ's spiritual singularity. The religious smorgasbord implies equality in the diversity: all are mutually good, depending on *our* evaluation. In American life, the argument used to be whether one church was as good as another. Now it's whether one religion is as good as another.

2. Christians cannot be indefinite about Christ's absolute authority when so many in society are convinced of their own leader's equal authority. The matter of authority in the spiritual life resolves itself into a single, simple question: who has the ability to determine acceptable

doctrine, forgiveness, morality and the composition of eternity? Who knows because he's been both in eternity and on earth—and in eternity before he came to earth? Only the person with both certifications in his portfolio can possess all authority over secular and religious life.

3.   That is the facility Jesus has in himself that's lacking in every other religious and secular leader. Others died and went to Heaven from earth; some were transformed on earth before they went to Heaven. But only Jesus came from Heaven to earth, Heaven being his eternal home and earth his temporary assignment at God's behest!

4.   The miracles, teachings, death, bodily resurrection, ascension back to Heaven and eventual return from Heaven, distinguish Jesus from every other leader in history. That's why Satan bitterly and constantly attacks the authenticity of the four Gospels! Gods and goddesses galore he loves; lords not a few he touts. But the concentrated intensity of God in Christ terrorizes him, for in their eternal unity he sees his eternal punishment.

5.   Consequently, Satan inspires liberal theologians to attack the integrity of Matthew, Mark, Luke and John, realizing what their integrity means: since Jesus is as they wrote, he alone matters in history—and no one even approximates him, let alone equals or surpasses him. Since the Gospels accurately record Jesus as he lived, died and rose again, even liberals are smart enough to know that no one but Jesus holds absolute authority over Heaven and earth. But what are they to do? They don't want to believe Jesus is so great. They want to believe others are as great. Since the four Gospels offer the only record that obstructs their foolishness, they create theories so fanciful they don't even make good fiction!

6.   Jesus is One, while many pretenders arise. But they need to be many, since they die; in each generation another claimant rises. He needs to be only One since the power of his indestructible life frees him from competition!

⌘   ⌘   ⌘   ⌘   ⌘   ⌘

Subject Idea:	Light
Scripture:	John 8:12; I Thessalonians 5:5
Visual Item:	Candle and matches with holder; small flashlight; high-powered flashlight
Truth Stressed:	No religious leader carries Christ's candle power.
Procedure:	Darken the room to the fullest extent. First light the candle and set in holder. Then turn on small flashlight. Then turn on powerful flashlight.

Applications:

1. The three kinds of light represent God's revelation of Himself through the patriarchs, Abraham, Isaac and Jacob; the Law of Moses and the person of Christ.

2. Note that the candle lights only a small area around it and produces nothing too strong for the eyes. The small flashlight can be seen farther away with steadier light and produces some harshness to the eyes. The third light billows as it shines, becoming a flood that demands adjustment as we gaze at it.

3. Like the smaller light, God's revelation of Himself through the patriarchs illuminates, but to a limited degree; through the Law of Moses, like the small flashlight, it exposes more of God than previously, without much discomfort to the eyes; but like the powerful light, Christ's revelation of God initially blinds before it enlightens.

4. Little wonder that no one in world history, especially in our society, refuses the validity of lesser religious leaders, while many attack the revelation of Jesus Christ. The very nature of the Master's illumination rouses such powerful opposition. Many take exception with His initially blinding claims.

5. The lesser lights taught the decency, morality and values God still wants embraced. Christ's light opened God Himself to appreciation, praise and obedience. Everything the patriarchs and Law revealed about God was true, if incomplete; everything Jesus revealed about God is true, without incompleteness or inadequacy.

6.   Once Jesus came, it was obvious that everyone preceding
     had been only preparatory to him. As courtiers they
     seemed important until the enthroned, Crowned King ap-
     peared. Then the distinction was obvious in the
     difference. Their essentiality vanished in the exclusivity
     of Christ's shining. They are seen as only the servants
     they always claimed to be, bearing faithfully the light God
     gave them in anticipation of the Christ's infinitely greater
     luminescence.

⌘   ⌘   ⌘   ⌘   ⌘   ⌘

Subject Idea:	Access
Scripture:	Hebrews 9:27-28
Visual Item:	Map with departure and arrival noted, with route to be traveled. Use two cities or places well-known to everyone (perhaps displayed on an overhead projector or large board).
Truth Stressed:	Jesus offers humanity's only way to reach God's presence.
Procedure:	Using a pointer if possible, show the audience how to go from point A to point B. Stress that we may be able to reach our destination by other routes, but this one is the quickest and shortest.

Applications:

This is a matter of contrasts between following a physical map
to go from point A to point B and following God's spiritual directions to go from an earthly to an eternal life.

1.   For many, the idea of a spiritual roadmap is superfluous.
     The twentieth century, they say, blessed with the ad-
     vantages of an information highway, medical advances
     and scientific underpinnings, knows well enough how to
     live in the only world we're given. In former times, in un-
     informed cultures, religion may have been necessary to

control behavior. But such artificial controls aren't necessary now. In fact, they're hindrances to our creative forces.

2. Scratch that veneer, and the ugliness of fallen, undisciplined twentieth century man proves it monstrously mendacious. No society ever demanded more spiritual direction than ours precisely because we're so arrogant. We've reached the dizzying height of self-acquired boasting that Satan knows portends our fall. But he'll never warn us!

3. However, for most, the other problem facing humanity isn't so easily settled: how to prove there's only one way to Heaven? After all, using the map as an example, there may be a best way, a shortest way, a more scenic way, etc. from point A to point B, but there is no *one* way.

4. Even there, however, the reason people take different routes as they travel offers spiritual lessons. They may be bored going the one way and need a change of scenery. Lots of people are bored with Christianity because of its implacable hostility to physical pleasures. (Who's to say, really, that sex between unmarried people is wrong if they love each other? How could that be so bad? Isn't it far superior to indiscriminate sleeping around?) Then there's the "better scenery" reason. It's nice to see new places. To many, other religions seem more attractive than Christianity because of its emphasis on self-denial and tithing and evangelism and community involvement. Then there's the "easier grade, fewer hills" reason. Such and such a route is less demanding on the car. Lots of people look for a religion that's less demanding than Christianity. And they're easy to find. They want a faith that has broader appeal by being more tolerant of differences in values and morals. Last of all, there's the "pure adventure" reason. It's good to get off the freeways and turnpikes to the by-ways and shunpikes where few go because they're afraid of the challenge. Spiritually, these are the people who refuse to "follow the crowd" by believing in just one religion, especially one so intolerant that it considers everyone else's inferior—including theirs, which they happen to know is as good as anyone's.

5. We can go out of our way to get from here to anywhere
    else. It may cost more, be more damaging to our vehicle,
    our kids, our marriage, but we can do it. However...and
    mark this well...no one gets to Heaven by going out of his
    way to avoid Jesus, ignore Jesus or deny Jesus. He's the
    inescapable person in history and eternity. We have to
    deal with him because he's unavoidable and inescapable.
    He's the One beyond life who determines our eternal
    destiny; one word of disapproval from him at judgment,
    and we're in Hell forever; one word of approbation, and
    we're in Heaven forever. Who wouldn't make peace with
    this essential Person?

6. The road from A to B may be out of use for repairs; a
    storm may have weakened bridges; floods may have
    carried some away. But the way to God remains open and
    unbarricaded for all who follow Christ's directions to get
    there. Whatever reincarnationists believe, we get one
    chance — and no more — to go from earth to Heaven.
    Because we're ignorant of the way, we must listen to our
    Guide and his Map Book.

7. Indeed, the singularity of Jesus eliminates the clamor for
    choice. It's God's Way or no way. It certainly isn't the
    highway, because no way but Christ's ever climbs the
    ascent of Heaven and enters the City of Gold! Yes,
    people will miss Heaven, but not because it doesn't exist;
    they simply took the wrong way to get there. They could
    have been saved, but will be lost, because they considered
    themselves skilled spiritual geographers!

⌘   ⌘   ⌘   ⌘   ⌘   ⌘

Subject Idea:	Perfection
Scripture:	Hebrews 1:3
Visual Item:	Lamp with bulbs of various wattages.
Truth Stressed:	Only Jesus Christ perfectly revealed God.
Procedure:	Put each bulb in, turn it on, show and note the various strengths.

Applications:

1. The difference isn't in the electrical current coming to the lamp, but in the capacity of the bulbs. The 25 watt, 75 watt and 200 watt produce the amount of light built into them—but no more. If you need more light, install one that can produce it. We can't blame the 25 watt for not producing 200 watts of light. It conducts electrical energy according to its manufactured limits.

2. God's divine presence has been pouring into humanity since Eden. Adam was the first person capable of conducting God's light to all generations. Since he failed, God called others to carry His illumination to theirs: Enoch, Abraham, Moses, David, Jeremiah, etc. They conducted all the spiritual light their fallen humanity allowed. Then Jesus Christ came, and in him everyone, even his declared enemies, saw the perfect conduit of God's spiritual incandescence. His followers said it was because he was God in the flesh. His detractors said it was because he made an alliance with Satan to deceive. But no one in his generation doubted that in him a tremendous, original Light shone!

3. There is a way we can overwhelm the electrical current coming to this lamp: by turning on more electricity than the breaker has amperage. Then the circuit breaker trips. Or we could put a high-enough wattage bulb in to melt the wires in the lamp. Spiritually, only Jesus Christ, of all people ever to live, has carried every ounce and every inch of God's Being to humanity, retaining everything and losing nothing and never being tripped by pressure and responsibility. In Jesus God found the one person ever to live who could express Him completely, absolutely, indefatigably, perfectly, unerringly—nothing lost or impaired!

4. After Adam and until Christ, God could find no one else capable of meeting that challenge. It would have blown the emotional and mental circuits of anyone who tried. It happens with insane people today who claim to be God or Jesus or the Holy Spirit. Only in their irresponsible condition do they make such claims.

5. In absolute control of all his faculties, Jesus claimed that he revealed everything about God that humanity can

grasp, that there's nothing about God that he hasn't revealed! And the interesting response is: believers bow and worship him while unbelievers declare him Satan's instrument. There is no third choice. If Jesus perfectly and absolutely carries every ounce and every inch of God's Reality to humanity, he is God in the flesh and must be worshiped. If he doesn't, he's a mental incompetent! He cannot be a "good man," without being God in the flesh, for good men don't deceive so many millions.

⌘   ⌘   ⌘   ⌘   ⌘   ⌘

Subject Idea:	Solutions
Scripture:	Romans 1:4
Visual Item:	Math problem on overhead transparency
Truth Stressed:	Jesus alone offers God's solution to our spiritual problem.
Procedure:	Have a math teacher draw up a complex problem. Ask if anyone knows the answer.

Applications:

1. Mankind has a horrifying sin problem. It alienates us from both God and each other. It terrorizes individuals with guilt complexes that lead to emotional and physical difficulties. Philosophers have written volumes trying to calm our fears, saying that guilt is a vestige from earlier generations that modern medicine and psychiatry can eliminate. These fools assure us that our ancestors, living in primitive conditions, had to resort for survival to procedures of violence we haven't yet outgrown, but will, given enough education and culture.

2. The Bible disagrees. We have a right to our guilt because we've violated God's law—not some primitive culture's! God is the author whose principles we have ignored, denied and broken. And the conscience He built into us verifies the guilt we must feel to be worthy of God's presence.

3. If we want a math problem solved, call for a mathematician. If we want the sin problem solved, don't call for a mathematician, a philosopher, a psychologist, a biologist, etc.—or anyone but God in Christ. It's against God that we sinned. And it's God who determines how the sin problem will be solved and its accompanying guilt removed.

4. We hear from many cultural and educational sources that we don't need to accept Christ's miracles, virgin birth, redemptive death or bodily resurrection to solve our sin problem. All we need is to appeal to "our better natures."

5. However, our fallen nature flummoxes every attempt to assist our "better nature." Our better nature can't be expressed until we crucify the old nature that's imprisoned it. And that's where Jesus Christ succeeds. If we deny ourselves, with our callous egotism, and confess his worthiness to save, he removes the old nature and, in the process, renews our better self with his perfect self—so that he in us can triumph over our still-fallen nature.

6. It takes no genius to see that we hire experts to solve problems within their expertise. And if we eliminate Christ's miracles, etc., we eliminate from him the very essence of what makes him capable of removing sins. We cannot dismiss all the evidences he offered to prove he could conquer sin, then blithely say he *can*, regardless of whether the evidences he offered are true or not, real or not!

⌘   ⌘   ⌘   ⌘   ⌘   ⌘

Subject Idea: Attractiveness

Scripture: John 12:32

Visual Item: Magnet; box of paper clips; overhead projector

Truth Stressed: Jesus will attract us if we get close enough to him.

Procedure: Sprinkle paper clips on the glass. Note that they remain inert and without reason to move. Place the magnet just close enough to make clips twitch but not move to it. Push it closer and watch clips "run" to the magnet, adhering to each other, but held together by the magnet.

Applications:

1. Jesus has the intuitive ability to draw to Him all who seek spiritual help, life and instruction. The word *draw* refers to a person who attracts others by the winsomeness of his nature and personality. In every way Jesus revealed a life-perspective that has excited and impressed billions of people.

2. Knowing that most people won't move to Him on their own, God has often approached us. In many ways, Jesus draws near—through adversity, achievements, a Christian friend's example, economic setbacks, death, a child's birth, etc. However it happens, Jesus has come, the kingdom of Heaven is at hand, and we're influenced by his presence and its existence.

3. However, not everyone feels his attraction or is influenced by spiritual thoughts or concerns, just as some substances aren't attracted to a magnet. For Jesus to draw us, we have to be within spiritual range—and some people have so short-circuited their spiritual nature they feel no attraction to him. He's a name, a person, a something or other in a strange, inexplicable volume, but nothing more.

4. Others feel initially moved, quivering like the clips as the magnet draws near. Momentarily impressed, they never permanently cling to him. They have occasional "religious sensations" and are sometimes challenged and impressed, but never convinced by and converted to Jesus! They love movies and books bout him and love discussing his electric effect on history, his impact on values—anything about Jesus that rouses occasional, gentle emotions. But not something they want to possess permanently; and not someone they want to accept personally as Lord and Savior. Influenced by him, they don't want to be *caught* and *embraced* by him.

5. This illustration challenges Christians to be Christ-honoring disciples, possessing and expressing the spiritual

optimism, mastery and loftiness he exhibited. Some may not pay attention to us; some may be impressed but not convinced; others will want to adhere to the Christ who could so powerfully hold us. Whatever their response, his presence in us offers them their spiritual opportunity. Jesus wants his life in us to be seen by all, though equaled by none; admired by many and imitated, if only by a few.

⌘   ⌘   ⌘   ⌘   ⌘   ⌘

Subject Idea:	Influence
Scripture:	Colossians 1:27
Visual Item:	Clear pitcher with water; grape Kool-Aid; long-handled spoon
Truth Stressed:	Jesus has to permeate our lives before we're real Christians.
Procedure:	Show the pitcher and Kool-Aid packet. Ask if their propinquity makes Kool-Aid? Would rubbing the packet against the pitcher? Would throwing the unopened packet into the pitcher? Would pouring the Kool-Aid into the pitcher? Some may affirm this last point, but others will say it must be stirred together before it's Kool-Aid.

Applications:

1. What makes a person a Christian? Growing up in a Christian family? Having a Christian mate? Associating with Christian people? Going to church? Praying? Thinking good thoughts? Following the Golden Rule or the Sermon on the Mount? Obeying the Ten Commandments? There are nearly as many answers as there are unsaved people.

2. Consider the illustration. The pitcher of water and Kool-Aid became Kool-Aid only when stirred together. Whatever else it was before—clear water, altered water— it became Kool-Aid only with the mingling of the two,

each indistinguishably becoming the other. In fact, the Kool-Aid is the distinguishing factor because it introduced to the water the element that turned it into something else. And Jesus becomes the distinguishing factor in our lives by turning us into his disciples, filled with his Spirit, producing his fruit.

3. If we want to be Christians, think of ourselves as a pitcher of water and Jesus as a packet of Kool-Aid. Invite him to pour all of himself into us, stirring in whatever it takes to lose us in his all-pervasive personality. Then we'll be a sight worth seeing, have a faith worth sharing and an example worth following.

4. Only Christ so thoroughly mixed in us that we're lost in him makes us a Christian. Others accept less, expecting to get more from their faith. But there's no substitute for the real thing. The Kool-Aid mixture immediately made its presence known, making an instant change in the water. Christ's presence will do that in us if we have the same property as water towards anything soluble—we'll soak up Jesus instantly.

5. What position have we allowed Jesus to occupy in our lives? Do we, like rubbing the packet against the pitcher, just stay close to the religious life—going to church, giving money, appreciating the minister, etc.? Or, like throwing the unopened packet in the pitcher, accepting Jesus initially, but keeping him under wraps, our daily life separate from and not influenced by him—letting him eventually "bleed" through to us? Or, like stirring the contents into the water, do we let him pour himself into us and mix himself with our lives so thoroughly that people see Jesus in us?

LEADERSHIP

Leadership is a necessity, not an option. Because humanity needs direction, guidance and encouragement, God recruits leaders in each generation. Because leadership runs the risk of becoming self-serving and self-perpetuating, God clearly outlined its function. Leadership is responsibility more than authority and privilege more than responsibility; it's always limited to decisions in harmony with God's word and in the best interest of those led.

In these illustrations is a challenge for leaders to work under the Good Shepherd in order to be trustworthy shepherds.

Subject Idea:	Influence
Scripture:	Matthew 10:16
Visual Item:	Glass of water; salt shaker with salt
Truth Stressed:	Leadership changes others into its likeness.
Procedure:	Take a drink of the fresh water; add salt and take another drink; add salt and drink until the fresh is turned to salt water.

Applications:

1. Leadership is to have on its environment the effect of salt in water, changing the environment into its own likeness. Like even a little salt in the glass, the least influence of leadership alters those associated with it.

2. Like salt, whose properties create change, leadership impacts wherever it's expressed. Having natural powers of influence, leaders should exercise them, not apologize for possessing them. Since most people are followers, they need leaders to offer positive, beneficial examples. As it's the property of salt to influence, without explanation, it's the nature of leadership to influence, without alibi.

3. As salt changed this glass from fresh to salt water, able spiritual leaders can turn any church into something it hasn't been before. That can be harmful if leaders forget their spiritual responsibility. It's certainly for the good

when they remember it. An extraordinary group of leaders produces a powerful church. The key to any successful body of believers is a Spirit-filled cadre of men and women out front, leading others on.

⌘   ⌘   ⌘   ⌘   ⌘   ⌘

Subject Idea: Maturity
Scripture: John 13:12-15; I Timothy 3:1-13
Visual Item: Dress pattern
Truth Stressed: Leaders must establish the spiritual life they want followed.
Procedure: Have a person come forward and help hold the opened pattern. Note that a dress will result from following the pattern.

Applications:

1. A pattern is necessary to offer some assurance that what begins as a dress doesn't become a skirt or blouse. Where God has been concerned with the absolute integrity of His directions, He offered a model to be followed. Building the tabernacle and temple are examples. Where He expected spiritual life in believers, He gave His Son, all to guard against His life in us being different from His life in Christ.

2. Leaders accept both the privilege and the responsibility of their position, knowing that higher privileges beget graver responsibility. While not overwhelmed to despair, they're quickened to faithfulness by the accountability involved.

3. God established in the leadership a habit He wishes to become the disposition of the membership. He expects leaders to model the behavior sought in the membership. The spiritual life that's idealized in the membership must be realized in the leadership as a whole, with strengths of one compensating for weaknesses in another and one's successes for another's failures.

4. Church members need various levels of modeling, depending on their spiritual maturity. Some need only a

clue and encouragement to develop; others need full instructions. Leaders need to know their people. Similarly, some Christians need little, while others demand strict supervision; again, leaders need to know. It's no merit if leader *control* is the object of his leadership. The ideas may sound like twin images, but they're not. *Control* creates puppets while leadership motivates servants according to their giftedness.

5. Like some amateur seamstress managing to butcher the clearest pattern, reproducing a skirt instead of a dress, it's possible that Christians won't reproduce what they're shown by the leadership. Not to despair: another function of leadership is to patiently try again, remembering one's own inability as a beginner; remembering one's continuing inability despite maturity.

⌘ ⌘ ⌘ ⌘ ⌘ ⌘

Subject Idea: Immunity

Scripture: Acts 24:24-25; III John 9-10

Visual Item: Teflon pan or skillet

Truth Stressed: Leaders can be above reproach.

Procedure: Ask how many have used such a skillet or pan. What foods do they like to cook in them? What is its most attractive feature? (Non-stick means little or no scrubbing after use.)

Applications:

1. As the coating protects the dishwasher from that dreaded "S" word, scrubbing, Christ's grace protects the soul from that fatal "S" word, sin. Though Teflon is used as a pejorative of a person immune to scandal or criticism, in a real and specific sense, Jesus is our spiritual Teflon cover. Consequently, all sin bounces off us. It may momentarily cling to, but it won't adhere to us. Let's delight in his impermeable cover over us!

2. Teflon can get scratched if the wrong utensil is used on it—say a stainless steel instead of a plastic spatula. In the same way, we're responsible for keeping Christ's covering intact. Only as we reinforce it with prayer, Bible study, church attendance, witnessing, etc., do we find it continually protecting. His immunity never fails to safeguard us if we don't allow Satan to scratch or crack it by carelessness, neglect, unconcern or unbelief.

3. Leaders should have a progressively stronger Christ-likeness that renders them increasingly impervious to Satan's attacks. No one, not even the finest Christian, can escape criticism; all who lead have charges thrown against them, sometimes by intentional enemies, sometimes by well-meaning, but mistaken friends. Jesus experienced both kinds of attacks. Whatever the accusations, leaders who persevere in Christ-likeness render them only rumors.

4. Should a leader allow cracks and scratches that give Satan entry, it's the responsibility of others in membership and leadership to rebuke the fallen. Mistakes happen; leaders fall, but forgiveness and restoration to grace, if not to previous leadership, should be the goal. Though a leader may forfeit his prominence in the congregation by an egregious sin, he never loses his position with Christ if he repents and prays for forgiveness.

5. The Teflon allows diffusion of heat while protecting the pan or skillet from the "baked-on" results that demand hard cleaning. It helps the object serve its purpose without becoming imbedded with whatever it cooks or bakes. In essence, it remains unscarred by its service. God's grace immunizes leaders against the special hazards hereditary to leadership: pride, ambition, lust, control, etc. It protects against the Diotrophes complex that seeks to rule and dominate; from the cowardice of Pilate, who let public opinion pressure him into the wrong decision; and from the procrastination of Felix, who could always find ways to delay a decision.

⌘   ⌘   ⌘   ⌘   ⌘   ⌘

Subject Idea:	Influence
Scripture:	II Corinthians 4:7
Visual Item:	Large magnet; pocketknife; box of paper clips
Truth Stressed:	God calls people to Himself through Christ-focused leadership.
Procedure:	Put paper clips in view; move the knife over the open box: nothing happens. Magnetize the knife by rubbing it against the magnet; repeat the action.

Applications:

1. Leadership should make a positive difference in the lives it contacts. Christian leadership goes beyond a positive to a powerful, Christ-centered difference.

2. Notice that the unmagnetized knife attracts nothing. It can stab or slice or cut, but not attract. In many churches leaders are trying to draw people to Christ without first being impacted by him. They're consequently expert at hurting, maiming and disfiguring people and the church's influence, thinking it's leadership. But it isn't; it's mutilation! The purpose of church leadership isn't to show how sharp or blunt it is, but to show how spiritually attractive it is.

3. Only by being magnetized does the knife attract the paper clips. Leaders have no originality that motivates people; that comes only from Christ. It's his purpose to attach others to himself through human leaders, but only to himself through them, never to them as their possession; always to him as his, and leaders as his stewards serving faithfully. The purpose of the spiritual leader is to remain in touch with Christ's power. Then, while Christ produces the power and tows others toward himself, he does it through the pull of servants devoted to him.

4. Leadership was meant to persuade the led. That's the nature of the leader. Where the Christian leader differs is that his power is borrowed from Christ's source; therefore, people are encouraged by the example the leader sets. People are drawn to the Christ who so em-

powers! By offering a scintillating example of Christ's presence, the leader activates and induces emulation!

⌘ ⌘ ⌘ ⌘ ⌘ ⌘

Subject Idea:	Purpose
Scripture:	Acts 20:28; Ephesians 4:11-13
Visual Item:	Tools: hammer, drill, tape measure
Truth Stressed:	Church leadership serves best that equips the membership to minister.
Procedure:	Show the tools and ask each one's purpose: pound nails, make holes, measure distances. Have a little fun: point out that we could use the hammer as a paper weight, the drill to pound nails and the tape measure to wrap a package, but that wouldn't be their purpose.

Applications:

1. Nothing is easier in church leadership than to select a slate of officers, then forget they're to be purpose-driven, not office-centered; function-focused, not self-centered; responsible, not honorific.

2. The first qualification in spiritual leadership is a Christ-honoring life, not administrative, intellectual or economic skills. The latter are necessary in the fulfillment of their role, but only with the spiritual undergirding. Since leaders are Christ's representatives to the congregation, they must be Christ-honoring disciples. Without it, no one should be selected as a church leader. No one!

3. The role of church leaders is to define the congregation's mission; to set goals to achieve the mission; to suggest procedures (programs) to achieve the goals; to achieve the goals; to oversee the implementation of the programs (recruiting and training the right people); and periodically to evaluate the effectiveness of the programs, altering, adding, abolishing as necessary. Through the entire process runs the necessity of keeping the congregation informed, while requesting its input.

4. Leaders should adhere to their purpose, whatever other demands call them aside. Without faithfulness to their God-focused role, they'll misuse their ability, waste their energy and divert their time. While there are many good things leaders can do in a church and things they would like to do for a church, only as they prioritize Christ-directed responsibilities will they fulfill their calling. From good things they turn to what's important; and from the important to what's essential in making the church a Christ-honoring body of believers that maintains its focus! Only this will stimulate lay people to accept their personal, God-ordained ministry.

5. Only a strong Christian is leadership material; but not every strong Christian is a leader. Those who lead God's people must commit themselves to a hard-headed faithfulness to what He expects the church to become, not what the people are willing to let the church be.

⌘   ⌘   ⌘   ⌘   ⌘   ⌘

Subject Idea:	Impact
Scripture:	Acts 20:28
Visual Item:	Saltine cracker; loaf of bread
Truth Stressed:	Leadership has a visible effect on people's lives.
Procedure:	Show both cracker and loaf; stress that yeast is the difference.

Applications:

1. Like yeast, leadership never fails to make its presence known.

2. Like yeast, leadership can be seen working in the body of believers. Visibility verifies it. It's seen most dramatically in individuals. The most necessary component is interest in persons, not just in people. Specific persons always offer more difficult challenges than people in general. That's why leadership is so demanding. Leaders

are called to lead individuals who may resent and resist every effort. To get the "people" He wants, God orders leaders to recruit and equip individuals. So it's to be individuals before goals, programs or production.

3. Like yeast, Biblical leadership's results are predictable. Leadership stirs confidence in people, stimulates their faith, enlarges their capacity for challenges, emboldens them against fear, encourages them in failure.

4. Leadership should talk to individuals: about God and through problems, questions and reservations as they arise, offering the local congregation steady, trustworthy, positive, long-lasting community impact.

⌘   ⌘   ⌘   ⌘   ⌘   ⌘

Subject Idea:	Responsibility
Scripture:	John 18:4
Visual Item:	Compass
Truth Stressed:	Leadership must provide direction to the church body.
Procedure:	Explain that a compass is built with a heading to the North Pole. We can deflect the needle, but it unfailingly returns to its original position.

Applications:

1. The purpose of a compass is to keep us pointed in the right direction. It can't force us to take that direction, but it makes excuses for losing our way groundless. Leadership sometimes can lead the way to a needed goal, but find few following. That happens. Then leadership has been poorly served by its constituency. The prophets had this ongoing problem with the people of Israel. Israel never lacked direction; she lacked obedience to the clear directions prophets outlined. They never ceased pointing the people to God; the people as consistently resisted the direction. In such a situation, leadership must remain true

to its responsibility, even when not accepted and followed. God doesn't release us from our task just because people won't follow us. If we're right in what we offer, His own experience encourages us to persevere. After all, God remains God, even if no one follows His orders.

2. Leaders can't sneak away when threats come; or elude hardships that others experience; or escape challenges that others face; or plead "executive privilege" exempting them from problems others necessarily confront. The leader is always on the point, leading: expecting attacks from the enemy and wearing the scars as marks of spiritual glory.

3. Leaders must know where they and the church are and where they and the church should go. Then they outline how to get there; lead the people to accept the goal; admit failure when they're not reaching it; seek other ways to achieve it; and persevere in attaining it.

4. It's a rare church body that won't confidently follow Christ-focused leaders—the people who have earned the confidence placed in them by exemplary living, consistent discipleship and personal integrity.

⌘   ⌘   ⌘   ⌘   ⌘   ⌘

Subject Idea: Essentiality
Scripture: Acts 20:28, 32
Visual Item: Cookbook
Truth Stressed: Open to any recipe and read it to the people. Ask which ingredient can be omitted as irrelevant or non-essential.
Procedure: None: cooks can change the amount listed or substitute other ingredients for something they don't have, but being listed in the recipe indicates each ingredient's importance.

Applications:
1. Leadership is the essential ingredient in God's recipe for

church growth. Whether they're unelected or formally recognized and installed, every church has these people. They're usually elders and deacons, but they can be people outside the recognized body of leaders. In fact, no congregation exists but has these people in place. The challenge is to identify, then organize them into a working cadre, producing a positive impact on the body, leading to a positive impact in the community.

2. Programs are secondary to leadership. Programs offer a means by which leadership expresses itself, but people follow individuals, not programs. Personalities expedite the passage of programs that would otherwise demand intensive filibustering to "sell." If people are sold on the leaders involved, they'll invest in leaders' dreams.

3. If weak, non- or counter-productive leadership exists, the pastor's first responsibility is to teach, train, educate, oversee and free new leaders to lead. It isn't a factor we can take for granted in any church. Christ-centered, people-friendly leadership will occur only by following the Holy Spirit's direction. Only in that way will we have a leadership loved by loving, reachable by reaching out, teaching by being teachable. It'll be a leadership accessible to, not aloof from those it wants to influence—for access offers opportunities isolation denies.

4. Even the best of God's people can mistake their interest for His—where our interests are at stake. We'll sometimes misdirect our interest and energies into lesser goals than our calling imposes. When that happens, it's good to know that the leaders we've chosen will always be looking after God's interests, that they'll call us back to the basic and essential ingredients of our faith and hold us accountable for our spiritual enfranchisement.

OBEDIENCE

When in Egypt, Moses thought God sent him to rescue Israel, he willingly killed the oppressor. When at Sinai, God specifically ordered him to deliver Israel, Moses dissented. Like him, our clearest commission may offer the toughest test of obedience. More likely, it will come when we're unsure of God's direction or unhappy with our own. Whatever, our obedience must have substance. In these illustrations, the challenge is to be faithful in, not just talkative about obedience.

Subject Idea:	Results
Scripture:	Matthew 17:3; Galatians 6:7
Visual Item:	Overbake-to-ruined box of brownies without ruining the pan; box the mix came in; knife
Truth Stressed:	God expects His word to be explicitly obeyed.
Procedure:	Bring the pan of brownies. Read the directions; confess that you cooked the mix twice as long (or however long it took to ruin it). Take brownies out and hold them aloft; tap with a knife; anyone interested in losing a tooth by biting into it?

Applications:

1. Who would be foolish enough to buy the brownie mix, read the directions on how to bake them and then disregard the directions and bake them as we saw fit? The directions and our oven may differ by a few minutes, but not by 10 to 20! Who should know how long it takes to turn the mixture into a gastronomic delight? And who's to blame if we follow our inclinations instead of the manufacturer's instructions and get this concrete slab as a result?

2. Refusing to follow God's instructions has the same consequence for life and eternal destiny as substituting our opinion for the manufacturer's instructions. Only here it's a box of chocolate that's lost and with us our eternal soul!

God intends for us to read and obey His instructions! He isn't like a lot of people, who have an insatiable desire to speak, whoever's there to listen. In fact, unwilling to speak unless it's essential, God's words are few, but each one packs an atom's wallop!

3. He's given us the right to disregard His instructions, just as (General Mills/Duncan Hines), etc. exercises no control over how we follow their directions. But God won't take the blame for our failure to follow His word, much as we want Him to! Many people refuse to search for God's truth, read God's truth, believe God's truth or embrace God's truth, but still want God to accept the blame for the failures following their choice. Even in the church, we weaken accountability by stressing God's "unconditional" love—as if God doesn't impose judgment on our behavior but accepts us whether we obey or not! The "I" is followed by the "not I" generation, and both are wrong. We reap what we sow because God won't be mocked. Obey His word and enjoy the results; disobey only if we want to suffer the consequences. We'll never reject Him and enjoy the results!

4. We'll mature or ruin our life depending on how closely and persistently we follow God's instructions. We all face instants of dispute between obedience to God and adherence to our opinion: obedience verses self-will. Growth to maturity or ruination of our Christian life depends on how we systematically resolve those conflicts, on whether God or we dominate the decision! In such instants, we need the habit of obedience, not the instinct of self-preservation!

5. However clearly our choices show in this life, they show definitively only in the next. We can never weigh the true worth of our obedience to God without the weight of eternal glory on the scales. The final day proves whether we've been an obedient Moses or a rebellious Israel; whether an obedient Elijah or a vile Jezebel! Would we choose *then* to have been consistently obedient or a born rebel?

⌘ ⌘ ⌘ ⌘ ⌘ ⌘

Subject Idea:	Instructions
Scripture:	Isaiah 35:8
Visual Item:	Candle; box of matches; card table
Truth Stressed:	God offers unmistakably clear teachings for our spiritual life.
Procedure:	You'll need mental flexibility for this illustration—i.e., the ability to play dumb. Remember that you're to follow explicitly the people's instructions—no more or less. First, ask their help in lighting the candle. A few clues: If they say, "strike a match," hit the box of matches with your hand. If they say, "take out a match," shake the box, turn it around and look at it, but don't do more without instructions. If they say, "push the end of the box," set it down and push the box across the table. Do nothing without specific instructions from them. The frustration will soon irritate them, but that's okay since they've frustrated you enough with their refusal to obey God's will. Finally, if they can't give you the instructions you need, do what it takes to light the candle!

Applications:

1. Did anyone think that such a simple act could be so frustrating? And why? Because I followed what you explicitly *said* while you assumed I understood what you *meant*. How, then, does God expect us to understand and obey profound spiritual truth when we sometimes find simple instructions too complicated?

2. By making all teaching essential to our forgiveness so simple even adults can understand, that's how. That simplicity underscores the reason for God's frustration with our refusal to accept what we can't deny and our reluctance to obey what we wholeheartedly accept. Our refusals are inexcusably blameworthy. Consider those who express dissatisfaction with Christian teaching about salvation. Then who will they find to die on the cross to

forgive sins and rise from the dead, conquering Satan? Or those who express discomfort over things Jesus said and did; then who else will they find with the authority to say and do whatever he pleases? Or those who feel God hasn't offered ample evidence of Himself. Then to whom will they ascribe the invariable faithfulness of equinoxes and solstices; of birds that sing, lions that roar and antelopes that leap; of seeds that die, only to multiply themselves through death and creatures that unfailingly reproduce after their own kind? When we've convinced ourselves that the author of integrity is himself dishonest, how shall we convince ourselves that integrity is superior to deceit? We must not add to our lengthy list of sins an egotistical declaration of God's incompetence to judge us for them, creating our own theology and expecting Him to subscribe to it!

3. Since God reveals only what we need to know, we can't consider unwanted parts non-essential. In fact, it's at the point of surprise at or disagreement with something God says that we prove our nature. We would never have known that Cain was an ungodly man if he hadn't offered sacrifice; in the act of doing what he felt was right, instead of what God taught, Cain expressed his unbelief. All the piety he might have felt disappeared when conflicting with God's demands. Then Cain's unsolicited, unwelcome but "considered opinion" interjected itself. All our devotion faces the litmus test at the point of our surprise at or disagreement with God's expressed, explicit word! Do we obey regardless, or do we temporize, seeking explanations, reserving obedience till *we're* satisfied?

4. If Christians are correct in ridiculing humanists who worship at their own altars, we cannot easily explain our reluctance to obey what we devotedly believe. It's hardly a compliment for us to accept the obvious fact that God has spoken. That's a necessity for us, not a compliment to God. Unbelief would be an insult to Him, with all the proofs He's offered. But how can we explain the disgrace of our continued disobedience despite our affirmations of Bible truth?

5. Like Cortez burning his ships at Vera Cruz, like Caesar crossing the Rubicon to fight Pompey, Christians must make the irreversible commitment to believe what Jesus did and to obey what Jesus taught—without question and with a great deal more consistency than we've customarily shown!

6. God patiently repeats some teaching He knows is harder to accept. This may explain why Jesus taught about financial obligations in one of every six verses of the Gospels and why the apostle Paul covered the subject so well in I and II Corinthians. Nothing jangles human nerves like sermons on giving, yet there's nothing more essential to discipleship than sermons on giving. Let the teaching continue!

⌘ ⌘ ⌘ ⌘ ⌘ ⌘

Subject Idea:	Examples
Scripture:	Matthew 17:5
Visual Item:	An expert in crafts: someone who makes silk flowers, crochets, knits, does tatting, embroidering, macrame, sewing, quilting, jewelry, wood crafts, etc.
Truth Stressed:	Jesus is the only authority when we want expert spiritual guidance.
Procedure:	This needs to be something that can quickly be done, or at least to get the idea quickly taught. This is done on cooking and craft shows. Let the expert offer brief, step-by-step instructions.

Applications:

1. Since I needed guidance in (whatever the skill required), I asked (name of person); I knew he/she would know. I wouldn't pretend to possess a knowledge and skill just to escape saying I don't know. Yet, though none of us knows how to build a life that pleases God, most people

refuse to consult Him for guidance, instruction or even an opinion! They want to be their own experts.

2. God's word is replete with both acceptable and unacceptable models: the examples of behavior He approves and what He condemns. No one reading it is ever left in doubt. Some have criticized the Bible for revealing sexual immorality, but no one can doubt the Bible's demand for sexual purity; or for revealing deceit and treachery, but no one can dispute the Bible's call to integrity and mercy. The Bible won't deny the depravity so evident in humanity, even in its main characters, but it always holds God's perfection as His ideal.

3. However, in positive ways the Bible provides a variety of people with a variety of experience common to humanity. Powerful visual tools teach us what to avoid to keep from displeasing God and what to embrace to warrant His pleasure. Bad people's sins are recorded as a warning to avoid their mistakes. Good people's virtues are offered as an encouragement to spiritual growth. Good examples are just as infectious as bad ones—and they're worth being caught.

4. Jesus is offered as the only perfect example of human nature. While we're glutted with information, we're starved for God's wisdom by not following Jesus! Error grows in the absence of following him as rumor expands in the absence of fact. Our society is so enthralled with error precisely because it's mortified by God's truth in Christ! Many people, not a few of them believers, never get the hang of delighting in Jesus because they never yield to him the deep-down allegiance of body and soul! Understanding of and obedience to Jesus work hand in glove: one now preceding, now following the other, first offering inspiration to, then drawing inspiration from the other, both inextricably associated with the other—but always initiated by a willingness to obey whatever Jesus demands!

5. As examples are powerful witnesses, the perfect example is the ultimate witness. As we are challenged by the

example of others, we're always commanded to keep our eyes fixed on Jesus, not on anyone else!

⌘   ⌘   ⌘   ⌘   ⌘   ⌘

Subject Idea: Instructions
Scripture: Genesis 2:16-17
Visual Item: Large, empty, closed box
Truth Stressed: Following God's instructions will protect our spiritual lives.
Procedure: Show the box. Explain the two ways people generally lift objects. First, the wrong way: bending from the hips, grabbing and lifting with the back. Second, the proper way: bending at the knees, grasping firmly and slowly rising, lifting with the legs.

Applications:

1.   The box is empty; if it had been full, I might have injured my back lifting it; had it been heavy, I would have risked serious injury by lifting the wrong way. As there's a right and wrong way to lift a box, there's an acceptable and unacceptable way to live. It's amazing how many people swear by the principles of math, economics and politics but think spiritual principles don't exist. We determine procedures and practices that expedite our life here but think that God has none to determine who shares His life hereafter!

2.   That accounts for the many not finding the life that pleases God. Since they don't think it exists, it isn't recognized when it appears. They mistake it for something else—usually an emotion they'd rather avoid, an intensity they'd rather flee.

3.   This also accounts for the life that many pursue, but never find; or possessing, fail to enjoy. Only God knows the life that pleases Him. His word is full of instructions from Genesis to Revelation, but one principle lies at the heart

of all His dealings with us: He expects obedience to His word. Hearing His word isn't sufficient; listening to it isn't sufficient; believing it isn't sufficient; explaining it isn't sufficient. Obedience isn't subject to any explanation or interpretation short of *obedience to* what we're told by the One in charge.

4. This means obedience whether we feel like it or not, whether we agree or not. God may explain why, but He usually won't. Whether or not He does, He expects and demands obedience. For us, then, it's obedience when God explains and when He doesn't; when it makes good sense and when it makes none. Obedience because God said it, and that settles it!

5. We'll always find, if we follow God's instructions, that we can safely lift burdens that will otherwise harm us; bear losses that will otherwise break us; suffer joyfully through experiences that will otherwise embitter us. We'll never suffer spiritual harm, whatever we're called to carry for Jesus, if we follow his directions for its conveyance. And, while incorrectly lifting this box could harm our backs, not even our sins will harm our soul if we consistently obey Christ!

⌘   ⌘   ⌘   ⌘   ⌘   ⌘

Subject Idea:	Compliance
Scripture:	I Timothy 1:3-5; Revelation 2:4
Visual Item:	Dirty plate; pan of soapy water; table; towel
Truth Stressed:	Obedience must be unconditional.
Procedure:	Show the dirty plate; anyone want to eat from it? Wash half the plate and dry that half. Anyone comfortable eating from it now? Immerse the whole plate, clean and dry it. Would anyone be uncomfortable using it for a meal?

Applications:

1. Obedience means an unconditional willingness to seek, hear and comply with God's word. Yet we find ourselves offering partial obedience to God—wherever we feel comfortable, in areas we please. If Jesus wants to remove something we abhor, we freely surrender it; if he demands what we want to keep, we resist. Then it's a contest between our will and God's demands: a mutually exclusive, hostile and incompatible mixture. Only as we surrender does peace with God come.

2. Strange as it may seem, the mere possession of God's truth can hinder obedience. For we begin to trust what we know instead of the Lord who teaches it. Then we're no different from the Jewish leaders who, Jesus said, knew the Scriptures but couldn't see him as their goal!

3. That's the burden of possessing God's truth: the mere possession can become a substitute for obedient growth, and that imposes its own severe penalty. "We have the truth" then becomes a condemnation of us instead of a proclamation for the unsaved. The very thing we trust becomes our snare. Let's never be satisfied with knowing less. Let's always demand more. But let's always pray that the knowledge will encourage, not block spiritual growth and enhance, not diminish our witness to the lost.

4. What is there that we're keeping out of the baptistry waters? What didn't we get wet in order to keep it for ourselves? Jesus suffered to death; he came off the cross a corpse. Do we really think he'll understand if we offer a partial obedience in inheriting the salvation it took his complete self-renunciation to gain?

5. We can also diminish our obedience by getting stuck at conversion; by thinking that no feeling is so intense as that which led us to Christ. As any couple married forty years can verify, that isn't true. They'll tell you that conversion love is like kindling compared to the Bessemer furnace love of obedient discipleship.

PRAYER

Prayer is a spiritual privilege we all intend to exercise but seldom adequately experience. While it puts us in touch with God and gets Him involved in our daily affairs, we often find excuses to justify our undeveloped, inconsistent prayer life. The following visual illustrations help us understand the relevance of prayer to our daily walk.

Subject Idea:	Perseverance
Scripture:	Daniel 6:10; Luke 18:8
Visual Item:	Phone with attached cord; phone jack
Truth Stressed:	The combination of Bible reading and prayer connects us to God.
Procedure:	Show each item separately; note incompleteness by itself. Attach cord to phone: still no communication. Plug cord into jack. (If possible, dial someone and put him on the microphone.)

Applications:

1. While God communicates to us through the Holy Spirit in the word, we communicate with Him through Christ in prayer. In the Bible God declares, "Here's what I want to say." In prayer we say, "Here's how I want to respond."
2. Both are equally important. We need the objectivity of God's word to educate us in spiritual truth. We also need the sense of dependence on and appreciation of God that prayer brings.
3. While undisciplined prayer is often, as President Polk said about office seekers, "More importunate than meritorious," prayer disciplined by Bible reading offers an opportunity to respond specifically to God's particular emphasis in the scripture: believe His promise, accept His encouragement, heed His warning, fear His threat, etc.
4. Retain in our Christian life all that God says keeps us connected with Him: church attendance, fellowship with Christians, witnessing, etc. Leave nothing out as unim-

portant or irrelevant. God's statement of a matter's essence, not our opinion or experience, determines our acceptance and practice of it.

5.   As David Brainerd noted in his *Diary*, "It is good,...to *persevere in attempts to pray*, if I cannot *pray with perseverance.*"

⌘   ⌘   ⌘   ⌘   ⌘   ⌘

Subject Idea:	Connectedness
Scripture:	John 15:4, 7
Visual Item:	Vacuum cleaner; electrical outlet
Truth Stressed:	Believers must remain connected with their spiritual power source.
Procedure:	Run the vacuum cleaner around the platform/room without plugging it in; then plug it in and push the machine past the length of its cord, pulling it from the outlet.

Applications:

1.   Spiritual life is possible only from personal connection with God through Bible study and prayer.

2.   Spiritual potential within the human instrument is activated only when we're personally related to Christ. Prayer is straight talking, not straight thinking. It's open, free, honest communication between a mortal and God Almighty, not a soliloquy with oneself.

3.   Power outage renders the highest horsepower vacuum cleaner useless, but a personal relationship with Christ in prayer never fails to activate the spiritual life needing only the ignition of grace to function.

4.   Those active in pursuit of hard-won goals may think themselves too busy to pray. As saints of God have verified through the centuries, however, the time taken sharpening the ax makes felling the tree easier.

5.   Prayer offers a foundation on which to build a lasting spiritual superstructure. Around the structure, it con-

structs a wall that protects life from Satan's ravages and rages.

⌘   ⌘   ⌘   ⌘   ⌘   ⌘

Subject Idea: Submission

Scripture: Zechariah 7:13; Mark 6:5-6

Visual Item: Metal saucepan with lid; transistor radio

Truth Stressed: We must remove hindrances that keep prayer from getting through to God.

Procedure: Put live radio inside the open pan. Put a lid on the pan; sound ceases because the signal can't be transmitted. Remove lid, and radio can be heard again.

Applications:

1. As the live radio in the open pan represents free communication with God, the cover represents obstacles we place over that communication, blocking its signal.

2. We should seek to live in free communication with God: to read God's word and pray; to correct whatever keeps us from developing intimacy with God; to remember that any malfunction is in us, not in God's desire or ability; and that God's closeness to or remoteness from us depends on our lifestyle. We, not He, develop hindrances to free, useful prayer. We need to eliminate the assassins of effective devotional life that, like a lid over the radio, silence effective intimacy with God: unbelief, unforgiven sin, pride, disobedience, activities, etc. and to acquire the traits necessary to activate an effective devotional life: faith, forgiveness, humility, perseverance.

3. All Christians want communication from and with God. But we need a habitual, not an intermittent relationship that is continually and spontaneously offered, not just when we have a hurt or a need. We need to see prayer as an exercise of our trust in God, not as a means of raiding God's treasure of gifts.

4. Personal peace begins in prayer when we place our cares in God's hands, not when the answers come. But how great God's adequacy is when we feel just as *full* after trusting Him as when getting answers from Him! That result teaches us that we don't need answers from God so much as we need merely His presence in our lives.

5. God knows the struggles we face, so He won't leave us alone. Like a shepherd listening to every bleat, He hears His lambs call. And as we call, He comes to us and lifts us into His arms. And gradually we forget what we called for because we find God loving us, finding He's the reason for our being there and the only reason that matters.

⌘   ⌘   ⌘   ⌘   ⌘   ⌘

Subject Idea: Listening

Scripture: Philippians 1:19

Visual Item: Radio

Truth Stressed: Prayer can be a learning as well as a listening time.

Procedure: Turn through radio dial; note the different receptions, static and blank spaces. As you get within range of a station's signal, the static diminishes, and voices or music become clear and resonant.

Applications:

1. We hear so much *noise* we sometimes find it hard to distinguish *sounds*.

2. If we aren't "within range" of God due to interferences we allow into our life, prayer may seem to produce only a lot of "static" with unclear results.

3. People need to "learn to listen," especially in a society that has all our means of expression. In prayer we can become so obsessed with sharing our thoughts that we forget to pause and let the Holy Spirit awaken us, create

awareness, offer a sense of direction, etc. Without listening for direction as we pray, we stifle the Holy Spirit, whose presence is sovereign at such intervals.

4. Quiet time is needed every day, but not to listen to self or to meditate with self, as the new- age gurus urge. Christians scorn self-delusion for the relaxation and peace of communicating with our Heavenly Father in Christ and receiving from Him assurance, forgiveness and wholeness.

⌘   ⌘   ⌘   ⌘   ⌘   ⌘

Subject Idea: Rejuvenation
Scripture: Mark 5:30
Visual Item: Car alternator
Truth Stressed: We can always be spiritually powerful, whatever demands we face or burdens we carry.
Procedure: Show alternator. Explain that the alternator allows the battery to recharge as the car's heater, air conditioner, radio, lights, wipers, etc. function. If the alternator malfunctions, electrical loss renders the car immobile.

Applications:

1. Prayer is the soul's alternator, recharging its batteries so we can continue to function spiritually. Prayer has accomplished its purpose when it develops awareness of God's presence and provision for daily tasks.

2. As Jesus experienced when the woman touched him, the demands of the spiritual life reduce our stamina, but contact with God repairs the loss and restores our ability to continue. Anyone dealing with the public in stressful situations needs the spiritual and emotional replenishment prayer provides. If each hour of flying military jets demands eight to ten hours of maintenance, personal involvement in people's lives demands the maintenance of continual reliance on God.

3. As winter or hot weather offers the car's alternator its stiffest challenge, trials, disappointments and unsolved problems often sap our spiritual energy until we have none left. Bible study and prayer offer the surest means of restoration to a full-time, high-speed spiritual life.

⌘ ⌘ ⌘ ⌘ ⌘ ⌘

Subject Idea:	Accessibility
Scripture:	Mark 1:35; Luke 6:12; John 6:15
Visual Item:	Cellular phone
Truth Stressed:	We always have access to God through Christ's high priesthood.
Procedure:	Show phone. Ask how many have one. Ask the strangest place from which they've placed or received a call or strangest request made or received. Point out that the phones are useful in accessing loved ones and in getting help for accidents or breakdowns.

Applications:

1. God is always available to us and more eager to help than we are bold to ask.
2. Christ's high priesthood enables him to mediate constantly our appeals to God.
3. Prayer remains effectual whatever time we call or our locality when we do, and unlike cellular phones, prayer doesn't have batteries that need recharging to operate.
4. Peace and security come to us when we pray because prayer changes the focus from our mortality to God's eternalness; from our sins to His grace; from our coming death to His endless life. He becomes the focal point, not we; what He has done, not what we haven't. This helps us realize that Christ's death to save outdistances any sin we commit, and that our certain mortality has been eclipsed by his immortality.
5. Everyone needs an escape from the uncertainties and stresses of life. What distinguishes the believer from the

unbeliever is the means of escape: believers seek God's face while unbelievers seek drink, drugs, sexual conquests, earthly pleasures, etc. Prayer offers two significant advantages the others cannot: one, a safe and positive escape; two, a sober, objective resolution to the problems faced.

⌘   ⌘   ⌘   ⌘   ⌘   ⌘

Subject Idea:	Mistakes
Scripture:	James 4:3
Visual Item:	Electric drill; tape measure
Truth Stressed:	Prayer must have proper motivation to achieve spiritual excellence.
Procedure:	Hold up both drill and tape measure. Ask the purpose of each. Ask what would happen if a carpenter used the drill to measure and the tape measure to drill holes. The carpenter uses the right tool for each task.

Applications:

1. Prayer can have the wrong motivation or have the right motivation in the wrong cause. Richard Berdin attended Christmas Eve midnight mass with his girlfriend in Alabama. It evoked childhood memories—and a desire to pray. But the object of his prayer was the drug money he'd hidden in a floor lamp of his New York apartment. He didn't want some American thief to profit from his own illicit activities.

2. The purpose of prayer is to express our praise of and dependence on God, to align our will with His, to deepen our commitment to Him.

3. Using prayer as a means of prying favors from God or as a means of escaping danger or problems or as a mere ritual, lessens its capacity and eliminates its effectiveness. While it's necessary for us to devote time to prayer, we

must never think that merit is measured by the hour or that repetition in prayer is essential. He who *believes* is answered as God wills, not as he who prays repeats himself.

4.   We need to test ourselves with a simple question: thinking back on all the times we prayed this past week, did we ask more for favors or for deeper commitment; for everyday benefits like job, family, safety or for more Christ-likeness and appreciation of the spiritual life?

5.   Prayer covers every subject important to us. But it reaches its greatest potential when we see it as a means of inviting God to create in us a clean heart and a Christ-like spirit. Will we use prayer as a measuring tape to drill holes or a drill to measure? Or will we let prayer fulfill its truest purpose by surrendering our life to God in Christ?

Subject Idea:	Discipleship
Scripture:	Ephesians 6:18
Visual Item:	Two Dustbusters: one fully charged, the other nearly discharged
Truth Stressed:	Only as we recharge spiritually can we remain spiritually active.
Procedure:	Run the Dustbuster that's nearly discharged; then run the freshly charged one. Ask what the difference is since both have the same components and purpose. Why does one softly growl and the other loudly roar?

Applications:

1.   The one has been worn out by use; the other is fresh from its transformer. The Christian life draws heavily against our physical and spiritual energy. Recharging by Bible study and prayer prevents our being weakened and enervated by the expenditure.

2.   Since the spiritual life is something we *work* to achieve, never something we *naturally* possess, the drag always reduces, not increases our reserves.

3.   God provides many support procedures to recharge any loss of spiritual energy and vitality: prayer, church at-

tendance, fellowship with Christians, Bible studies. All are spiritual resources that reinvigorate us for our work.

4.   As we would use the charged Dustbuster to clean, God uses the recharged disciple in His work. Only those replenished by grace have the capacity to carry the burdens placed on their time and energies. Prayer offers a quiet time where God empowers us so that, when times aren't quiet, we can draw from the grace gained in the quiet time. We always stand tallest from our knees.

PURITY

Living by influences invisible to and unfelt by those outside faith, Christians acknowledge the need of personal purity. Most people, however, feel an uneasy ambivalence toward the word. They admire the concept but deride its particulars. They love its presence in others but fear its personal ramifications. They applaud its embrace by saints but, as sinners, flee its appearance. Consider how the following illustrations clarify the definition of and demand the presence of purity in the Christian's life.

Subject Idea: Influence

Scripture: Psalms 138:3; Matthew 5:13

Visual Item: Salt; bowl; other ingredients (sugar, baking powder, spices)

Truth Stressed: Letting ungodliness into life weakens our spiritual influence.

Procedure: Pour salt into the bowl. As you talk about its purity, add other items. Stress that, while the salt remains, other ingredients contest its presence.

Applications:

1. Like salt in the bowl, Christianity remains in many people who have contaminated it with competing religions, goals, beliefs, habits, etc. This brings a diminution of Christ's distinctive persona and appeal. To function at its highest level, Christianity must remain separate from every other doctrine, faith, persuasion and behavior.

2. The danger fusion brings is that it weakens Christianity to improve other perspectives without making them distinctly Christian. This is especially dangerous in a society that views as "spiritual" *anything*—a surfer's shack on the seashore, crystals, a decent TV show and, yes, even faith in God through Christ.

3. Christianity focuses on and is absolutely dedicated to the singularity of Jesus Christ. It's Christ-focused, Christ-

honoring, Christ-driven. Losing that solitary emphasis by combining Jesus with other religions and religious leaders elevates them but debases him. Like the soldier acquiring Christ's sandals at the cross, other religious leaders can wear, but never fill his shoes.

4.   People demand the right to choose from all religions what pleases them; then, from the potpourri, they formulate their religious philosophy. This offers no harm to other religions, which are man-made. But it fatally demeans the Christian faith by maintaining aspects of Christianity without its Christ-centered genius, by retaining Christian values while denying the unique person in whom they originate.

⌘ ⌘ ⌘ ⌘ ⌘ ⌘

Subject Idea: Pollution

Scripture: John 15:3

Visual Item: Oil/air filter

Truth Stressed: God's word keeps spiritual pollution out of life.

Procedure: With cut-away, show how the filter traps impurities before they enter and damage sensitive engine instruments and parts.

Applications:

1.   Without the Bible, we're like an engine without a filter: open to persuasive influences of an enemy skilled in overcoming our good intentions and using our bad habits to corrupt us.

2.   The Bible cleanses us by eradicating sin's corrosive power. Under the Holy Spirit's influence, working through God's word, we change, eliminate sin, outgrow our limitations, etc. In essence, the Holy Spirit confronts Christians with God's truth and challenges us to walk our talk.

3.   A difference exists between the filter and the Bible. The filter *catches* the debris before it enters the engine; the

Bible *destroys* sin before it infiltrates our mind and, if it finds sin there, extricates and banishes it.

4. Since our Christian life is a gift bestowed, not a wage earned, we intend to preserve it on behalf of the Giver. We see ourselves as stewards of, not as owners of our renewed life. As God's visible expression of Himself to our generation, we commit ourselves to withstanding whatever dishonors Christ and to acquiring whatever exalts him.

⌘   ⌘   ⌘   ⌘   ⌘   ⌘

Subject Idea: Fruitfulness
Scripture: Matthew 7:15-20
Visual Item: Various seeds, some helpful, some harmful
Truth Stressed: What we plant mentally and emotionally grows spiritually.
Procedure: Show the seeds and ask people to identify them. Would they intentionally plant harmful seeds, knowing they produce problems in the garden, field or orchard?

Applications:

1. Fruit grows according to the seed planted. We're not surprised to find an apple orchard where apple seeds were planted. Yet, many people who sow cynicism, anger, worry or other baleful negatives in their lives, are surprised when unhappiness, broken relationships and high blood pressure result. Whatever virtue we want developed is what we must plant and nurture. Unlike vice, righteousness is the product of our *design*. We sin naturally; we become righteous only by intention.

2. Sometimes like the plant-world, spiritual seeds die before effecting good or bad in our lives. For reasons we can't always determine, they don't develop. Not every anger eventuates in murder; not every forgiveness brings improved interpersonal relationships. Sometimes parents

plant the same righteous seed in two children, only to see one grace and the other disgrace Christ. However, as chance favors the prepared person, the law of averages remains true in the spiritual life. Most of what we plant grows, reproducing itself. That's why we must commit ourselves to faithful spiritual husbandry, trusting God for the harvest He's pleased to give.

3.   Most seeds need a particular climate or soil to develop. Palm trees need warm air while watermelons need sandy soil. The spiritual life blossoms only with the Holy Spirit as God's gardener. As it's useless to plant palm trees in International Falls, Minnesota, it's useless to hope for spiritual development where people lack a basic understanding of God. The person ruled by the flesh not only doesn't understand, but despises God and resists any appeal of the Spirit.

4.   However, when that person ignores the spiritual life as irrelevant or maligns it as useless, he's revealing his incapacity, not Christianity's weakness. The Christian faith is always defensible, if some interpretations of it aren't. But no defense of agnosticism, atheism or humanism exits. They're frauds that can never be true.

⌘   ⌘   ⌘   ⌘   ⌘   ⌘

Subject Idea:	Escape
Scripture:	Hebrews 12:14, 16
Visual Item:	Plate of food; container of dirt
Truth Stressed:	Sin ruins the perfect forgiveness Christ provides.
Procedure:	Show the plate of food, perhaps fruit since that would be more appealing. As you sprinkle dirt, ask how many believe you're making the fruit better. How many want to eat it covered with dirt?

Applications:

1. God declares righteous only those whose goal remains and whose behavior exemplifies Christ-likeness. The purpose of Christ's forgiveness is *new* life, not a remake of the old in new forms or with a mixture of old and new. Newness means creating an entirely different person from the old fleshly version. That's the only acceptable result of conversion.

2. Attractive Christian lives are rendered unsightly when we mix faith with worldliness. Contaminating the spiritual life inevitably diminishes its worth to the believer and ruins its appeal to the seeker.

3. The holy Christ, however blameless for our failures, receives the blame from unthinking unbelievers. So our willingness to allow corruption into faith harms the One we claim to honor.

4. To be Christ's witnesses, not his detractors, we must resolve to keep ourselves pure from admixture. More importantly, making that resolve possible, we must more basically resolve to remove all evil *influences* from our primary spiritual interest—and adamantly retain the distance, never letting them cross the invisible line we've drawn to protect Christ's purity.

5. Because our present Christian experience offers a preview of eternal life, we live as if we're already in Heaven. Destined to be exactly like Jesus then, we're getting into practice now. Since we know that God doesn't discard imperfect Christians but forgives them till He can perfect them, we resolutely nourish Christ-likeness, focusing our attention where we seek to focus our affection.

⌘ ⌘ ⌘ ⌘ ⌘ ⌘

Subject Idea:	Hypocrisy
Scripture:	I Samuel 16:7
Visual Item:	Gift-wrapped box filled with scraps or a white elephant gift

Truth Stressed: Christians need to be as inwardly attractive as we are outwardly appealing.

Procedure: Show everyone the box. Have someone come and closely examine it, giving an opinion of its contents. Have him open and reveal the contents.

Applications:

1.   We would think something so exquisitely wrapped would contain an equally attractive gift. Like this box, Christians sometimes advertise integrity, holiness and spirituality while producing insincerity, profanity and sacrilege. A castle in appearance, we're a ruins on inspection!

2.   While gifts may not always equal the beauty and care of their packaging, the Christian life must be as inwardly attractive as its appearance boasts. Professed faith promises Christ-likeness. Confessed faith cannot betray the promise, proving it a lie.

3.   Since we claim the privileges of, we accept the responsibilities of our spiritual enfranchisement. We seek to be a show-window, displaying the overflow of an unsounded reserve. Knowing that Christianity is a lifestyle, not a symbol, our personal content must match its slogans. We work to achieve a righteousness that appeals to, not repels the sinner and a merciful rectitude that arouses the conscience of, without alienating the sinner.

⌘   ⌘   ⌘   ⌘   ⌘   ⌘

Subject Idea: Uselessness

Scripture: Hebrews 12:1

Visual Item: A few household items we've broken but never discarded.

Truth Stressed: We need to eliminate useless habits and behavior so productive ones can grow in us.

Procedure: Ask several people the week before to bring a useless object. Show the objects to the

audience and have the owners explain why
they only fill space.

Applications:

1. Like these items, we all have attitudes, behaviors and
    beliefs that obstruct spiritual excellence. They serve no
    useful purpose; they only occupy space—until, when we
    least expect it, they negatively influence us.
2. Some useless things we keep on shelves and in cabinets
    may also be harmful: certain chemical compounds or
    paint supplies. Spiritually, these sins must be eliminated
    with no questions asked or excuses made. Sins must go
    immediately. Others may merely occupy space, giving
    the impression that our house or garage or shed is too
    small—when the only problem is that we've left too many
    unusable objects there. Spiritually, these are hindrances to
    excellence. We might carry these weights and remain
    Christians, just as we can run with them in our pockets,
    but not as fast or far and not without diminishing results.
    Our goal is the riddance of any offensive factor, retaining
    only what's strictly necessary for the Christian life. An
    ultimate choice confronts us, the inevitable choice that
    we've avoided in our rush to make lesser ones. Do we
    choose to keep useless habits and attitudes or release them
    to construct the admirable Christ-life?
3. God's people must as thoroughly refuse spiritual medi-
    ocrity as they despise immorality. Loving righteousness
    has hatred of sin as its antithesis. And many Christians,
    claiming to love righteousness, retain an apathetic tol-
    erance of anti-Christian attitudes, behaviors and beliefs.
    How can we *say* we love Christ's perfection while we
    silently suffer a proliferation of the godlessness that
    mocks him?
4. One difference shows our inconsistency. If we have too
    small a shed, garage or room, we find time to rearrange or
    discard the useless items to make room for the new.
    Spiritually, however, many of us decide we don't have
    enough room for spiritual growth because we're too full.
    It doesn't occur to us to eliminate the worthless to acquire
    the worthy. We simply find increasingly less time for
    God because we're so involved with self!

SELF

By accepting as disciples men whose only qualification was their willingness to follow, Jesus urges us to come to him as we are. By changing the hapless disciples into stalwart apostles, Jesus urges his impact on our personal Christian life. Accepting the latter is the key to tolerating the former. None of us is yet all we want to be and not even close to what Jesus intends to make us. In these illustrations, examples help us take the look at self we'd rather ignore and the look at others we'd rather avoid.

Subject Idea: Hypocrisy

Scripture: Matthew 21:19

Visual Item: A book with a cover different from the contents

Truth Stressed: Hypocrisy is in the intent to deceive.

Procedure: Show book and cover; cover declares the book's content. Then read a short paragraph that shows you're reading from an entirely different book.

Applications:

1. Being a weak Christian isn't hypocrisy. It's possible to make mistakes without being a hypocrite. Intent is what turns weakness into hypocrisy. Peter was a weak disciple, not a hypocrite, when he betrayed Jesus; his failure came despite his announced intention to be faithful. Judas was a hypocrite, not a weak disciple, when he betrayed Jesus. While posing as a disciple, he had become a traitor and sealed the betrayal with an act exchanged only in friendship. Hypocrisy is an army without reserves; a boxer without a counter-punch; a golfer with no follow-through: pretense deprived of the very nature of being.

2. We instinctively expect substance in profession. We may not practice it, but we want to see it in others. Nowhere is this clearer than in the unbeliever's attitude toward the Christian: the non-disciple may lie, but he expects integrity from the believer. Our life must not demean our

witness. Enough offense comes from the Gospel message, for the world hates to hear God's truth. Christians shouldn't give added, baseless excuses for pre-Christians to refuse their message by being personally unkind or offensive.

3. Believers live in two worlds, each mutually exclusive. *In* this world we are *of* another, and God expects that other world's lifestyle presently to possess and inspire His people. If we remain faithful to Him and consistently obedient, even the unsaved will view our sins for what they are: failures caused by the flesh, not by an intent to be one kind of person while advertising another.

4. Wearing crosses or mustard seeds as symbols of faith is perfectly acceptable; they can be an unspoken witness. But it's possible to wear large crosses, fill our houses with Christian literature and attend church every Sunday and still be devoid of that faith which saves.

5. Virtue is superior to sin. Most people want to be known for some goodness, even when they're really bad; few want to be known for some evil, even when they're really good!

⌘   ⌘   ⌘   ⌘   ⌘   ⌘

Subject Idea:	Pride
Scripture:	Matthew 23:5
Visual Item:	Phylacteries 1" x 2" and 5" x 12", with string attached; tassels 2" to 3" and 18" to 20" long made from yarn, with a blue cord enveloping.
Truth Stressed:	God despises any effort to call attention to one's self, away from one's faith.
Procedure:	Put on the small phylacteries. (Use Velcro to apply tassels to suit coat.) Explain Biblical purpose of both phylacteries and tassels: Exodus 13:9, 16 and Numbers 15:38-39: to have God's word before their

eyes; to follow His commandments, not
their own heart.

Applications:

1. Jesus would have worn both phylacteries on his forehead
and tassels at the corners of his robe, each wrapped in a
blue cord. That made them acceptable accouterments.
The phylacteries could be rolls of parchment containing
scripture; more often they were small boxes containing
scripture. These were tied to the forehead by a string.

2. The Pharisees, who couldn't resist tinkering something
good into ostentation, enlarged those boxes and tassels.
(Remove small phylactery and tassels. Put on the large
phylactery and long tassels.) This ostentation angered
Jesus and provoked his uncompromising condemnation.

3. Faith in God has obvious, external expressions. Jesus said
we should let our light shine because he wanted discipleship to be seen! Both secrecy and sincerity are factors
in discipleship: the former in preparation, the latter in
public expression. And while Jesus expects both secrecy
and sincerity, he demands a public witness, with no
attempt to reduce our lofty faith to spectacle instead of influence.

4. The Pharisees would have said they enlarged their phylacteries and tassels to set them apart from others. But what
God meant as symbols became expressions of faith to
them. God despises bravado that struts before Him and
hates hypocrisy that boasts before others.

5. Any good has the danger of bad applications. Human
frailty is always the weak point. Pride corrupts the two
relationships we must keep pure. First, with God: it
makes us think we're worthy of Him and—truth to tell—
equal with Him. Second, with others: it makes us think
we don't need them because we're better than they.

6. Any act of faith must be a symbol of our inner commitment but never a proof that we're saved. The worship
we offer is an indication of faith but not the end of faith.
As something we offer God, yes; as something we trust to
save us, never. Self-pride abolishes the servant attitude
and lifestyle God demands.

7.   We can dress as Christians but still act like worldlings. If
     we do, our dress becomes a source of ridicule of us and of
     the God we claim to represent.

⌘   ⌘   ⌘   ⌘   ⌘   ⌘

Subject Idea: Hypocrisy
Scripture: Matthew 7:3-5; Galatians 6:1
Visual Item: 2 x 4 lumber, about 3 feet long
Truth Stressed: We must be free of the sin we correct in
                   others.
Procedure: As you hold the 2 x 4 to one eye, close the
                   other and walk towards a person in the au-
                   dience; tell him you see a speck in his eye.
                   Ask him to remove it.

Applications:

1.   Calling for an action we ourselves won't perform destroys
     the effectiveness of our witness. We see how ridiculous it
     is for me to ask a person to take a speck from his eye
     while I have a 2 x 4 extending from mine. How can I see
     what's in his eye with mine covered? That's what Jesus
     condemned: assuming the right to correct another whose
     fault we share.

2.   Instead of being an excuse to let sin go unchallenged and
     uncorrected among Christians, we need to see Bible
     teaching as an opportunity for all believers to grow
     beyond their sins! Since the Bible assumes our need to
     correct each other, we need to improve our personal life in
     order to admonish another effectively.

3.   However, we can't use another person's involvement in a
     sin to justify *our* continuation in it. If someone guilty of
     my sin rebukes me for it, he may have no validity, but his
     rebuke remains appropriate. Jesus won't allow another
     person's hypocrisy to justify our sin!

4.   Jesus doesn't encourage indiscriminate acceptance of all
     behavior—"We're all sinners, so we have no right to
     judge." He didn't say we shouldn't be realistic in eval-

uating behavior in others—"Who am I to say what's right and wrong?" He does demand that we strive to have overcome the fault we want others to correct, both to retain our integrity and to serve as an overcomer. (After all, the Master always has the positive end in mind. A conquering life is an indisputable witness to the one still conquered by life.) Knowing that we make demands for others as we make exceptions for ourselves; that we offer forbearance for self as quickly as we express condemnation of others; that we overstate their wrong while understressing ours; and that we infamously minimize criticism of self by diverting it to others, Jesus insists we look within before staring at others and to teach ourselves what we want them to learn.

5. Above all, he won't have his people considering anyone else unfit for salvation, perhaps unable to be saved. That isn't our role. Also, he wants us to judge a sin purely on its demerits, not from our like or dislike of someone. He knows how much harder we are on our enemies than on our friends.

6. Since people need to be reproved when wrong, and since it's done by people often as guilty, the former can't use the latter's sinfulness to deny the reproof; the latter can't be blind to self-sin and condemn others.

⌘   ⌘   ⌘   ⌘   ⌘   ⌘

Subject Idea: Knowledge
Scripture: Psalm 139:1-6
Visual Item: X-ray
Truth Stressed: God's absolute knowledge keeps our life perfectly open to Him.
Procedure: Show the X-ray; ask how many in the audience have had one; ask several for what purpose. Explain that the X-ray reveals something in our bodies not otherwise seen.

Applications:

1. Though humans are infamous for inability to keep secrets, God is known for revealing the secrets we want kept. We

can't invoke the right to privacy when He searches our hearts. We may, like governments and magicians, successfully keep secrets from others and even from ourselves at great cost, but we keep nothing from God. As the dead reveal secrets to autopsies, the living reveal themselves to His omniscient eyes.

2. While X-rays can tell if something exists where it shouldn't in our body, it may take surgery to identify it. God's word *knows* on seeing, without further analysis. And any further discovery proves the accuracy of its initial diagnosis.

3. Certain fraternal organizations retain secrecy in ceremonies and procedures, not because they're dangerous or unusual, but to make them mysterious and, therefore, more attractive. God declares the glory of His secrets in Christ by revealing them to the commonest person many would think unable to appreciate them.

4. Motives may be known only to God, though they may sometimes be clear to us. Because we lack definitive, let alone perfect knowledge of a person and circumstances, God refuses to acknowledge our condemnation of a person's spiritual life.

5. God's diagnosis of our natural condition invariably hurts because it reveals us as instinctive, inexcusable rebels against grace. This offends many, who can't fathom God's condemnation of well-intentioned humanity. God won't be deterred. He makes it very clear: in the Edenic fall humanity committed an inexcusably vile offense. It was no mere peccadillo when Eve ate the fruit and Adam joined her, taking her side against God. It was a catastrophe that brought Satan's savage influence into a race so easily deceived, willingly misled and compliantly misinformed. The appalling violence, bloody warfare and egregious immorality in history resulted from that betrayal of God's word. Until we accept God's diagnosis and admit the rectitude of His anger against us, we'll never understand the need of Christ's sacrificial death on our behalf.

⌘ ⌘ ⌘ ⌘ ⌘ ⌘

Subject Idea:	Fruitfulness
Scripture:	Matthew 7:16
Visual Item:	Can of hair spray—or any spray can with the product inside; a container to hold the spray
Truth Stressed:	We prove the contents of self by our life and actions.
Procedure:	Display the can; ask how anyone can be sure the can has something in it. Spray some of contents into the container.

Applications:

1. Anyone can appear to be a Christian. The world's definition of religion has become so indistinct that many who don't accept Christ's deity still claim to live in Christ-honoring ways. Christianity first declares Christ's deity, then replicates his earthly life in human behavior.

2. Actions, always louder than words, prove the content of life. That's why Christians must accept the challenge of proving faith by their life! It's important, not only that we bear fruit as disciples, but the Holy Spirit's fruit! That expresses the content of our heart and mind.

3. We daily prove the thinking and content of life in the normal activities of speaking, making decisions and relating to others. We sometimes feel it's in the great moments that we prove ourselves. Nearly always untrue. It's in small ways—the way we answer inquiries, ask questions, respond to accidents, criticism, praise—that we automatically reveal self.

⌘　⌘　⌘　⌘　⌘　⌘

Subject Idea:	Expectations
Scripture:	I John 3:2
Visual Item:	A can of vegetables with its contents and weight; a variety of other cans and boxes for comparison

Truth Stressed: Christians must measure themselves by God's word.

Procedure: In one hand hold the can with the contents and weight you choose as your standard. This represents God's paradigm of belief and behavior. Pick up the other items individually and "weigh" each against your model. Some may be smaller, larger, weigh less or more, contain similar or different items. The point is, they're different from what you've chosen as the judge of everything else you've brought.

Applications:

1. Unlike the illustration, there isn't an arbitrary, capricious standard by which all belief and behavior are measured. I could just as easily have made the smallest can my paragon, or the heaviest. Though many people want to postulate such uncertain spiritual and moral patterns, God has fixed forever, based on His own inflexible life, the ideal of right and wrong. We determine only whether we personally accept or reject what God posits as the judge of everything else.

2. Christians are called to a distinctive lifestyle because Jesus lived a distinctive life. He remains God's pattern and our example. As we reproduce his life in us, we conform to God's standard. Since no one perfectly reproduces his life, Christ's perfection compensates for the failure, despite the effort. But as much like Jesus as possible God presently expects us to be, and exactly like Jesus God shall one day make us.

3. God's prototype is clearly revealed, like the content and weight of this can are revealed. If someone wanted corn, and this can advertised peas, would we blame the manufacturer if the buyer misread or carelessly chose any can he pleased? Yet many foolishly and groundlessly criticize God for condemning those who refuse to read His directions, or, after reading, refuse to believe He's really serious about what He's said.

4. We need to discern the belief and practice of other religions that claim equality with or superiority to

Christianity. Just as cans could have words on the label we don't understand, other religions have words unfamiliar to, or in direct contradiction of God's word. Their very existence should warn us to put them aside. Only what God planted survives the Fire!

⌘   ⌘   ⌘   ⌘   ⌘   ⌘

Subject Idea:	Modeling
Scripture:	Hebrews 12:1-2
Visual Item:	A monster #10 can of vegetables or fruit you'll label, "Christ's Life"; half a dozen smaller cans you'll label, "Human Examples".
Truth Stressed:	God insists that we measure ourselves by Christ's life, not by human examples.
Procedure:	Display the can labeled "Christ's Life"; put on either side of it the others. Note how insignificant the rest are compared to the #10.

Applications:

1. Jesus is God's ideal and our model. Only as we perfectly imitate Jesus is God pleased with us, for only to him did God ever say, "I am well pleased with you," a word declaring God's election of Christ based on his obedience. Abraham was called God's friend, David a man after God's heart and Daniel one highly esteemed. But only Jesus received God's accolade: well pleased! That ideal never changes; his model remains eternally in place.

2. Intimidated by a perfection they can never reach and ignorant of the grace that compensates for our flaws, many people adopt lesser models as their ideals: "If I can't be a #10 can, I'll be a 4 ouncer." This immediately satisfies their personal goals but further alienates them from God. As no can here comes close to equaling the monster can, no other life is an acceptable substitute for Christ's.

3. Of course, it's easier to choose another model for our life. First, we can pick someone with whom we'll feel com-

fortable; whose outlook on life is similar to ours; whose interests parallel ours. They're like us, so we like them. The trouble is they have the same problem we do: they're sinners needing forgiveness. So, however much above us they are intellectually or morally or socially, they're at the same level spiritually. And God won't accept spiritual substitutes for Jesus!

4. The problem with choosing fallen humans as our model is the wide divergence in models. We'll always find someone faster, wealthier or prettier than our choice—increasing our despair. Or someone slower, poorer or homelier than our choice—increasing our egotism. We can't be trusted to choose our own models of behavior! That's a deceitful game we play with each other to discourage them or justify self, but it won't fool God.

5. God declares our human diversity good because He loathes uniformity in creation. But in developing people He one day welcomes into His presence, He's absolutely focused on Christ's singularity as His ideal and our model! Every other standard is a counterfeit that He discards. All who choose a life outside Christ's own bring heartache to themselves now and endless misery to themselves later!

⌘   ⌘   ⌘   ⌘   ⌘   ⌘

Subject Idea: Salvation
Scripture: Mark 12:34
Visual Item: Expired sales ad from a newspaper
Truth Stressed: We must accept Christ while forgiveness is being offered.
Procedure: Note the sale prices listed and the date they're honored. Note that after the listed dates prices return to normal.

Applications:

1. The flaw that reduces all to a common denominator—sinner, opens all to a common opportunity—salvation.

What God alone derives every person can accept. Now, while the kingdom of God is near, is the time of salvation.

2. God demands our willing involvement in the process. To save us, apart from our willingness to embrace it, would perpetuate the chaos of which we're thoroughly disgusted but can't eliminate because we adamantly refuse His grace. Only the intentional penitent can be saved and live in harmony with God.

3. The time of forgiveness will lapse, just as these sale prices lapse. Just as we would have no success buying at the sales price after the sale is past, however much we plead, we won't receive forgiveness when the time of repentance has gone and judgment has come. What folly to wait till one is dying to seek the One who overcame death! What folly to possess throughout life what offers gain only for the body, then seek at death's door what can profit only the soul!

4. Yet, as $300,000 ad campaigns can't convince people in flood plains to buy flood insurance, fervent, expensive evangelism can't convince people so absolutely sure to die that after death comes God's judgment. So many, finding the Christian life too demanding, mistakenly plan to skip its pain to embrace its pleasure. They'll then find that the saddest words of tongue or pen are not, "What might have been," but, "Depart from me, you workers of iniquity, I never knew you." Come to Jesus, now, while he offers salvation freely. No...run to him. No...it's much too important...FLY to him!

⌘   ⌘   ⌘   ⌘   ⌘   ⌘

Subject Idea: Deception

Scripture: II Corinthians 6:11-13

Visual Item: Mask that covers the entire face

Truth Stressed: God sees us as we really are.

Procedure: After putting on the mask, wink, scowl, smile, etc. Then ask the people if they could identify your expressions.

Applications:

1. Our witness in court would be inadmissible if we took an oath to identify precisely what a person under the mask was doing. The mask fulfills its function by hiding the one wearing it.

2. We often don masks to protect those we love: we don't share a hurtful comment someone made or our true feelings of despair or grief. Doctors routinely withhold bad news from terminally ill patients.

3. Sometimes we mask our real intentions and motives from others, wanting to steal an advantage. Every professional baseball game is a contest in deception, with managers and third base coaches flashing a single truth to the batter and runner hidden inside a pack of lies. Nations routinely put on masks when at war, knowing the importance of deceiving the enemy to save the lives of their own troops. We sometimes intend to keep self hidden from others, as if we have that much they would care to see or mimic or possess.

4. We often have dual personalities in our interpersonal relationships. We act one way toward those on whom we're in some way dependent and another toward those who can't help us at all. With the former we're friendly, helpful, attentive; with the latter we're curt and inattentive.

5. We often find it hard to be honest with those whose opinion of us matters most. We're afraid we'd lose their love and respect if they saw us as we really are, not as we'd like to be when with them. We're such good actors in this farce that we carry it into our relationship with God. Most Christians have no problem admitting they're sinfulness to God; that's a problem the unsaved have. But the believer often has a problem absent in the non-Christian: he's afraid to be honest with God when he feels lonely or abandoned by God; when he's hurt because God hasn't answered prayer; when someone close and essential has been injured or killed. We think to hide those feelings from God, as if He wants only our praises, not our questions. As if He's offended with the honesty that life forces on us. Honesty with Him, however brutal, is

acceptable so long as it's offered within believing obedience. Jesus really didn't want to die on the cross! When, in the Garden, he asked for exemption from Calvary, it was an intense instant of humanity recoiling from terror, yet completely acceptable to God because Jesus submitted his will to God's! God wants us to be comfortable enough with Him to take off our masks and be real with Him.

6. Taking off masks with each other is essential for accountability in the body of Christ, and accountability within the body is essential before the church can positively impact society. There's little need for us to condemn in the unsaved behaviors tolerated in the Christian body. Within a small group, where we gradually learn to share and trust, we admit weaknesses and sins that we want their love to help us overcome. True, we run a risk by uncovering ourselves: of betrayal, of misunderstanding, of mockery, even the loss of friendships with people who refuse to get involved. We run a greater risk if we don't: of continuing to betray Jesus. Will we risk humbling ourselves before other Christians to escape disgracing ourselves before Christ?

⌘   ⌘   ⌘   ⌘   ⌘   ⌘

Subject Idea:	Promises
Scripture:	I Samuel 15:29
Visual Item:	Can of "Instant Hair" hair spray; thin wig on a Styrofoam head
Truth Stressed:	We need to be careful whose promises we believe.
Procedure:	Explain that this product claims to cover bald spots and to thicken thin hair. While it obviously doesn't work, enough interested people buy it to make its manufacture profitable.

Applications:

1.   There's massive false advertising in the world, despite laws against and occasional punishment of it. Manufacturers shout the value of their products, boasting their worth, dismissing the competition's, assuring us that using theirs specifically enriches life. The motto of the consumer always has to be, "Buyer beware." While there is recourse if the buyer isn't satisfied, it's often not worth the effort. We've been victimized and hopefully have learned from the experience.

2.   The world outside God's will never stops recruiting followers, promising fulfillment of our dreams if we buy its perspective. This is especially seen among those who consider creation the key to interpreting themselves. Understand: creation never lies but liars often misrepresent creation to us. Creation knows its place and rejoices in it, but humanists ceaselessly manufacture claims for creation that it never made. It sees itself as our servant, not our equal or master; as dependent on us for its renewal, not we on it for our purpose. Beware of anyone who thinks we discover our meaning by studying nature.

3.   If we were suddenly to change our outward status, what effect would it have on *us*? If we were to be instantly rich or famous or powerful, how would that improve *us*? Would it automatically eliminate problems? Would it guarantee a long-lasting marriage? Would it exempt us from death? Beware of thinking we can change our depths by improving our surface life.

4.   Promises aren't the truth; they're merely someone's declaration of the truth. The truth may be 180 degrees different from what's promised. The Bible is the only book, and God the only being in the world, to tell us the truth about ourselves and Himself. God knows we don't want to hear the truth about either one; that self avoids truth, rejects truth and, if truth insists, attacks truth. But God won't lie just because we believe liars. We can always find someone to agree with us; to minimize our evil; to maximize our few virtues. As our real and only Friend in this world, God won't lie just to make us feel good. We can trust Him because of that. He wants us to be at peace

with Him, not one with nature; at peace with Him, not content with self! God is the truth. Therefore, His claims are always so; His salvation always real; His joy always deep; His presence always constant; His promises always sure!

⌘　⌘　⌘　⌘　⌘　⌘

Subject Idea:	Genuineness
Scripture:	I John 4:1
Visual Item:	Two cans of pop: one regular, one diet
Truth Stressed:	Christians are to define spiritual reality personally.
Procedure:	Have each can's identity concealed. Ask a volunteer to come forward. Pour pop from each can into a separate glass. Ask the volunteer to identify each. Ask how he knew the difference.

Applications:

1. Since tastes differ, different colas exist to satisfy differing consumers. No one can say, "This is the real cola" except as a personal choice. It may be their favorite, but that doesn't make it the only worthwhile cola.

2. Spiritually, we're not drinking colas. Spiritually, we can't say, "One religion is good as another; it's all a matter of personal preference." Satan sells that view to society, and many buy it. It's especially attractive in a diverse America. So many refugees, particularly from the Arab world and Southeast Asia, have brought their religions with them and demand the right to exercise their faith. Which is fine. America was built on tolerance of competitive religions values. (It is interesting, especially among Arabs, that they *demand* the right to practice Islam here while the nations they left *proscribe* Christianity, won't let it be publicly taught and persecute those who do. Nevertheless, it's important to allow each person to practice his own religion as a protection for all religions.)

3. However, advocating religious freedom isn't the same as admitting religious equality. Christians affirm the former but vigorously deny the latter. Let America be the haven where all people can practice their faith, but don't let anyone, anywhere in America think that Moses, Buddha, Mohammed, Joseph Smith, Mary Baker Eddy, Ron Hubbard or Brahm comes within shouting distance of Jesus Christ! Until other religions have a verified historical personality who publicly lived and taught, then died for the sins of the world, lay in his tomb until the third day and then triumphantly rose bodily, no religion competes with Christianity!

4. Christians are commanded to test all religious spirits to determine their factuality or falsehood. This warning begins with doctrinal content. False teaching may stress certain values that impress people: strong family life; abstention from alcohol; impassioned patriotism. The unsuspecting consider the doctrine pacific because its behavior is positive. That's part of Satan's deceit: to mask lies with obvious truth, the kernel of truth giving credibility to the lie!

5. Our society has so badly forsaken Biblical truth that we have trouble knowing true from false behavior. Ethics being considered unnecessary to our national survival, it hasn't recently been taught in the universities or in businesses. As a result, stock scandals, business failures and unprincipled rivalries blacken the American character. We need to have virtue defined to have ethics delineated for us. And now colleges and businesses are back at the business of teaching ethics. Christians shouldn't need courses in ethics taught by secular sources. Virtue and ethics are defined for them throughout the Bible. Discernment is innate in the believer who knows God's word. We can instinctively know if a doctrine or behavior is flawed or permissible, harmful or innocuous.

6. The challenge facing Christians is to prove that *real* Christianity does exist—and they're examples of it! By spending time with Jesus in his word, in prayer and in the fellowship of believers, God's people offer an example of

the resurrected life that's an irrefragable evidence of
Christ's deity.

⌘   ⌘   ⌘   ⌘   ⌘   ⌘

Subject Idea:	Reality Versus Illusion
Scripture:	Galatians 4:19
Visual Item:	Artificial and living plants of the same variety
Truth Stressed:	Only genuine disciples achieve Christ-likeness.
Procedure:	Show both plants. Can they tell the difference? Why? Why not?

Applications:

1.   The artificial looks good but fails to produce the results of
the real plant. True, it offers beauty without work and appearance without caretaking. But it won't reproduce
itself; blossoms won't ever appear, or fruit hang from its
branches. Its leaves won't flutter in the wind; no perfume
will waft from it. In fact, the artificial can be too
complete, with everything manufactured to perfection.
Only the living plant can survive with leaves split or
darkened and petals hanging or lost. (However, plastic
plants *are* now being made complete with the brown
marks of a living plant.) There is a religiosity that
appears artificial: all stiff and formal, categorized and circumscribed; living within defined, legalistic boundaries;
hard to the touch, unresponsive to need, unyielding,
priggish. And, obvious to anyone who gets close enough
to see and experience it, not at all real! Lacking the
energy, bristle, excitement and creativity of reality, it just
stands there lifeless!

2.   If you want the decorative appeal of a plant without its
cost, buy the plastic. It costs more initially, but less in the
long term. Living plants initially cost less but exact more
investment as time passes. It takes effort, expense and at-

tention to keep living things alive. You can leave something artificial for months, and it will only be dusty when you return. Leave a living something for that long, and you'll find it dead on your return. But, then, the plastic *is* dead. That's the price you pay for romancing life, not flirting with plastic! People complain about the expense of keeping a church program going. Well, do they want the church to be alive or dead? Would they be satisfied without the results that demand the expenses? Dead and dying churches invariably cost little, but they produce even fewer results. There's usually someone willing to bankroll the church in exchange for the right to make the decisions. Is that what people want? Surprisingly, the larger the church gets, the more expensive its demands and the more precarious its existence. But that's the price we pay to GROW! It cost Jesus real blood to produce a real salvation: how can our real discipleship come free of charge?

3.   If we want particular kinds of plants not indigenous to our climate, we may have to buy the artificial ones. But we need never be artificial Christians, for Christianity flourishes in any moral, social, economic or political climate. It's as much at home in slave hovels as in Caesar's palace. Soldiers as well as diplomats embrace it. The first as well as the twentieth century comprehends it. Real Christianity can and must exist and flourish within us. Its reality produces real Christians. Jesus really did overcome the world. He really does live forever! That's reality, not theater; it's everyday joy, not pretense!

4.   What kind of self are we producing: a living spiritual or an artificial religious self? Be forewarned: the self we build is the same person we become and live with twenty-four hours a day. Does what we build have an attractiveness that appeals and multiplies itself? Or does it just sit or stand there, unmoving, uninspiring and unconvincing because it's really pretense?

SIN

It isn't that our culture doesn't believe in sin: it's merely trivialized it. Sin is fat in milk and sugar in cereal. To enjoy all the "sinful pleasure" without the "sin," use Fat-free Mocha and Equal. By adopting evil, Madison Avenue invariably sells sin's "sizzle" but never its "stake" into the human heart.

However, as the following illustrations show, ignored or underrated sin scars the human soul the way untreated blemishes pock-mark the body.

Subject Idea: Adhesion

Scripture: Romans 12:9, 12:21; I Thessalonians 5:22; III John 11

Visual Item: Glue; mousetrap; action figure (GI Joe, etc.)

Truth Stressed: Distancing ourselves from sin offers the only sure escape from it.

Procedure: Describe how the mousetrap works. Hold the trap perpendicular to the floor; throw the action figure into the air and catch it on the mousetrap. Stress that getting *close* to the trap presents the danger.

Applications:

1. Since sin contaminates by its very presence, avoiding the appearance of evil is necessary. Evil has a way of blackening even those just getting close to it, without getting involved in it.

2. Since bad company corrupts good character, Christians need to choose carefully those with whom they have intimate relationships. This isn't the same as social or witnessing relationships, but people whose values we at least respect and perhaps emulate.

3. It's as easy for good behavior to be demeaned by evil companions as it is difficult for good behavior to convert evil companions. Therefore, Christians must always follow a single rule in all relationships: if their association with the unsaved draws them to Jesus, continue it; if it

draws Christians from Jesus, sever it. Sin's sticky nature attracts and entangles anyone close to it. Many formerly strong disciples, who thought they could resist the temptations their friends offered, instead found themselves surrendering and becoming like the people Jesus wanted to become like him. Never underestimate sin's adhesiveness.

4.   By concentrating on the bait, the mouse misses the danger; by our concentration on what we think is the pleasure of, we miss the deadly pestilence of sin, but as danger doesn't miss the mouse, sin doesn't miss us!

5.   The trap will close on anything that trips it; made to trap mice, it fatally adheres to the animal closing with it. Like the trap, given the opportunity to close on us, sin closes! It's alert to any opportunity to adhere.

⌘   ⌘   ⌘   ⌘   ⌘   ⌘

Subject Idea:	Weight
Scripture:	Colossians 1:13-14
Visual Item:	Backpack; articles to put into it, some quite heavy
Truth Stressed:	The more we let sin accumulate in our lives, the more oppressive it becomes.
Procedure:	Have a person don the empty backpack. Ask if it would be hard to carry. Add items to the pack and ask if he feels the increasing weight. Insert two or three small but heavy items; ask how he would like to carry the pack all day, every day, everywhere.

Applications:

1.   Many people allow a "little sin" into their lives and find it tolerable, even easy to carry, to handle, to discipline. It never asks for much from us, as C.S. Lewis said, "Just the right to exist"; it promises to never get in the way; we won't even know it's there.

2. Sin lies. It's never satisfied merely existing in us. That's its "entry excuse": "I'm so little I won't bother you." Not so; by its very nature because of our weakness, it grows, then multiplies. It's like germs in a warm, moist host: hidden at first, but multiplying alarmingly to sickness or disease!

3. Sin's burden always grows increasingly oppressive, never lighter; more tyrannical, never more pliable; more demanding, never more docile. At first it's no problem at all; at last it's insufferable and intolerable—but constantly more demanding! Sin is always that way: we start having it; it ends possessing us. At first we're in charge and it's in our thrall; at last it's the harsh, incapacitating, damning master, and we're helpless before it!

4. The good news is: any time we want, we can remove the burden, just as we can make the backpack tolerable by removing objects. Jesus' conquest of Satan guarantees our own. He never fed Satan even a crumb but starved him to death for us.

5. Since no human can live without serving either God or Satan, Jesus imposes his own yoke when he removes Satan's from us. The difference: his is a burden that increasingly frees us as we carry it and weighs less as it grows heavier. It's a burden we can joyfully carry every day!

⌘   ⌘   ⌘   ⌘   ⌘   ⌘

Subject Idea:	Consequences
Scripture:	II Samuel 11:1-27
Visual Item:	Hammer; nail; piece of wood
Truth Stressed:	While grace forgives sin's penalty, life may unavoidably retain its results.
Procedure:	Show the unmarked piece of 2 x 4 lumber. Hammer in the nail part-way. Then remove the nail and show the print.

Applications:

1. There's hardly a sin so weak it can't leave a mark even after we overcome it. The spiritual struggle with Satan is eminently winnable, but it may inflict scars that remain.
2. God forgives the penalty of sin: we won't die. He doesn't remove the results: we have to live with the memory of the mistake and failure.
3. That scar/result can be a source of victory if the sin remains, not only overcome and in our past, never to return, but a constant encouragement *never again* to let it happen.
4. Even Jesus suffered scars, but only in conquering and destroying Satan. Since Satan wanted Jesus to avoid the cross, but Jesus went there anyway, despite Satan's every effort to prevent it, those scars will be the source of eternal praise and adulation for our Master. But he's the only one to glory in his scars. We *rue* every one as a reminder of our failure to overcome sin.

⌘ ⌘ ⌘ ⌘ ⌘ ⌘

Subject Idea:	Pervasiveness
Scripture:	James 1:13-15
Visual Item:	Packet of yeast; loaf of bread
Truth Stressed:	Sin naturally penetrates every part of life once given access.
Procedure:	Show loaf of bread and packet of yeast. The ounce of yeast changed the entire amount of dough, even altering its appearance.

Applications:

1. It doesn't take a big sin to harm our spiritual lives because sin naturally *grows*, as it's the nature of yeast to expand in whatever dough it's inserted. Contrasting the predisposition of sin's growth is our prejudice against spiritual growth. That takes a work of grace.

2. Yeast's natural leavening power is the reason scripture sees it as a symbol of sin and an evil force to be avoided, and why it must be removed from our lives before we can fellowship with the Holy God. This is why Jesus halted sin in the mind, where it begins and why we must halt it while it's only a thought, before it becomes a deed.

3. Don't let sin get started in life. Before we know it, like the yeast in this loaf, sin will penetrate every nook and cranny of life. *Confining* it puts it where it does the greatest damage. Hiding it, thinking we're rid of it, turns it monstrous!

4. Hiding sin may seem logical to those who want involvement with no publicity. But while we may keep others from seeing the actual commission of sin, they will certainly see its results.

⌘   ⌘   ⌘   ⌘   ⌘   ⌘

Subject Idea: Restriction

Scripture: I John 3:6

Visual Item: Handcuffs and key

Truth Stressed: We remain captive to our temptations only because we refuse the key that liberates us.

Procedure: Have someone come forward. Place handcuffs on him. Hold key aloft and ask how many would prefer to be manacled when they could be free?

Applications:

1. The presence of unforgiven sin automatically restricts the Holy Spirit's influence in our lives. However positive some want the Gospel message to be, the Christian life emphasizes strong negatives. Since we don't have room in our lives for everything, we prioritize development of the Holy Spirit's fruit, thus effectively minimizing the flesh's carnality.

2. Entertaining sin is like wearing handcuffs in daily activities: it can be done, but not without a compensating

effort that could better be expended in positive, Christ-honoring acts. Do we want to spend our time and effort overcoming obstacles we allow to invade our lives or in building Christ-honoring behavior?

3. Sin's presence confines us to a lifestyle needlessly imposed because it's unnecessarily allowed. Satan has no power over us that we refuse him! He can't keep us bound a second longer than *we* allow. Jesus holds the key to our release; we need only let him access the lock.

⌘   ⌘   ⌘   ⌘   ⌘   ⌘

Subject Idea:	Hindrances
Scripture:	Hebrews 12:1
Visual Item:	Bed sheet
Truth Stressed:	The disciple must strip to holiness to compete successfully as a Christian.
Procedure:	Describing the robes worn in Biblical times, have someone wrapped in the bed sheet. Explain that, while the robe made some daily activities difficult, it severely limited ability to run. Tuck in the bed sheet at the waist and explain why "girding up the loins" was necessary if one wanted to race.

Applications:

1. Since unlimited spiritual growth is our goal and destiny, any hindrance we allow into life mocks God's plan and our potential.

2. We must strip to essentials to compete successfully in the Christian life. Satan loves nothing more than to overwhelm Christians with burdens, involvements and cares that sap our spiritual energy and divert attention from our daily walk. Losing concentration on our goal serves his purpose as well as intentionally avoiding it.

3. Since the Christian life is really more a steeplechase than merely a race, the obstacles we must overcome will defeat us unless we strip down to holiness. Since the Christian

life is a 10,000 meter contest, not a 100 yard dash, removing hindrances is essential to our comfort and progress as we compete.

4. When only patient endurance succeeds in the race before us, can anyone "with patience" run the Christian race if he's uncomfortable, unsettled or distracted? To assure our eventual success God demands the removal of all sins and frailties, for while sin *suffocates* us, frailties *limit* our spiritual effectiveness.

5. Sin specializes in destroying the sinner, but it's just as willing to cause the righteous to fall. Anyone who concentrates on its appeal, its beauty, its size—or anything about it except its lethal danger to the soul—is a potential victim!

6. Are we stuck in a counter-productive or harmful relationship, one eventually, if not immediately deadly to our marriage, family or Christian life? *Get out now* before we're in deeper and find it increasingly expensive to extricate ourselves; before even more major disruptions occur in all our holy, meaningful relationships. Remember, we're not flies, and Satan's glue can't keep us stuck if we choose freedom in Christ!

⌘   ⌘   ⌘   ⌘   ⌘   ⌘

Subject Idea:	Definitions
Scripture:	II Corinthians 13:9, 11
Visual Item:	Target (archery or gun)
Truth Stressed:	Sin is any less-than-perfect behavior.
Procedure:	Show the target. Ask what part would be easiest, even for an amateur, to hit? What would be hardest, even for a professional? What amateur could hit the bull's-eye every time? What professional could hit it every time?

Applications:

1. Perfection is God's goal for us. Nothing else and nothing less. Whether we subscribe to it or not; whether we aim to achieve it or not.

2. That's why we must *make* it our discipleship goal. To say we may as well not set perfection as a goal because we won't reach it, undervalues the positive effect goals have on people.

3. Not every goal is 100% achieved; perhaps most aren't, but in the effort expended to achieve, people produce at a level they hadn't thought possible. Besides, to achieve anything in particular, we need to plan particularly. By a fluke we might shoot at the target blindfolded and hit it; by a greater fluke, the bull's-eye. But would we want to wager our house and savings account on either, especially the latter?

4. Whatever failures mar our efforts should be from trying to succeed, not from forfeiture of the match.

5. Perfection is the goal of all Olympic athletes. Yet, in the 1996 Games, the American Gold Medal winner in archery didn't score 100%. In the end, he was closer to the bull's-eye than his competitor by only a millimeter.

6. Spiritually, occasionally hitting something in the target is considered sufficient for us; to come close to the bull's-eye a major achievement. To hit it once or twice in a lifetime means we're a super-star Christian. But which of us hits the bull's-eye every time, 100% of the shots taken, time and again, 10,000 times out of 10,000? Of course, we wouldn't expect new Christians to hit the bull's-eye, just as we would forgive an amateur archer entirely missing the target. But what Christian, even the most mature, ever shoots perfectly?

7. Where does that leave us with God? His perfection allows only perfect beings in His presence. How can we ever stand there, imperfect as we are, whatever our efforts? Aah...the Master Marksman shot for us while he lived among us. And Jesus, carrying the fate of God's entire kingdom on his shoulders each time he strung the bow and pulled back the string, took aim and...struck the target dead center on bull's-eye! Every time! Every

moment of every day for 33 years! His perfection remains the difference between God's demand of perfection and our desire to reach it and our failures, despite trying. By trusting Jesus Christ, we put our hand on the string, but he pulls it back and shoots. And while that's happening, God sees *him* standing in our stead.

Subject Idea:	Danger
Scripture:	Romans 7:14-25; I Corinthians 15:56
Visual Item:	Blow dryer with warning label on cord or dryer
Truth Stressed:	God warns us away from sin by stressing its danger to our soul.
Procedure:	Read the warning label as you show the dryer. Ask if there's anything unclear about the warning. Would anyone but someone suicidal intentionally drop the dryer into a water-filled tub or basin?

Applications:

1. Dangers to the spiritual life exist. God's mercy, not His wrath or cruelty, motivates His warnings against a life of sin. The greatest, dead-level certainty is that we'll eventually go to Hell.

2. Why would we take seriously the word of a manufacturer of a hair dryer, but not the warning of the Immortal God? Why would we think the manufacturer serious and God jesting? And while the manufacturer warns us in order to protect itself from litigation, God unwaveringly opposes sin because it interrupts and abrogates our fellowship with Him.

3. The need to remain positive keeps some leaders from denouncing sin. That ignores the fact that Christianity stakes its reputation for holiness on some adamant negatives. If Jesus warns us against certain behavior, only a fool would make a virtue of affirming it! In that reference, God is unwaveringly positive about our need to flee from dangers to our soul!

4. God takes no pleasure from the death of the wicked—or in seeing the righteous fall. His only pleasure derives

from seeing all humanity rescued from sin by being brought into the name and under the blood of Jesus. If we resist and deny His appeal, however, and refuse to let God have His pleasure, God's justice will be satisfied! Do we want God to satisfy His pleasure or His justice?

⌘   ⌘   ⌘   ⌘   ⌘   ⌘

Subject Idea:	Enticement
Scripture:	I John 3:7-9
Visual Item:	Hunting call—turkey, duck, deer, etc.
Truth Stressed:	Only the Holy Spirit enables us to discern between Christ's and Satan's appeal.
Procedure:	As you show the call, explain that it's used to lure an animal into range. Demonstrate the sound: explain that while it may mean nothing to us, manufacturers have invested large sums in research and testing to produce a call that works for particular prey, whether for mating between adults or offspring calling for help from parents.

Applications:

1. Sin seems as attractive as virtue and most always more appealingly presents itself to humanity. The reason is simple: sin's only standard is deception, where virtue's sole standard is God's perfect holiness. Sin invariably stresses beauty and fulfillment in its allure; it never speaks of cost, penalties and failures!

2. God and Satan have opposite perspectives on yielding to sin. God says it brings death; Satan swears it's the only way to enjoy life. In fact, Satan brazenly lies that only interesting people are in Hell since they had the courage to live as free spirits, lacking in the boring and lifeless in Heaven.

3. Only the spiritually discerning individual detects the often fine distinctions between God's and Satan's call, partic-

ularly in areas of scriptural silence on behavior and values: movies to attend, TV shows to watch, entertainments we patronize are examples.

4. Satan wants us to believe that his call is as good, as appropriate and as helpful as God's—but the fact that God is Satan's standard of measurement, not vice versa, means that God is the original and Satan the imitator. While the imitation intends to sound as much like the original as possible, a difference exists in the spiritual realm, if not in the animal world. Satan can imitate much of what God does, but can never imitate God Himself!

5. Employing the imitation means using deceit to harm one's prey, which is fine for calling animals to slaughter, but deadly when following Satan's lure to spiritual destruction.

6. Since good can become evil even in the hands of good people, we need to learn the call's usage to determine its origin. Origin determines usage. Love is necessary in humanity, but if our call says to love self first, that usage instantly reveals its source!

7. If we're drawn to Satan by his call, we should pray to discern his presence and immediately withdraw! For, while being *drawn* to him may not be deadly to us, *remaining* in the danger zone is 100% effective in killing our spiritual life.

8. The Holy Spirit's influence gives us the discernment we need. We walk into Satan's trap only by refusing to consult or obey the Spirit's guidance. Why would we ever settle for imitation, however much like the original it is, when God provides the only original and eternal call in our world?

⌘   ⌘   ⌘   ⌘   ⌘   ⌘

Subject Idea:	Deceit
Scripture:	I John 2:15-16
Visual Item:	Hunting decoy or fishing lure

Truth Stressed: Fixation on sin's attractiveness endangers our spiritual walk.

Procedure: Show decoy and lure, explaining that while they can't fool us, they're made so colorful and lifelike that they can fool the hunted prey: the duck because of the distance, the fish because of the speed.

Applications:

1. As advertisers depend on their ability to attract attention by appealing to our senses, particularly the eyes and nose, Satan knows how to "package" his appeal to us.

2. Movement is the key to a lure as looks to a decoy. Something looking flashy draws people's interest. The drug dealers in their expensive cars and clothes appeal to street kids. It creates an allusion: "Looks like they're going somewhere, and I want to go along." Or "looks like *they* matter—see the people deferring to them—I want that power."

3. Being similar to God in Christ is often enough to fool people into thinking the imitation *is* God in Christ. The emphasis on "spiritual" in our culture can mean anything from mediums consulting the dead to new age philosophy to Biblical faith—the only real spirituality. But many people, who balk at the cost Christianity imposes, accept a substitute for it at none of its cost—and mistakenly consider it equal to Christianity!

4. Satan continues to create fraudulent facades of God to keep humanity from seeing the real God in Christ. Christians know that a decoy may look good, but only while the reality absents itself! Beside the Real God, every imitation looks every inch and ounce the dead illusion it is!

5. Christians have the obligation to present the real Jesus to people, so his reality can mock the pretenders looking something like him. Then the unsaved can realize the truth Christians have long embraced: imitations may be cheaper and reality more expensive, but only reality is worth the price paid!

⌘   ⌘   ⌘   ⌘   ⌘   ⌘

Subject Idea: Forgiveness

Scripture: I John 1:9; Exodus 8:1-15

Visual Item: Throw rug; whisk broom; dirt/objects

Truth Stressed: Forgiveness of guilt, not hiding guilt, removes its power from our lives.

Procedure: Ask if anyone has, in an emergency, hidden dirt or crumbs under a convenient rug or chair? Putting all the objects under the rug, ask if they would hide so much there it would be obvious to anyone?

Applications:

1. Refusing to accept misbehavior as sin, many consider it a neurosis. Instead of calling for forgiveness, they seek psychiatric explanations and assurances.

2. That's why Christians must stress human sinfulness to unsaved sinners. Every sin can be forgiven and removed because God specializes in forgiving sin. But neuroses can only be managed or controlled, not banished, meaning *they* remain as others accrue. Soon we have a stack of things tormenting our lives because we've enabled them to pile up instead of being carried off one by one.

3. Acknowledging our guilt before God keeps life from being a piled-high complex of problems over which we stumble. It keeps us free from accumulated problems, enabling us to be good examples and stepping stones to the unsaved.

4. Only the easily deceived or willingly deceived think we banish interpersonal problems by hiding them. Facing differences, even if we find it necessary to have others mediate for us as we discuss them, offers long-lasting solutions. Without clearing the air over our differences, the feelings we've developed often make themselves known in negative behavior. With the very people we've always treated well we show irritation, impatience and disrespect. All because they've offended us, and we're too cowardly to confront them over it. But *they* know the difference and wonder why. Kind, patient honesty better serves our long-term relationships than deceit-covering cowardice. Often the excuses we use for not confronting people over

our differences—don't want to hurt their feelings, don't want to make a fuss—become stumbling blocks to healed relationships.

5.   All of that is a big problem with human-to-human relationships, but it's a monstrous difficulty between humanity and God. The problem always becomes *our* problem with God; He becomes the tyrant, trying to harm us, or He's unkind for imposing guilt because guilt is negative! As a result, we withdraw from God, in essence crawling under the rug intellectually, emotionally and spiritually; thinking that our withdrawal settles the matter for us, we've resolved the issue by denigrating God and denying His right to charge us with guilt. That's like piling all our household dirt under this rug. No one else is fooled, not even our friends, and certainly not God.

6.   There's one other person who sweeps dirt under the rug: the lazy person who feels it's just too much trouble to remove it! Spiritually, it's the person who intends to accept and confess his guilt sometime—but not just yet; he wants his piled-up life a little longer. Or it's too costly in time or emotions to confess guilt; or he'd have to make too much of a change to admit guilt; or a thousand other excuses that keep people accumulating sins only God's grace in Christ can forgive. As there's no answer to a lazy housekeeper, there's no answer to spiritual procrastination. While a family may have to tolerate the lazy housekeeper, God won't tolerate the spiritual procrastinator. Guilty we are, and admitting and seeking its removal we must, or God banishes us from His presence.

⌘   ⌘   ⌘   ⌘   ⌘   ⌘

Subject Idea: Pervasiveness
Scripture: Hebrews 12:1-2
Visual Item: Two glasses of water: one clear, the other filled with debris.

Truth Stressed: God uses disciples who live in forgiveness, not in sin.

Procedure: Ask for a volunteer. Show clear glass of water. Would he drink this? Show contaminated glass. How thirsty would he have to be to drink it?

Applications:

1. The very appearance of our Christian life either invites further investigation or terminates further interest. God uses appearances to arouse curiosity, not to convince people; to attract attention to us and, consequently, past us to Him. Maybe all that appearance does is recruit a second look from the unsaved. If so, it's done well; it's often the outward attractiveness of life that draws questions and comments from seekers. It matters what impression we make on people. Often they won't get past the impression to the reality of faith unless the impression pleases them. We need, therefore, to be careful what initial impact we have on people, for we may never get a second chance.

2. Christ builds such beauty in the Christian that our authenticity is as pleasing as our appearance. Jesus delivers every product he advertises.

3. A Christian life adulterated by sinful practices, habits and possessions is no more attractive than the glass of water with debris in it. Not all that's in this glass is harmful, but it's foreign to potable water and detracts from its purpose. Certain factors in our Christian life may not be strictly sinful, but they're unsightly—and, thereby, render us less usable as an instrument of grace.

4. Even should we hide our sinful nature from others and practice it only in secret, our lives are transparent as clear water to God. Since He pours anointing oil through holy to unsaved souls, Christians necessarily seek the *holiness* that makes their lives a conduit to the lost. Since our first responsibility as Christians is service to the Christ we love, we owe him the privilege of a sinful, but forgiven vessel. That he's pleased to use.

SPIRITUAL LIFE

Settlers in America filled the eastern half of the continent, through the woodlands and prairie to the Great Plains. There they stopped until emigrants overleaped the Great Plains to reach Oregon and California. They left the Great American Desert to the Indians because they couldn't imagine a use for it. Christians know that we come from Eden and will one day live in Heaven, and between is what we often consider an inhospitable, arid spiritual wasteland. However, we refuse to see the Christian faith purely in terms of "other worlds." Right now Jesus lives and overcomes, and we because of him! In these illustrations is a view of how the spiritual life refuses to give an inch or an ounce to Satan and how it turns even the wilderness of life into a garden of spiritual exotica!

Subject Idea:	Cleansing
Scripture:	II Timothy 2:21; Acts 22:16
Visual Item:	Glass dirty inside and out; pan of soapy water; bowl of clean water; towel
Truth Stressed:	Accepting God brings inner cleansing.
Procedure:	Show glass. Would anyone care to drink from it? Stand glass in the water, then wash and rinse outside of glass. Would anyone care to drink from it? Immerse glass and wash it inside and outside and rinse. Would anyone be uncomfortable drinking from it now?

Applications:

1. The Old Testament demanded sacrifices without emphasizing motive in the worshiper. The New Testament demands conversion in those claiming discipleship, without stressing ritual. Punctilious observance of ritual remains essential in religious faith where the demand of conversion is absent or minimized. The Pharisees could always claim ceremonial cleansing by washing up to the elbows after being in public. But

what could cure their pride, hypocrisy and objection to Christ? That's why Jesus demanded a change of the heart (in the Bible sense as the center of being) as essential to conversion.

2. It's our will, not our sins, that keeps us from God. Sins He can forgive, one by one, but He refuses to force it on us. Nothing exists in us so hideously bad that God won't forgive, if we seek it. But only we can will that forgiveness by seeking it.

3. Like the glass, we remain the same after conversion: a human being with all the same personality, ability, limitation, possibility. Like the glass, we may continue in the same career, but like the glass which is now clear and capable of use, we're cleansed and capable of being used. In that sense, though the same component, we have a different potential. A new intention is the key to our spiritual life. However attached to our past, we escape it by living for tomorrow.

4. Conversion demands that newness: the turning from one lifestyle to another. That's foundational to Christianity and the spiritual life. Unlike the glass, *we* become someone different from previously. Conversion, then, is both an end and an open-ended beginning. It's a door into a new life—and we shouldn't get stuck in the door. It's a hinged door that we open and walk through to somewhere else, not a revolving door that keeps spinning us around, going no place. Reinforcement of our new life offers the best proof of our conversion.

5. Immersion in water isn't, as some say, an outward sign of an inward grace—as though we're already forgiven—but an outward work with an inward effect, cleansing what repentance has loosened in our soul.

⌘   ⌘   ⌘   ⌘   ⌘   ⌘

Subject Idea: Transformation
Scripture: Romans 12:2

Visual Item:	Foam sofa cushion; Shop-Vac; clear garbage bag
Truth Stressed:	Christ's grace transforms us into his likeness.
Procedure:	Remove the cover from the foam cushion. Place the cushion inside the bag and seal it by wrapping the opening around the hose and holding it. Turn vac on and watch the cushion shrink; turn vac off and remove the cushion. In a few seconds it returns to normal size.

Applications:

1. You've just seen a transformation—a marked change in the size of the cushion. Change doesn't always involve transformation, but transformation always demands change in appearance, size or content.

2. A transforming experience occurs to them when sinners repent, confess Christ and are baptized. It begins unnoticed but soon becomes obvious. It starts within and expresses itself in changed attitudes, values and behaviors. It's called conversion, turning us from one kind of person into another, eliminating old perspectives and creating new ones.

3. And it has every potential of being permanent. The cushion regained its former size with the air restored. Saved people never need return to being unsaved. They can continue developing their initial conversion into permanent discipleship by welcoming the Holy Spirit's influence. As surely as wolf pups can learn to protect, not prey on the sheep, saved sinners can decreasingly resemble their old ways by increasingly reflecting the Christ-life.

4. The purpose of spiritual transformation is to become more like Jesus. Becoming a Christian may not make us a better general or president or singer, since these are areas of giftedness, but it certainly brings spiritual insights not previously possessed, grants honesty we never before expressed and self-control previously absent. It realizes that the change has to be constant, if deliberate; Christ-

centered, if faulty; and progressive, if irregular. For, while we might otherwise tolerate our humanity, we know God wants it renewed; while we could excuse our sin, God wants it removed. We know that Christ brought us his new life by sacrificing his own. Since our new life comes through his death, we refuse to trample on that sacrifice just to resurrect an old life we now despise, from which we derive only shame. We'll gladly trample Satan underfoot as we let Christ transform us into his image, but we'll not walk over our Savior's love to be again what we have previously been! To impede the re-emergence of our old state we'll gladly accelerate the emergence of Christ's new life! Indeed, while the pillow will never be anything but a pillow, even if sealed permanently in the bag, we're destined to become someone entirely different once freed from baptistry waters.

⌘   ⌘   ⌘   ⌘   ⌘   ⌘

Subject Idea:	Content
Scripture:	Galatians 1:23-24
Visual Item:	Raw egg; hard-boiled egg; table; paper towels
Truth Stressed:	The truth of Christianity is in its results.
Procedure:	Put both eggs on the table. Ask if they can distinguish them. (No, because they look the same.) Spin the eggs. The raw egg won't spin because it has liquid at the center; the hard-boiled will because it's solid at the center.

Applications:

1. We need to distinguish the Christian faith from our Christian life. The former may not be reflected in the latter; the latter may bear no resemblance to the former. The Christian faith is God's objective revelation; the Christian life is our subjective effort to duplicate it. What

unbelievers often condemn as poor Christianity is really a poor example of a magnificent Christianity. What is, in itself, graceful, helpful and meaningful appears weak, insipid and irrelevant through our inadequacies. Since "practice is the final test of theory," as Will Durant wrote, while our failures don't make Christianity less true, they do make our efforts to convince people less easy.

2. The word "Christian" has become so generic it's often equal to "moral" or "benevolent." Many who deny Christ's deity appreciate the humanitarianism he inspires. They consider those non-threatening results alone the essence of Christianity. We can't afford to be confused. Christianity begins with Christ's deity; a Christian is a person who intentionally and consciously replicates Christ's life. Many lost people incidentally do Christ-like things, but only intentional effort makes a person Christ-like.

3. In its simplest definition, the Christian faith consists of the life of Christ energizing his people: his life in Galilee continuing on the Main Streets of the world in those who claim his lordship as subordinates, thinking and acting as he did when living here. That draws him near to all others and draws them to obedience. As he made every person better by being with him, we make every neighbor better by associating with him, and every neighborhood better by our presence there. That's the essence of the Christ-life.

4. Lifestyle—the place where faith meets life—always tells the truth about our claims. It proves that Christ's faith is a palace to be seen and inhabited, a garden not only beauteous but redolent, a field not only ploughed but productive.

⌘   ⌘   ⌘   ⌘   ⌘   ⌘

Subject Idea: Removal
Scripture: II Peter 1:5-9

Visual Item: Naval jelly; a rusty tool and one cleansed by
                the jelly
Truth Stressed: The spiritual life begins with the removal of
                our past and continues with the generation
                of Biblical virtues.
Procedure: Note that naval jelly is a highly acidic sub-
                stance used to remove rust. It usually works
                in a few minutes. Show the tools, the one in
                its rusty, the other in its restored state.

Applications:

1. God begins by calling us sinners. Accepting His eval-
    uation is essential to forgiveness. We've betrayed God,
    and we have a right to the guilt it brings. There's no need
    to change the nomenclature hoping to escape the
    presence, power and penalty of sin. Justifying our misbe-
    havior merely extends and deepens the problem. Sin must
    be the basis of our appeal to the lost because it's God's
    appeal to humanity and the reason for Christ's death.
    Many want forgiveness apart from admission of sin. It
    can't be. Whether of omission or commission or ig-
    norance, whether of the soul, mind or body, all have
    sinned and continue to fall short of God's perfection.

2. In Christ God removes our past with its sin. Like the
    naval jelly removing the tool's rust, Christ's grace
    removes our sins. His blood cleanses us from every sin,
    all removed, none remaining. That removal redirects our
    life from vanity to substance, from novelty to quality.
    Seeing it removed, we understand the meaning of the
    freedom granted: we're no longer threatened by wrongs
    too frightening to face or stained by indelible terrors or
    haunted by guilt. By referring backward we comprehend
    the value of our present and future.

3. While the naval jelly works, in time rust will return to the
    tool. Knowing that our past is always closer than we
    admit and not as far removed as we think; knowing that it
    easily returns, beckoning our re-involvement, how do we
    escape carrying over our old into our new life? How do
    we outdistance the old so it never catches up? By under-
    standing the future of conversion. Righteousness

flourishes with sin removed! Only by delaying and denying spiritual growth will sin's rust reappear in us, making an *ongoing* spiritual life necessary. It alone eliminates any corrosive impact. We'll still sin, but it won't accumulate and corrode. Righteousness keeps rubbing out the sin that enters so it doesn't get attached to our life. We're always like new to God!

4. Our escape offers others their hope. What God did for us He'll do for them. Christ's grace extends to all who trust his sacrifice, not to a few God *chose* to be saved.

⌘ ⌘ ⌘ ⌘ ⌘ ⌘

Subject Idea: Newness

Scripture: Romans 6:21

Visual Item: New clothes with price tags on; old, faded clothes with holes, paint, grease spots, etc.

Truth Stressed: The privilege of living for Christ should inspire our willingness to try.

Procedure: Show both sets of clothes. (If possible, have different people model them.) Point out that our activity determines our wardrobe. Digging in our garden and attending a garden party may both be done in back yards, but each demands specific clothes.

Applications:

1. On becoming a Christian we pledge new life to the Christ who removed the old, with its pain and penalty. The old life is now unacceptable to Christ. It doesn't fit, it isn't appropriate and it won't be tolerated.

2. If we wonder why American technology fuels so many economies, militaries and governments world-wide while our missionary enterprise is copied by none; why billions are impressed by our politics but unmoved by our religion, it's because we're better citizens than believers!

Why would our political and economic model be the dream of so many and our Christian faith the goal of so few? Because while our genius in cyber-tech astonishes, our tolerance of little ethics and lower morals incenses others. Like people in all ages, they copy what appeals and reject the discordant; they buy what fits and refuse the incompatible. Thus, they take from an American society what makes this life better but refuse the Christianity they think irrelevant to improving any life, present or future. We've been talking new but wearing old! And thinking people everywhere know the difference and aren't fooled!

3. Let's vow that, since we're in the forgiven life, we'll wear its wardrobe, knowing God won't make any exception to this rule! Everyone who comes to Him kneels at the cross, and claiming to be under Christ's blood makes us new creatures living a new way. Let's despise what we *were* and love what Jesus makes us! Let's look back at our past with regret and to Christ's life with longing! Let's realize that all we previously thought worth our time was useless and worth our involvement, foolish. And let's delight in the Christ who lets us live guilt-free by becoming Guilt for us, who lets us escape our past by accepting its penalty, who frees us to God's love by accepting God's wrath, who guarantees that all our flaws and failures are overwhelmed by his perfect worthiness! Indeed, how could any Christian, once free from his past garments ever return to them, given the alternative of wearing Christ's righteousness?

⌘   ⌘   ⌘   ⌘   ⌘   ⌘

Subject Idea:	Christ
Scripture:	Acts 10:37-38; II Corinthians 5:5
Visual Item:	Puzzle, with a few pieces out
Truth Stressed:	Jesus is the essential person in life.
Procedure:	Mount the puzzle on a cardboard on an easel. Secure it with tape or glue. Add the missing pieces as you speak.

Applications:

1. Obviously the puzzle is incomplete—like every one of us in some way, whether it's unreached goals, unanswered prayers or unforgiven sins. While we may have fruitful, happy lives without every incompleteness being eliminated, we risk our future by leaving other areas deficient. In fact, as nature abhors a vacuum, none of us tolerates a deserted life. We fill it with something, however worthy or ineffectual, because we hate to feel incomplete.

2. Since God formed Himself as the essence of our humanity and as the center of life, we must welcome Him to be completed human beings! If we're in Christ, we're complete, whatever else we lack, and if he isn't our Savior and Lord, we find ways to compensate. Into this life-space (add a few pieces to the puzzle) people put careers, companions, causes, etc. Just as the puzzle is complete only when I add the last piece (add it), our life is complete only when Jesus Christ is Savior and Lord! While the last piece in this puzzle may not be essential to appreciating its picture, it's essential to *completing it*. And Jesus is essential to completing life. Putting in all the other pieces to life won't make us complete until Jesus fits in!

3. In reality, it's necessary to put him in first, then build life around him. Then he gives meaning to every dimension we add, and each finds its proper place. People who wait till later in life to add Jesus invariably find it difficult to make the room he naturally occupies. As a result, they often decide they have no room for him. Young people have the chance to build him in first, then construct the rest around him, letting him direct the house they live in. Either way, whether we accept Christ sooner or later, we find him giving proper value to everything else. It's just that the older we are when we let him in, the more we have to move out or shuffle to give him space. But make no mistake, whether sooner or later, we need to accept Jesus! Refusing him is the worst mistake we'll ever make.

4. Be forewarned, however. Either way, Jesus never "fits in" to whatever place we make for him. Jesus *rules* wherever he is. Everything else fits around him, not he around it!

When he comes into life, everything else shrinks to allow his expansion, getting out of the way, accommodating his presence.

5. Jesus is God's Model Man. At the very least, his life offers God's ideal for everyone else to emulate. For it says, "This is what life can be when God rules you!" Hardly a person alive doesn't admire that life. The problem is, does it offer everyday relevance? Many people say no, that they're perfectly satisfied without Jesus. They obviously don't understand self. While at the very least God offers Christ's life as our paradigm, by sending Him as His Son, God demands our submission to him on the threat of eternal damnation if refused! Now that's not much of an alternative, but it's the only one God gave. Take Christ into our life and be saved now and forever or refuse him and deceive ourselves now and die eternally. The rule is God's, only the choice is ours.

6. That other people find satisfaction in someone other than Christ doesn't make him less relevant and them more intuitive. It certainly doesn't make them right and him wrong. They've just settled for less when they could have more; little when they could have much; part when they could have whole; and illusion when they could have reality! As sure as he's the only one to bring us into God's presence, he's the only one now to give us an overcoming life! Will we accept, as the focus of our life, goals, causes and relationships that inevitably perish in the Burning? Those factors, worthy as they may be now, don't relate to eternity. What will we do, then: Bolster our ego to justify our denial of Jesus Christ or boost our humility to admit our need of him?

⌘   ⌘   ⌘   ⌘   ⌘   ⌘

Subject Idea: Winsomeness
Scripture: John 3:17
Visual Item: Pitcher of water with unsweetened Kool-Aid mixed in

Truth Stressed: Love makes righteousness winsome.

Procedure: Have a volunteer come forward. Ask him to drink from a glass of the Kool-Aid. Have him identify the kind, then face the audience. Pour a glass and let him take a deep swig. The effect should produce a laugh. Ask him what it lacks.

Applications:

1. As the drink was incomplete without sugar, the Christian life needs love to render its demands and expectations attractive and compelling. One reason Bible teaching seems so harsh is the crustiness of those proclaiming it. The life of Jesus proves how *agreeable* holiness is, even to sinners...no, especially to sinners! While the Pharisees delighted in making others feel unclean compared to them, Jesus drew sinners with an iron hand "in a velvet glove." How could the perfect person so strongly appeal to consummate sinners who made no pretense to righteousness—when sinners today carefully avoid church services, pastors and Christians? Why do they flee us while others just like them pursued Jesus? Here we are, just like the sinners who elude us, while he, different from all, had long lines of people waiting to see him! Why the difference?

2. Because they sensed his spiritual gentility—the cultured grace only the perfect being can possess! That grace called sinners close so they could be forgiven, not judged; empowered, not condemned! Even the Pharisees, with whom Jesus had only doctrine in common, continued inviting him to their banquets, and he continually accepted. We understand why he accepted; he wanted to love them, not argue and dispute endlessly with them. They forced that issue, not he. Their hypocrisies roused his wrath, and their pretensions his hostility, but even there his criticisms were agreeably stated. We might find it hard to think of Jesus smiling while calling them hypocrites, but how else do we explain their continued association with him?

3. Love sugars Christianity without sugar-coating it! Harsh judgments need not be expressed with a frown; strong

words need not be couched in hate. We have no choice, as Jesus made clear. By our love people identify us with him, and they instinctively expect us to express the love we claim to possess.

4.   In any church are distinct personality groups: the extroverts and the introverts; the Type A and Type B; the communal and the monastic, etc. Each group possesses God's love, even if it impacts them in different ways. But each group must express that love to make its faith as agreeable as it is true; as positive as it is true; as welcome as it is true. Jesus attracted sinners because they knew he would receive them, his love for them was so obvious. Do we repel sinners because they know we won't, our lack of love is so palpable?

⌘   ⌘   ⌘   ⌘   ⌘   ⌘

Subject Idea:	Growth
Scripture:	Mark 3:13-15
Visual Item:	Dot-to-dot picture (A more sophisticated picture from a GAMES magazine works best; put picture on an overhead transparency, if possible.)
Truth Stressed:	The Christian's goal must be maturity in Christ.
Procedure:	Show the half-finished picture and ask them to identify it. It isn't always easy to tell. Then finish the picture for the people.

Applications:

1.   Growth in ever-maturing discipleship is God's goal for each disciple. The Christian life is a journey from growth to growth, one point connecting another on and on continually till death. God didn't demand our maturation without providing the means. The problem comes from our reluctance to accept the commission Christ gives everyone he calls and the empowerment he gives all he commissions.

2. Our desire to grow precedes any success in its pursuit. We may grow physically without much thought—but hardly any neglect the fuel of physical growth! Every other kind of growth—mental, social and spiritual—comes from intentional effort, fueled by the proper motivation and substance.

3. Persistence is also necessary to spiritual growth. Intermittent efforts spurt us ahead; only dogged perseverance keeps us there. Many Christians fail here. They lack the tooth-and-nail commitment spiritual warfare demands, finding submission to temptation much easier than resistance of it.

4. That's where a hunger for growth intercedes and saves us from our natural spiritual laziness. Making a throne of our heart, from which Jesus can rule over us, provides the fixed core of motivation to continued improvement. It sidetracks what would otherwise derail our efforts and silences distractions that continually clamor their appeals. It insists on finishing the picture Jesus started painting when we emerged from the baptistry. Back to that motto we go when tempted to settle for less than our best or when we grow weary of virtue's demands.

5. Any part of Christianity we possess and live is appreciated; that's the nature of the spiritual life. It naturally uplifts, encourages and emboldens. If its parts are attractive, the sum of its parts is magnificent! An immature Christian life declares Christ's beauty in prospect; a maturing Christian life declares it in reality; a mature Christian life declares its future glory. Who would stop part-way through his journey with Christ when, with each advancing stage, he keeps getting better and better?

SPIRITUAL PREPAREDNESS

It isn't because the Christian faith is a military institution or because writers have a military complex that the spiritual struggle between God and Satan is often seen in terms of war and battles. It's because the spiritual struggle is as remorseless, as dogged and as consequential as war between opposing armies. It's also because of something else: while the conquered make excuses, the conqueror boasts—and Christians find themselves in the unenviable, inconsistent role of the conquered explaining failures while society boasts of its conquest of spiritual values! These illustrations offer hope that God's people will lay claim to the spiritual preparedness that's our birthright and reclaim the world lost by our inattention to it.

Subject Idea: Readiness

Scripture: I Corinthians 10:12

Visual Item: Can of pepper mace

Truth Stressed: Spiritual preparedness means being ready before it's needed.

Procedure: Show the can and explain that it's used for protection if attacked. However, it must be armed to be useful; most pepper mace containers have a button or handle that needs to be activated for use.

Applications:

1. To prevent accidental discharges, the safety feature is in the off position. If we're in danger, however, leaving the safety off benefits only the attacker. If we wait to arm the can when needed, it's probably too late.

2. To understand the urgency in arming ourselves spiritually, we must think of life as a battleground and our personal life as a war zone. Christians must first guard what Christ has entrusted to them, then keep that trust primed for action. Satan loves sneak attacks and knows where we're most vulnerable, where we'll almost certainly be shocked, terrified, intimidated and panicked. We may live for years

and not have any of our weaknesses assaulted by him. But like "moles" in an intelligence service, those frailties lie open to his exploitation any time he considers it necessary. We can respond in one of two ways to our frailties, then. One, since they haven't been exposed yet, they won't soon be; two, since they haven't been exposed yet, they're soon bound to be. Only the latter meets the definition of *preparedness*.

3. Christians are recruited to fight moral and spiritual battles, not to waste their weaponry and ammunition in lesser wars. We're unprepared to engage Satan politically or militarily when Jesus has equipped us solely as a spiritual host. So much of society has been plundered by Satan because God's people didn't see the danger coming, didn't arm spiritually against it and haven't shot the ammunition the Holy Spirit equipped us to use! Confronting Satan with any weapon but the Sword of the Spirit amuses him; only wielding that weapon with abandon terrifies him! For us to discard that Sword in favor of some church growth principle to make the church grow, or to ally it with a political party, guarantees our ultimate defeat, whatever our initial victory! God knows the armor we need to protect us spiritually and the weapon with which we wage successful warfare on His behalf. If we determine that weapon isn't essential because we have more up-to-date ideas and methods, we find ourselves unarmed just when we need to attack!

4. We're almost always like soldiers at the front—in furious, short-term action, followed by periods of rest and relaxation. During the in-between times, Christians need to prepare for the next battle. If we'll consider each week from Monday through Saturday as our war zone, viciously contesting Satan, we'll understand the value and need of retiring Sunday to education and worship services to be re-fitted for the next week-long battle. Be forewarned: as an unarmed weapon hazards the soldier's life, an unarmed faith hazards the Christian's witness in his weekly struggle for Christ.

⌘ ⌘ ⌘ ⌘ ⌘ ⌘

Subject Idea:	Constancy
Scripture:	II Corinthians 2:12-14
Visual Item:	Umbrella
Truth Stressed:	Faith in God must constantly be exercised.
Procedure:	Show umbrella. Ask if they've ever been one place and the umbrella in another just when they needed it?

Applications:

1. The umbrella protects us from the rain. But only if it's with us, at the time needed, does it serve its purpose. Like the umbrella, the Christian faith offers invincible protection from Satan's attacks. But like the umbrella, it can't make the decision to cover us; we make the decision to seek its protection. Jesus overcame the world to equip us to overcome it, but what good is an overcoming faith that isn't practiced? What value is Christ's lordship if we make a habit of exercising only his saviorhood? Do we think he vanquished Satan so we could easily fall to him? When he made Satan his floor mat and wiped his feet on him, does Jesus expect us to surrender supinely to Satan and let him walk all over us?

2. God's protection is like an umbrella: so long as we stay under it, we're safe. It's only when we consider ourselves immune to Satan's attacks and stake success on our personal efforts, that we find how vulnerable we are. Under God, never careless, always armed, vigilant and ready, Satan has no power over us. We're a fortress he can't storm; he's in a defensive position helpless against our overwhelming assault! But it's God's grace empowering us, not our own wit and wisdom.

3. Most Christians have a workable, sometimes expansive knowledge of God without its corresponding application to life. It isn't that we can't apply it, we just don't. We reveal it in the worship services, then secrete it in the pew when we leave, to be taken up next time to "glorify Almighty God." Admirable, except that unexercised knowledge soon becomes legalism. We learn to spout slogans instead of taking action; we substitute "church work" for witnessing; we even use Bible studies as an al-

ternative to outreach. How cleverly Satan deceives us into considering knowledge about God as an end in itself, not as an irresistible power to change us and all others he wants to receive it.

4.   We might prepare for years, waiting for our time to come, and it doesn't. But if we know God's word and practice it, God always has a role for us. If we're willing to take God with us, wherever we go, He'll send us where He's needed most and where we can most effectively represent Him.

⌘   ⌘   ⌘   ⌘   ⌘   ⌘

Subject Idea:	Protection
Scripture:	II Corinthians 10:5
Visual Item:	Construction hard hat; hammer
Truth Stressed:	We must carefully guard our lives from spiritual harm.
Procedure:	Put the hat on. Talk about the OSHA requirements to wear it in all construction areas. Strike the hat with the hammer hard enough to give the people a laugh and yourself a thumping, but without harm.

Applications:

1.   The helmet of salvation is the Christian's spiritual hard hat, Ephesians 6:17. By wearing it—meaning it's covering our most essential bodily part, where all behavior originates—we're protected from thoughts and perspectives that harm, that fill our lives with trash and trivia. We have no room for them because we're filled with God. We must prioritize in life; we don't have room for everything that attracts our attention. So we honor what graces and disregard what disgraces our Savior's holiness. Sometimes we feel guilty about having evil thoughts that appear, then pass through our minds. On sober reflection, however, what better response to an evil thought than to let it *pass through* without being feted!

2. No one's mind is empty, despite daily experiences with people we swear are air-heads. They could very well be mentally deficient; more likely they've simply failed to focus and discipline their minds. Against that carelessness, we need to judge carefully all we hear from the perspective of our forgiveness. Does it fit the righteous lifestyle? Is it harmonious with Christ's presence in us? Satan loves to introduce extraneous but harmless thoughts just so we won't focus on thinking Christ's thoughts after him. Satan even entices us with thoughts necessary for maintenance of this life—but only to prevent thoughts essential for both here and hereafter! Just as construction hard hats became necessary to avoid otherwise deadly accidents, our salvation is necessary to protect us from all the ideologies Satan creates to waste us in Hell.

3. Often, simply giving sound thought to a problem prevents mistakes and failures. Acting hastily, without that preventative, embroils us in behaviors we'll regret and sins we'll repent. Just so, judging any temptation in the light of our Christian calling encourages us to sacrifice what we won't ultimately want to keep and to keep what we don't ultimately want to lose. Christians must commit themselves to the behavior of the God in whom they trust, not to that allowed and encouraged by our perverted age. A question poses itself to us, often disturbingly so: for what cause do we reserve our best thoughts, our most refined thoughts, our deepest thoughts—the thoughts we want to be remembered for?

4. There's a company that makes construction hard hats to look like Stetson's—with all the appearance of a Stetson and all the protection of the steel. Our salvation is attractive that way: while protecting us from evil, forgiveness dresses us with dignity and panache! God's people add zest and flavor wherever they live. And we can thank God that, when He clothes us in beauty, it's still all protection, not just show; all content, not just form. For we know that, by being very sure that we want to think Christ's thoughts after him, we invite Satan's wild, ruthless assaults that would dissuade, weaken and destroy anything less than the salvation protecting us!

⌘ ⌘ ⌘ ⌘ ⌘ ⌘

Subject Idea:	Resistance
Scripture:	I Peter 4:4; James 4:7
Visual Item:	Pair of ear plugs; blindfold
Truth Stressed:	We honor God by refusing to think in anti-Christian ways.
Procedure:	Show both plugs and blindfold. Plugs are used by factory workers, shooters on gun ranges, fans at rock and roll concerts and husbands with yakking wives—to protect the ears from loud or extraneous noises. Blindfolds are used by day sleepers and by Felix Unger of TV's Odd Couple.

Applications:

1. Spiritual preparation involves the elimination of harmful factors. We don't let them into life; we pull the welcome mat from under them, then slam the door in their face. This response to evil really works. A drug slogan, introduced years ago, remains popular: "Just Say No," a good concept generally, but often weak specifically. Deeply-rooted problems may need resolution before a person can confidently refuse drugs. In the Christian life, however, resisting evil works. Just say no to Satan, and he flees! Temptations may be different, more difficult, more demanding than when James wrote. But his formula still works. Resist Satan, and he flees because he cannot withstand Jesus' powerful name and the Christian life dramatizing the Christ who overcame Satan.

2. Whatever those thoughts, relationships and possessions are, we need to react ruthlessly when they come expecting a welcome. They're up to no good and to great harm! Any welcome we extend them brings negative results. In contemplating this fact, there are obviously certain TV shows and movies we won't watch because they blatantly mock all we proclaim and defend. And we can't find any reasonable way to explain to God that we love Him, then laugh at shows that ridicule Him. We have no time for them; none! Maybe that's the way we once lived, but not now. Maybe we once thought them hilarious or enter-

taining, but no more. We refuse them because we now honor Christ. If former friends wonder how we could have changed so much, *so do we*. We never dreamed it possible. If they think it strange that we could now embrace what we previously abhorred and abhor what we previously embraced, only their experiencing Jesus as we have will convince them. Our witness is real and worthwhile, but *their* personal experience alone will alter their thinking as it did ours. In this sense, Christianity is absolutely a faith personally experienced. It can't be dubbed into another person's life, with their mouthing but someone else saying the words.

3. If we carelessly take into our lives attitudes and behaviors that are potentially or decidedly anti-Christian, we're making a lot of unnecessary work for ourselves. Those things cannot remain if Jesus is Lord. We face the choice: remove them to please him or retain them and guarantee his wrath. In addition, if we carelessly build what should be soundly built, we'll find it unequal to the demands of discipleship. And what will we do, then, when what we unnecessarily let into our lives betrays Christ and weakens our witness? Will we afterwards love Christ enough to re-do what we loved him too little at first to do right?

4. Being deaf and blind to sin has an unusually positive benefit: we don't have to repent what we do right! We'll not commit adultery if we refuse to lust; or murder if we refuse to hate; or theft if we refuse to covet. Eliminating the sinful thought eliminates the sin! Behavior is predicated on thinking; we think, and so we are! If it's true that bad behavior more easily follows bad thoughts than good behavior good thoughts, that doesn't disprove the axiom. All it proves is that we naturally *do* evil but have to *learn* virtue. Either lifestyle begins with thinking! In addition, by refusing to build wrong into life and insisting on building righteousness, we'll discover more time to construct righteousness by needing less time to tear out the sin.

5. We've become so accustomed to mocking the three monkeys who saw, heard and did no evil that we equate

denying evil with escaping reality, as if there's no value in refusing to see evil; in refusing to invite it into our heart. True, there's no virtue in denying evil if it exists, but there's certainly no virtue in embracing it just because it does! Since it's a short trip from the ears and eyes to our brain, we determine not to let gossip, coarse talk, slander or lust—all the things that easily and instantly make the journey—travel that path. Refusing all such sins and failings, we'll express a positive witness to others; more importantly, we'll prove the truth of the confession that Jesus Christ is Lord!

⌘   ⌘   ⌘   ⌘   ⌘   ⌘

Subject Idea: Protection
Scripture: Luke 21:18; Ephesians 6:14
Visual Item: Bulletproof vest
Truth Stressed: God's armor protects our spiritual lives.
Procedure: Show the vest. Explain that it protects the wearer from penetration by, but not against bruising by the bullet. But that's its protection: the policeman might get bruised, but he won't be killed.

Applications:

1.   God outfits us in armor to protect our spiritual lives as we contest Satan. As policemen are required to wear vests, God commands believers to wear His accouterments. A policeman won't keep his job if he refuses; while a disciple won't be fired, he'll soon be harmed enough to turn in his resignation.

2.   God makes no false, misleading promises to recruit our interest and discipleship. The fact that He prescribes particular gear implies the danger faced in contesting Satan. Not to take God's instructions seriously will expose our vulnerability to Satan's attacks. Because wounds in spiritual warfare are inevitable, protection against their

turning lethal is necessary. While we're sure to be wounded, it never has to be fatal. Even if we're protected, the wound can be so severe it kills further interest in being a disciple. Without protection, God's people have no chance of surviving their collisions with Satan.

3. There's a cost to discipleship, if it's nothing compared to the gain; there's an investment, if its nothing compared to the dividend. The point God stresses is that it will often be painful to serve Him in this fallen world. We shouldn't be surprised at the ferocity of the conflict! It's real, it's savage, it's demanding. We cannot embrace the glory without paying its price.

4. In spiritual, as in physical warfare, people get wounded. It can't be helped; it won't be changed. In spiritual warfare, unlike physical warfare, our wounds never have to endanger our spiritual life. They can; they sometimes do. Just as some men have lost faith in God in the experience of war, seeing the slaughter and waste, some Christians lose faith in God by serving in the spiritual life. They figure that if God wanted them to start, He shouldn't have made it so hard to stay. They reach the end of their ability to accept criticism, to lose friends, to stand alone. It becomes too high a price to pay. Their wounds have become fatal. The experiences that deepened their sorrows evaporated their faith. Their suffering lacerated trust to death, despite God's promise that our spiritual life is secure, that Satan has no ability to overcome us! It has happened to others; it can happen to us.

5. The vest assures the officer that he'll be around to boast of his bruise! God's armor assures the disciple that he'll be around to boast of the wounds received while on active duty against Satan. He counted on paying the cost before reaping a reward; on farming before reaping a harvest; on standing against the tide and resisting the wind before establishing spiritual truth and on wearing slaves' garments before elevation to rulers' linens. Any wound is an honor, not a disgrace and quickly shown, not hidden. It's always a greater privilege for Christians to say their faith cost them much than to admit it cost them nothing. At least we put it out there, where it could be tested and de-

tested, criticized and attacked and refused. Indeed, the wounds gained in holy causes have the capacity to enlarge the soul suffering them.

6. Unlike this vest, God provides his warriors with Satan-proof coverage everywhere—except in the rear. Like Roman soldiers, we're covered in the front, but uncomfortably vulnerable behind. But, then, like them, we're expected to advance, not retreat, to pursue the fleeing foe, not leave the field in his charge. God expects us to wage an offensive war, not a defensive struggle against Satan; to carry his strongholds, not defend ours from him. Church buildings aren't to be what they've often become—fortresses where we hide from life. They're to be what they most often aren't—oases where we spiritually refresh ourselves for the next battle. And that makes what goes on inside a church building on any Sunday infinitely more important than anything going on in the world at the same time.

⌘   ⌘   ⌘   ⌘   ⌘   ⌘

Subject Idea: Check-ups

Scripture: Hebrews 2:1; 10:25

Visual Item: Fire extinguisher with a pressure gauge on top

Truth Stressed: We need periodic check-ups to be sure we're ready for service.

Procedure: Show the extinguisher. How many have one? How many haven't checked it the past week; past month; past six months; past three years; ever?

Applications:

1. It's possible to find our fire extinguisher failing us when needed because we failed it periodically. It produces what we pressurize into it. The last problem we want is a useless fire extinguisher while fighting a fire. The

spiritual life is like the fire extinguisher: if we neglect fortifying and reinforcing it, it shouldn't surprise us by failing in a crisis. There are members who feel disappointed with the church when the real problem is their own oversight. For while we'd abuse only ourselves for not checking our fire extinguisher, we often criticize others when our Christian life crashes. Why do we easily fault ourselves for not pressurizing the fire extinguisher and so quickly condemn others when *our* faith fails? Do we expect them to be responsible for our Christian life?

2. Without a crisis in everyday life, others will know the condition of our spiritual life, even if we don't. They'll know whether we're pumped up or flattened out; pressurized or fizzled; exalted or depressed. It won't take a crisis to determine that, just a greeting or normal conversation. How interesting that what's often hidden from us about ourselves is so obvious to others.

3. God knows how easily punctured our spiritual life can get and how naturally it loses its impact. Quite innocently, first getting pushed aside by, it's next buried under everyday affairs, soon to be forgotten in the rush to cook meals, attend Little League games, get the children to the babysitter, play that round of golf. And our Christian life? Oh, yeah, that's something *I used* to practice. And the church? Oh, yeah, *I used* to be active there. To prevent a *used-to-be* discipleship, God designed periodic check-ups. They're called worship services, held every Sunday! And if worship doesn't recharge our spiritual batteries, blame the church for uninspiring services, the preachers for dull sermons or self for not being awake to God's call, but don't blame God. He designed worship, in part, to keep us from straying far away by drifting there a little at a time.

4. May we never have to use the fire extinguisher. When we must, menace and destruction threaten! But let's consistently use our Christian life; that means life to the world! Where fire extinguishers serve to extinguish a destructive force, our witness encourages and enlarges spiritual life in others! May we always be ready, primed, charged and pressurized, ready for the Holy Spirit's use.

⌘ ⌘ ⌘ ⌘ ⌘ ⌘

Subject Idea: Defense

Scripture: I Peter 5:8-9

Visual Item: Deadbolt lock

Truth Stressed: We need to use our God-given defenses against Satan.

Procedure: Show the lock. How many have one? Explain that the dead bolt fits into the door frame, making difficult any unauthorized entrance.

Applications:

1. We need defensive mechanisms to protect our spiritual lives while at rest. However offensive-minded businesses and armies are, they employ defensive measures. Stores may want unlimited members of people thronging their aisles, but their security forces discourage criminal action. Armies may assault enemy lines, but need sentries to guard sleeping troops. Christians can't always be in an offensive mode, though they're often safest when trusting God and engaging the enemy. And it's afterward, when at rest, that God's warriors are most vulnerable to Satan's probes. Indeed, success in service renders us vulnerable when at rest, the degree of the danger inversely proportionate to the success.

2. God has provided specific defensive measures to guard us from Satan's surprise attacks. The Bible, prayer and fellowship are three useful strategies. Like the deadbolt, however, which must be engaged to be useful, these measures must be activated before they protect. Indeed, these measures stand as sleepless sentries guarding us, but are we familiar enough with them to call for help when attacked? Do we know enough Bible passages and examples to call to our side when tempted? Is God such an intimate friend that we pray as easily as we breathe? Do we cultivate Christian relationships that offer unfailingly objective counsel and correction?

3. We can also establish personal defensive measures. One would be periodic examinations of our faith. Like quizzes and tests, the quarterly or semi-annual introspections reveal our progress or reverses, whether we're courting

the content or flirting with the form of faith. Any church could profitably establish one-day retreats and invite willing members to probe and be probed by others involved in their common calling. A second would be establishing defensive zones around life, beyond which we won't go mentally, emotionally, physically or spiritually; across which we won't let Satan intrude without attacking him like killer bees. The farther from the essentials of faith we establish the zones, the safer our resolutions are.

4. As successful as we can be in any particular battle against Satan, that engagement alone is the only one we win—not the war. We may best him in any number of conflicts, but he's never defeated. He'll retire, but only to regroup for a riposte, seeking by a new what he lost with an old strategy. If our Lord whiplashed him so brutally in the wilderness that Satan lay a mangled chaos, yet left Jesus only until a more convenient time, we dare not think we've conquered him once and for all. He'd love us to believe that; then he's able to get inside our ammunition storage while we think he's still outside the fort.

5. God's help in crisis should teach us what we're slow to learn and often don't want to know: He must be in our lives daily because we can't make it successfully and victoriously through everyday experiences, let alone through adversities, without His sustaining grace. Don't wait to invite God into life when an emergency comes—when we have to ask a total stranger for help. Invite Him into life now and live faithfully in His love. Then we'll know His prophylactic presence against life's anxieties and worries and His deliverance from life's disasters and challenges.

STEWARDSHIP

We might wonder why God gave Solomon so much wealth when he asked only for wisdom to rule well. If we think about it, however, who's better qualified than a wise person to gauge wealth's potential and limitation? As Solomon's acquisitive nature grew, his wisdom shrank until accumulation obsessed him and wisdom departed. The following illustrations show the worth money has when given to God.

Subject Idea: Decisions

Scripture: Luke 16:10-12

Visual Item: Four two-liter pop bottles with caps; utility knife; five-gallon bucket

Truth Stressed: We alone determine our generosity in giving.

Procedure: Put all four water-filled bottles on display. Since they represent levels of giving, beforehand drill a small hole in the bottle to be used second.

Applications:

1. The first bottle, lid on tight, represents the person who refuses any financial appeal to church, to missions, to Bible colleges, etc. Hold bottle up and shake it—no way any can get out. Strange as it seems, many live as if they owe only themselves for their prosperity, education and achievement. Of all they may owe to others, they feel no indebtedness whatever to God.

2. The second bottle represents the token giver. Shake this bottle enough and trickles fall from it into the bucket. But who can devote energy or time getting pennies out of a bottle so obviously full of resources? This is the $1 giver who's neither widowed nor poor.

3. The third bottle, cap removed and contents poured into the bucket, resembles the more generous giver. Note that the bottle *neck* remains, making a characteristic glub-glub of too-much supply at too-small an orifice. This rep-

resents the person who gives more than he ever has but still can't bring himself to tithe. He can't imagine giving away that much money. He's invested too much time and energy making it, and it is, after all, *his*!

4. The fourth bottle, the entire neck cut off, represents the tithe plus giver. The water pours from the unblocked bottle. This is the person who recognizes and accepts God's ownership of all he has, whether money, time or talents. Whatever he gives is the least he can do to thank God for Christ. In truth, the gift may not be in excess of the third giver—but if the resources out of which the fourth person gives are less, his gift is really more.

5. Question: Which of the four stewards has opened his life to in-depth spiritual understanding?

    Question: Which bottle represents our personal stewardship?

    Observation: It's barely possible to be a good student of God's word without being a generous steward. It's nearly impossible to be a generous steward without an in-depth appreciation of spiritual truth.

⌘   ⌘   ⌘   ⌘   ⌘   ⌘

Subject Idea:	Submissions
Scripture:	Exodus 3:21-22; 36:3-7
Visual Item:	A plumbing gate valve that can be opened and closed
Truth Stressed:	God knows whether our gift represents an open or a closed heart.
Procedure:	As you show the valve, open and close it, demonstrating complete closure through partial to unobstructed access.

Applications:

1. In giving, as in every Christian activity, we decide the extent of God's accessibility to our life. We crank our will wide open or closed or somewhere between, so that every gift represents both money and motive.

2. God's first expectation is that we'll be the mirror image of His generosity; having modeled it, He expects us to emulate it. The first question that confronts us in giving is: does the act represent a heart stirred and a spirit moved by God's love? Is the force dictating the act from within, making it unthinkable not to give? Or is it a pressure applied from the demands of our church budget, friends and pastors? The answer to these questions determines the outcome of our stewardship and, consequently, of our church's finances. It's possible to give generously, but grudgingly, if the gift doesn't come from our personal openness to God's will.

3. We need to understand that God unmistakably understands our motives and our financial capacity. He accepts the smallest gift if financial restriction, not our refusal to tithe, limits the amount; He sees the valve opened to His will. But any gift, even the largest, is an abomination to Him if it's only a token of our financial statement; He sees the valve closed to His will.

4. As we give, ask ourselves: does our gift express a life closed or open to God? Does it represent a life that willingly accepts God's stewardship teaching or one partly or completely closed to it?

5. We know from Exodus that the result of giving with a willing heart was an abundance that evoked a "cease and desist" order. Is our gift one that, if multiplied by everyone's *willingness* to give, would bring the church a surplus or a deficit? If our church suffers a financial lack, it means that too many of our hearts are only partly open to this significant spiritual exercise.

⌘   ⌘   ⌘   ⌘   ⌘   ⌘

Subject Idea: Tithing
Scripture: Genesis 16:18-20; Hebrews 7:1-2, 8-9
Visual Item: One hundred $1 bills; ten $10 bills
Truth Stressed: The tithe belongs to God.

Procedure: Show the money to the people. Count out ten $1 bills or one $10 from the $100.

Applications:

1. Under Mosaic law, the Levitical priests received tithes from their brothers. However, Melchizedek, priest of Salem, received tithes from Abraham almost two millennia earlier. As the earliest Biblical account of the tithe, it still impacts us today. As surely as the Levites were in Abraham's loins when Melchizedek met Abraham, Abraham's action obligates all his descendants. The existence of the tithe previous to the Law of Moses is the precise reason it survives the passing of the Old Testament as our rule of faith.

2. The tithe is a debt we pay, not an offering we give. We can say we love God enough to pay our tithe, but we cannot say the tithe is a love *offering*. Any love offering exceeds the tithe the way sacrifice exceeds generosity.

3. God's tithe is the first debt we have to pay since we owe Him before anyone! The popular fallacy is that we pay self first out of our income: put aside so much for savings and investment. The Christian cannot be deceived. God's tithe comes first (from our gross income), then, from the rest, satisfaction to savings and bills.

4. This acknowledgment of God's priority is based on two convictions: first, God is our security, not any amount of money saved or invested. (This doesn't deny our need to save or invest; it's simply an acknowledgment of a fact too often overlooked by Christians.) Second, it's as important for us to have God's blessing on what we keep as on what we give. Tithing our firstfruits develops a spiritual mindset that controls our sense of need while it severely diminishes our sense of want.

5. Paying $1 out of every ten to God is hardly exorbitant when He already owns the other $9! Instead of thinking of our obligation to pay Him $1, we should thank Him for the privilege of keeping the $9.

⌘   ⌘   ⌘   ⌘   ⌘   ⌘

Subject Idea:	Blessings
Scripture:	Luke 6:38
Visual Item:	Large package of rice; small bowl
Truth Stressed:	God returns far more than we give.
Procedure:	Set the bowl where everyone can see it. Begin to pour rice into it, in stages. Make applications as you do.

Applications:

1. Our offerings are like these grains of rice. A token offering—something we give by impulse or out-of-pocket, is like a few grains. A tithe of our firstfruits is like many grains. A tithe plus love offering is like many more grains. Notice that I have more than three-quarters of a sack left over.

2. It represents God's return to us. (Pour the bowl full until it overflows. Remember to have something to catch the surplus.) Any faithful tither will agree that he's received more in financial resources and spiritual benefits than he's ever given, however generous his gifts. God's deeper resources guarantee that his benefits fill, press down and overflow in our lives. Some people here have given small fortunes in cash to God through the years. And each one will witness that he's richer for it!

3. Tithers have found that the faith tithing demands activates trust in God's promise to supply their needs. They've found His promise warranted by God's own unshakable bond.

4. It doesn't take a lot of people to support a church. It takes only a lot of commitment from the few. However, as the overflow of rice illustrates, it takes all of God's people to contain the spiritual benefits He gives in return—with sufficient affluence to meet the needs of as many more who trust Him enough to tithe.

⌘ ⌘ ⌘ ⌘ ⌘ ⌘

Subject Idea:	Greed
Scripture:	Matthew 6:19
Visual Item:	A "monkey trap"—a glass jar big enough to insert your hand but too small to retract a fist; a shiny object
Truth Stressed:	Greed blinds us to its danger.
Procedure:	Explain that Indonesians trap monkeys by drilling a hole in a coconut, putting a shiny object inside and attaching the fruit to a tree. The monkey comes, looks inside the coconut, sees the bauble and reaches in. However, the clenched fist can't be retracted. Not even the hunter's approach with nets, in full view of the animal, will distract it from its fixation on the bauble, rendering it an easy capture.

Applications:

1. This jar is today's monkey trap. Notice that, with an open palm, I can insert and withdraw my hand without difficulty. It's only when I grasp the object, making a fist, that I can't retract it.

2. Knowing our acquisitive nature, God has repeatedly warned us against acquiring possessions as symbols of our worth. While He honors the acquisitive nature—He bred it into us—it's only to seek, pursue and retain spiritual values. Any other purpose traps us even as we reach for it.

3. Like the monkey, many people refuse to see the danger presented by their pursuit of things. It may cost them family, marriage, friendships and health, but the *pursuit* is all important to them; possessing objects so blinds them that they care for nothing else, regardless. Objects become so strongly their point of identity that not even the certainty of losing significant relationships changes their perspective—only to get things they crave!

4. Unlike the monkey, who is only an animal after all, we are spiritual beings, created to think through foolishness to reason. Only by turning from God and the freedom He brings, do we turn to things, heedless of the incarceration they inflict.

5.   Greed traps, enslaves and darkens perspectives. It turns everything 180 degrees from reality. It blinds us to spiritual grace, kindness, patience and generosity. It enlarges ambition, egotism and tyranny. It destroys as it lures to hope. It's never possible to be trapped by possessing spiritual values; it's never possible to be free by pursuing possessions.

⌘   ⌘   ⌘   ⌘   ⌘   ⌘

Subject Idea: Returns
Scripture: Exodus 4:2-3; Mark 8:5
Visual Item: Apple seeds
Truth Stressed: Given to God, our combined gifts multiply.
Procedure: Show a dozen seeds. Ask people what they're seeing. Most everyone will say "seeds." In reality, you're holding twelve apple trees.

Applications:

1.   Like the single apple seed producing a tree that produces many apples, the essence of the Christian life is the multiplication of itself into many other Christians.
2.   The same principle applies to our combined, concentrated stewardship. Unlike the single seed, containing in itself the entire history of the apple, no single Christian can support the local church. If God had wanted that, He wouldn't have established the local *congregation* of believers.
3.   In some churches, we are one of a few; in others, one of many. Don't be deceived by the numbers. God sees only the individual, not the few or the many. We are no more hidden among the many than we are exposed among the few. But if we let God start with our individual financial potential—what is that in *your* hand?; how many loaves do *you* have?—our combined tithe multiplies astonishingly. Every church has the capability, in itself, of

supporting local pastors and programs, in addition to world-wide missions, with the capability of reproducing itself in another congregation, all because our combined gifts far exceed the actual worth of any single one.

4. Will God find us as fiscally responsible as He is spiritually generous? In that way the Infinite Multiplier of our gifts amplifies them as they're spent, expands them as they're subtracted and extends them as they're diminished.

⌘   ⌘   ⌘   ⌘   ⌘   ⌘

Subject Idea:	Priorities
Scripture:	Haggai 1:3, 8
Visual Item:	Plate of attractive leftovers under plastic wrap
Truth Stressed:	Only by giving God the firstfruits of our income do we comply with His stewardship demands.
Procedure:	Show the plate. Explain that, as good as the meal was, the leftovers wouldn't be considered acceptable for invited guests.

Applications:

1. Perhaps, if someone unexpectedly visited, we'd feel free to offer leftovers. But, if we had made previous arrangements, we'd plan a meal appropriate to the value we place on that friendship. It might not be fancy, but it would be original and fresh.

2. We've all heard about people giving their last $10 to God; better that than nothing. But the Bible principle stresses God's priority in, not His addition to our life. On impulse a miser might be moved to generosity. From momentary penury a philanthropist might give nothing.

3. God's priority in giving establishes three important factors of faith. One, the principle of faith: God is first in our life. Someone is—either God or us. The tithe prioritizes

God's rule. Two, the challenge of faith: we can trust God to provide our needs if we put Him first in our giving. Three, the essence of faith: our best goes to God—the original part of our career, our energy, our time.

4. Only planned, intentional, faith-driven stewardship willingly subtracts each pay period what can be substantial sums to support spiritual values that many ignore or demean. But to His people those values represent the God who loved us enough to give His best when we were helpless. We can feel nothing more personally satisfying than to take the firstfruits of our endeavor and put them in God's hands.

5. Whatever belongs to God must be given to God. No other use sanctifies it, not even giving it to the impoverished or homeless or hungry. All these are demands on us, but God's tithe is to be given to the church to evangelize the lost and edify the saved. This endeavor alone prevents the scourges of homelessness, hunger and impoverishment we often feel compelled to alleviate, but find ourselves unable to prevent because evangelism offers the only prophylactic against them.

⌘   ⌘   ⌘   ⌘   ⌘   ⌘

Subject Idea: Mistakes

Scripture: Luke 12:15; John 12:5

Visual Item: Have several people bring items they've purchased but never used.

Truth Stressed: Any money given to God is productively invested.

Procedure: The display of items will bring a laugh, as people consider their own mistakes in purchasing clothes, shoes, furniture, tools, etc.

Applications:

1. Never is the Christian's perspective more at odds with the world's than in giving money to God's church. The world can't imagine a more useless, or we a more useful place to invest it.

2. We've all wasted money on things we thought we needed, but didn't; would use, but haven't; would value, but don't. If it teaches us to be more careful shoppers, it's not a total loss. But does it? Be honest now—how many times since we bought that useless object and vowed "never again," have we repeated the mistake?

3. Whatever we give to God is kept, never lost; always enlarged, never abated. Churches can sometimes misuse the money given because we carry the frailties of our humanity into church leadership. However, that doesn't diminish the worth of the gift to God. He honors the giver, even if responsible stewards misapply it.

4. No lust for gold consumes God, but He does use it to teach spiritual values and security. He does warn us that we lose all we spend on self, except as it equips us to serve Him, and we keep all we give Him to reach others.

5. Holding the earth in trust for God gives us the freedom of choice we adamantly esteem. Holding us accountable to Him for our stewardship of that trust gives us a warning we'd rather avoid. However, free to use or abuse our personal lives and the resources of the earth, we're still accountable for all we possess. And God has warned us that only the money given to Him has lasting, then eternal value.

STRESS

Everyone eventually experiences stress. The experience itself isn't necessarily negative or adversarial. As athletes have learned, stress helps keep them sharp and focused. As writers and artists have learned, creative processes flourish under pressure.

However, stress that remains unharnessed and unchanneled wreaks havoc. While we can keep the existence of stress private, its results soon publicly express themselves. Unknown marital difficulties can bring chest pains to superbly conditioned men and intolerable migraines to otherwise healthy women.

The following illustrations show the positive and negative nature of stress.

Subject Idea:	Origins
Scripture:	II Kings 19:14-19
Visual Item:	Full can of pop
Truth Stressed:	Stress must be released or it endangers life.
Procedure:	Thoroughly shake the can. Ask if anyone is brave enough to come forward and pull the tab.

Applications:

1. Like the pop can, our life isn't usable if we retain unrelieved stress. Unlike the can, which can be shaken repeatedly without weakening, human life constantly shaken by stress eventually breaks into demented incoherence. Like the pop can, outside forces create stress within. Unlike the can, *we* determine the extent to which outside forces unnerve us.

2. While life certainly convulses us, God builds into our constitutions restrictions against any permanent influence. While there are other positive ways to relieve stress—exercise, dialogue, even breathing and many negative ways—work, drugs, alcohol—God invites us to seek Him in prayer as the long-term answer to demoralizing situ-

ations. He promises that prayers garrison our hearts like pickets safeguard their fellow soldiers.

3. His relief is essential because, should we remain under strain, our focus invariably shifts from God and others to self. That at once compounds our problem and wastes energies that could more profitably go to career, family or friendships.

4. Like the pop can once shaken, it takes time for the effects of stress to diminish, but we can be confident of a return to normal, given enough time.

5. Jesus was a man of sorrows and acquainted with grief — an amazing revelation since no one knew it, watching and listening to him. Obviously free of anxiety and tension, his eyes glistened with an inner peace, and he lived unmolested by the struggles he faced. Like Jesus we also can suffer but never show it because from him we derive the peace that soothes our wounds and stills our turmoil. Submission to him brings us the same vivacity his obedience to God brought him.

⌘　⌘　⌘　⌘　⌘　⌘

Subject Idea:	Necessity
Scripture:	John 6:15
Visual Item:	Pressure cooker, rocker
Truth Stressed:	By relieving stress we're able to continue serving productively.
Procedure:	Describe briefly how the pressure cooker operates and the value of the rocker in gradually releasing steam as the cooker prepares food.

Applications:

1. Should the rocker become clogged, the steam will eventually blow the lid off the cooker. Then, whatever was in the pan will be on the kitchen walls and ceiling. The rocker is the key to the cooker's continual use, just as finding productive ways to release stress is our key to continual service.

2. Stress comes to us in many ways: an adult child with marital trouble; an X-ray with a suspicious spot; rumors of downsizing at work, etc. Any tension increases the heartbeat and breathing and boosts the blood pressure. None of these is necessarily bad; all of them can be useful and helpful if controlled and quietly released, so we're not eventually overwhelmed with emotional or physical explosion, or, as so often happens, with psychosomatic diseases.

3. Life is unforgiving. If stress hasn't yet, it's going to harm us. Once we resolve a problem, another lurks, menacing and intimidating. New deadlines always confront us, unpleasant people are always present, unsought difficulties always appear.

4. We need to find emotional, spiritual and physical "rockers" that release the strains gradually so the inevitably continuing tumults won't overwhelm us. Maintaining fellowship with fellow Christians, praying and quoting or reading scripture are three such "rockers" that relieve building stress. The more spiritual "rockers" we build into life, the more likely we'll relieve stress *as* it builds rather than letting it accumulate to a damaging explosion.

⌘   ⌘   ⌘   ⌘   ⌘   ⌘

Subject Idea: Methods

Scripture: Philippians 4:6-7

Visual Item: Pressure relief valve from hot water heater

Truth Stressed: God provides ways for us to release stress before it harms us.

Procedure: Explain that the valve detects unacceptable levels of pressure in the heater and releases hot water to prevent an explosion.

Applications:

Stress, like hot water in an enclosed heater, will damage our lives if we let it accumulate. The following are examples of many ways we can concentrate on God's presence and simultaneously keep stress manageable.

1. Talk to a Christian friend who can listen and empathize. The act of sharing often offers a catharsis, and nothing more needs to be done. Like bombers over Germany in World War II, we're vulnerable to attack; like fighters accompanying the bombers, friends help us break through misery into buoyancy.

2. Accept interruptions and changes as opportunities for growth in unexplored areas. Jesus used such occasions to reveal magnificent truths. Luke 12:13 ff, Luke 10:25 ff and Mark 10:17 ff are such examples. Hardly anyone's life goes according to an invariable schedule. Those who enjoy diversions most see them as opportunities to create unexpected pleasures.

3. Take time to do nothing. Mark 6:30 ff tells us that Jesus took his disciples away for quiet and rest. (They didn't get it since the crowds followed, leading to the feeding of the 5,000, but Jesus saw the need and acted to bring physical relief to his men.) No matter how carefully we program our day, we need daily diversions to unstring our emotions and intellect. The time we spend doing nothing is as important as organized effort.

4. Accept our humanity, with its limitations, frailties and sinfulness. Hebrews 4:12-16 assures us that God's word reveals all that we are—an unsettling thought—then assures us that Christ's High Priesthood makes possible our bold and confident access to God's presence anyway.

5. Learn to accept ourselves as unique individuals whom God loves as we are, not because we're like someone else. In II Corinthians 10:12 Paul discussed the spiritual danger of comparing ourselves with other mortals instead of with the perfect Christ. Berating ourselves because we're not like someone else or congratulating ourselves that we're not like someone else has the same risk: we consider others, not Jesus, as our standard.

⌘   ⌘   ⌘   ⌘   ⌘   ⌘

Subject Idea:	Relief
Scripture:	Psalms 105:1-6
Visual Item:	Baby's pacifier
Truth Stressed:	Praising God offers escape from stresses that otherwise keep us in turmoil.
Procedure:	Hold the pacifier and ask how many parents have used one to calm an infant's distress. It seems to have a magical effect on babies, as if the very act of sucking reduces their anxiety.

Applications:

1. Of all the "spiritual pacifiers" at our disposal, praising God in a time of turmoil or disappointment offers a guaranteed escape into joy.

2. The focus of the praise must be the person of God and Christ. (It delights the Holy Spirit to help us praise the Father and the Son, without himself being praised.) Consider God's creative genius; the Old Testament miracles on Israel's behalf; His sovereignty over kings and nations; His long-suffering compassion for recalcitrant people; Christ's personable concern for individuals; his easily-aroused pity for the suffering; his courage under duress; his invincible integrity; his loving sacrifice; his triumphant resurrection and ascension.

3. Praise God wildly, if we have the need, quietly if we have the impulse; praise Him continually without stopping to think what we're saying. Let adulation for God pour like rivers of delight: words, scripture verses, hymns, choruses. As it flows, contentment grows! Calm replaces restlessness; insouciance replaces mental and emotional turbulence.

4. A baby lulled to sleep from previous tears offers proof of a pacifier's worth. A tense, fatigued child of God, finding peace by praising his Creator offers the world an argument for discipleship it can't refute and an invitation many in it won't refuse.

⌘ ⌘ ⌘ ⌘ ⌘ ⌘

Subject Idea:	Testing
Scripture:	Proverbs 24:10; I Corinthians 10:13
Visual Item:	Empty pop can; full soup can
Truth Stressed:	Stress determines the content of our personal lives.
Procedure:	Have a youth and an adult come forward. (Be sure the adult isn't a two-ton or with a vice-like grip.) Ask the youth to crush the empty can with his hand. Ask the adult to crush the full can with his hand(s). Have him put one foot on the upright can and apply pressure.

Applications:

1. Since no one is exempt from the pressures of life, our response determines their positive or negative impact, whether we withstand or collapse. Since each person has a different stress threshold, some will collapse sooner or withstand longer.

2. Just as we can crush this soup can by standing on it lengthwise, nearly every human can be broken if enough pressure is applied in the vulnerable area, whether psychological, intellectual or emotional. Some finely cultured people have been known to break when godless interrogators spewed vulgarities in their faces.

3. Scripture assures us that we never need reach the point of breaking under duress. The verse we often use as a comfort really offers a challenge: God knows at what point we break and, to prevent it, provides a way of escape. Our trouble is that we become so obsessed with the problem or situation that we don't look for the escape.

4. Building Christ-honoring virtues strengthens us against the inevitable testing. The Master's own temptations prove Satan's inability to abase a person wholly committed to God's will. It's given to Satan to test and sometimes to flog us, but God has reserved to Himself the power to overcome all such testing and flogging.

5. Unlike this can, we need never collapse under Satan's stress. His pressure has no power we disallow! He can never apply enough tension to break our personal place

and peace with God if, in the testing, we mentally and emotionally fling ourselves into God's everlasting arms. We never expect to find Satan less powerful than he is; he should always find us more formidable than he expected.

⌘   ⌘   ⌘   ⌘   ⌘   ⌘

Subject Idea: Pressure

Scripture: I Kings 22:13-14

Visual Item: Oversized shirt; undersized hat or cap

Truth Stressed: We need to work and serve within our personal talent and temperament ranges.

Procedure: Put on the shirt and hat. If you can bear the witticisms, ask if it "looks" like you. If you're up to more embarrassment, ask what it would take to show the real you. (After taking as much raillery as necessary, be sure to remove the cap and shirt, or they'll pay no attention to the applications.)

Applications:

1. It's essential that we honestly and objectively arrive at spiritual convictions and determine our spiritual giftedness. Deprived of either, we'll always be at the mercy of well-intentioned but mistaken friends or malicious enemies.

2. Regarding our belief in God: read God's word and, based on the facts revealed, anchor ourselves there, Daniel-like. Know what we believe, for there's always someone willing to talk us out of it, substitute something in its place or encourage compromise.

3. Regarding spiritual giftedness: through Bible reading, prayer and a thorough inventory of our personal lives, discover the abilities God gave us at birth that we can return to Him as service. Christian friends can *verify* our giftedness, but *we* must discover it. They can assure us whether we're right or wrong, but we initially exercise it.

4. Without personal convictions, both in our basic beliefs
    and ways to serve Christ in the church, we'll be wearing
    oversized spiritual shirts and undersized spiritual caps.
    We'll have people teaching who should be students and
    others following who should be leading. What's far
    worse, we'll have people who *wonder* why they believe
    instead of *knowing*; who stutter uncomprehendingly when
    asked why they're Christians instead of rattling off ten
    reasons without a breath.

⌘   ⌘   ⌘   ⌘   ⌘   ⌘

Subject Idea: Positives
Scripture: Jonah 1:17
Visual Item: Ten-pound sledgehammer
Truth Stressed: God uses stress to both negative and
                positive ends.
Procedure: Explain that construction workers call a
                sledgehammer the "Persuader," using it to
                move stubborn building materials into tight
                and hard-to-reach places.

Applications:

1. A whack or two with a sledgehammer will drive plywood
    sheets or heavier lumber exactly where the carpenter
    needs them. Stress acts as such a "persuader" in our lives,
    particularly to a Christian, if we're open to God's grace.
2. Whenever we feel the persuasion of God through the Holy
    Spirit, we better pay attention, listen carefully and obey
    explicitly. Many Biblical examples offer pleasant or un-
    sightly results, depending on the person's response when
    God came knocking. As Jonah's life shows, God per-
    suaded him to preach in Nineveh; as Paul's life shows, the
    Holy Spirit persuaded him not to enter certain mission
    fields. As Jesus told his disciples, the word of God would
    persuade them to be holy vessels.
3. Stress persuades us through negative responses to our ac-
    tivities: guilt; failure; defeat; a sense of dissatisfaction,

however much others want to assure us it wasn't our fault—a down-deep conviction that we should have done something different; criticism from others, even if it derives from the constant critic. Even critics can sometimes be right. Our first response to such should be a question—is their criticism valid?; not a declaration—just what I'd expect from that source!

4. Stress also persuades us through positive responses to our activities. Success is the greatest approval; so is a feeling of achievement in overcoming difficulties. Even a moral victory in defeat can be, knowing we didn't succeed in the effort but did better than we anticipated. This stimulates renewed, more assertive effort. The assurance of objective friends is also invaluable: people we know who verify our result if we're right and correct it when we're not—but who always stand by as helpers and encouragers.

INDEX AND CROSS-REFERENCE

STRESS

VISUALS